HIGH SCHOOL THEATRE OPERATIONS

for
Architects,
Administrators
and
Academics

Elizabeth Bracken Rand

© Elizabeth Bracken Rand, 2015

TABLE OF CONTENTS

PART 2 - OPERATIONS

INTRODUCTION

These days many junior and senior high schools are being built or re-modeled with a state-of-the-art theatre on campus.

Architects who normally specialize in educational facilities have been appointed to design theatres, and administrators who normally specialize in education have been appointed to manage a theatre, as a part of their duties. One district administrator commented that he had never had to think about school theatres so much in his career as he has to now. Having to *design* a theatre without having an understanding of how it functions is like being charged with painting the lines on a football field without knowing how the game is played. Having to *manage* a theatre facility without an understanding of its operations is like coaching a football team by just letting them get on with the game themselves, making up their own rules and safety procedures. Of course all of the shortcomings would be obvious to the football players, and operational and safety issues could put them in dangerous situations. The same is true for the functions of a high school theatre.

So how can you design and manage a theatre if you've never "played" behind the scenes before. This book will take you behind the scenes and show you situations that theatre people experience, which will give you insight into what matters to a high school theatre's operations. Once you understand the functionality of the theatre, you are more likely to apply the correct operations. For instance, it's no good me telling you that you need a headset jack in a certain place, without first letting you know the function it serves.

So, who should be reading this book?

THIS BOOK IS WRITTEN FOR...

ARCHITECTS

* Architects
* Educational Facility Planners
* Theatre Consultants (many specialize in places of worship and home theatre systems)
* Contractors
* Subcontractors who spec and install high school theatre systems
* Suppliers who supply equipment for high school theatres

ADMINISTRATORS

- School District Superintendents
- School Boards
- Principals
- District Facility Maintenance and Custodial Directors
- District Business Managers
- District Human Resource Directors

ACADEMICS

- District Learning and Education Directors
- Performing Arts teachers and directors (drama, band, choir, dance, etc.)
- School custodians, maintenance and any other school staff who will be involved with the maintenance of your theatre
- University students studying architecture, construction or building management
- University students who are studying entertainment industry management
- University students in a teacher training program
- High school and college performing arts students

and also....

ARTS EMPLOYEES

- Theatre Managers/Technical Directors
- Theatre designers, technicians and staff
- Stipended professionals, volunteers, and members of the community who design and build for high school plays

TO ARCHITECTS

Because it is becoming more and more popular these days for new or renovated high schools to be equipped with a state-of-the art Performing Arts Center (theatre), more and more educational facility planners (EFPs), are being thrown into designing theatres.

In your personal life you go to restaurants, hotels, shopping malls, doctor's offices, perhaps even hospitals. You've cooked in your own kitchen and possibly run your own office. In your younger years you may have had a job in one of these facilities, and you've certainly set foot in schools. For the most part, you know how these types of facilities function, as enough of the "behind the scenes" operations are apparent and common knowledge. However, when you go to see a play, ballet, concert, opera or other performance, what has been going on and what is going on behind the scenes is not apparent at all. All you see is the magic of the performance. If you don't have a practical working knowledge of theatres, when you've never worked behind the scenes, or haven't worked behind the scenes since you were in high school yourself perhaps, it's nearly impossible to anticipate what today's end user may need in terms of functionality.

For this reason most EFPs hire "theatre consultants", when it comes to designing a high school's performing arts center. But even this is not a panacea, because many companies that offer theatre consulting today are staffed by people with no practical and functional experience working in an actual live theatre. In fact, a lot are from the home theatre or places of worship industry. Or, they worked in the theatre a long time ago, started their company, and haven't worked in the theatre since. Many of them have no practical or current experience in the theatre industry. If you look at the websites of many theatre consultants, you will see that they are system designers and equipment installers with a wide range of experience working in churches, halls and home theatres. This does not necessarily indicate that they also have the specialized knowledge to properly outfit a high school theatre appropriate to its specific functions. In addition, school districts – to their long-term detriment - usually go with the lowest bidder, who tends to be the one who will bid any job, and therefore is the one with the most generalized knowledge. I once spoke with someone who had designed a system in a theatre I was working in, and he commented that he thought it would be fun to work in a theatre. He had never worked in a theatre, yet he was spec'ing out equipment and systems.

This book primarily addresses the operations of the high school theatre once the keys have been handed over and the doors are about to be opened. It is not the intention of this book to address designing and building theatres. However, if you are an Architect or other professional working in Educational Facility Planning, then reading this book and learning about the functions of a high school theatre, will help determine the design decisions you make.

As an example, how do you know if you want to spec an analog sound board or a digital sound board? There are pros and cons to both, and the choice depends on the primary functional use of the theatre. Will the theatre be primarily used by students who come and go each year? Will there be formal vocational training for students using the equipment? How many students a year will want to learn to be sound technicians? Will the theatre be staffed by professional technicians? Will the technicians run the theatre, and/or work with the students? Will the theatre be rented to outside users? Who will staff outside events - professional staff or students? Or will outside users be expected to be able to run the sound board themselves? Will outside users be permitted to use the theatre's equipment unsupervised? Who will restore the equipment each time in preparation for the next user (school or outside)? The answers to all of these questions will determine if you want to spec an analog sound board or a digital sound board. These same questions can be applied to a lot of situations in your theatre in order to help you make your design decisions so that the managers (the school administration) of your theatres have the tools appropriate for the intended use.

The design has to be appropriate in the first place before the keys are handed over, because the type of equipment installed directly affects building functionality, student learning and faculty retention. I've seen too many theatre designs go to complete waste and not used to their full potential because the design was not suitable to the users abilities or budget. For instance, one school I worked at had a (mega overkill, ultra expensive) state-of-the-art light board installed with a complete system of programmable LED lights in their 100-seat theatre. I suspect the architect was concerned about energy and environmental design, and rightly so, but the system was so complicated that no one had used the theatre's lighting system for the first year and a half of the school's operation. For a start no one knew how to turn off the stage lights (all of the lights had been left programmed to come on when the board was turned on and they didn't know how to create a blackout) let alone operate the lights individually. So my techs and I re-hung and focused the lights and programmed the whole system for them in a simpler format. That system will never be used to its full potential in such a preliminary learning environment and cost the school district hundreds of thousands of dollars. This is a classic example of where simpler technology (a "two scene preset" manual board with standard manually focused instruments) trumps state-of-the-art technology when it comes to building performance affecting academic performance, as well as staff ability and retention of knowledge.

FORM VERSES FUNCTION

A word about form and function. I know the artistic side of you wants everything to look "warm" or "attractive" or "inviting" or "pretty" or "dazzling" and so on. As a Lighting Designer, I completely get that. But don't let form rule at the expense of function in a high school theatre facility. Remember, techies wear black and skulk around in the dark backstage. If they haven't been seen or noticed then they have done their job. Techies have that same mentality about their theatre building too. It's ok to make the lobby and house attractive for the audience, but not at the expense of taking away from the thing the audience came to look at – the show.

Some functionalities to take into consideration include:

- Traffic patterns, doors, locks, room configurations
- Efficacy and practicality of the equipment - is the equipment obsolete, overkill or just right?
- Placement of equipment
- Optimal amount and quality of equipment needed in order to efficiently run a production
- The layout of the backstage area for optimal functionality
- Optimized communication system to fulfill the needs for the operation of a production
- The function of auto lighting and sound controls
- Headset positions
- Scene shop location
- Storage needs for sets, props, costumes and people
- Counterweight system or winch system, or a combination
- Drapes, their purposes and placement
- What equipment should go in the booth, what should go backstage
- Placement of air-conditioning units so that drapes don't ripple during shows
- An office space for the theatre management and staff - a window please!

Form should stop at the proscenium and function should take over. We don't care how pretty things look backstage; we only care if they serve to make the show work. At one high school theatre I worked at, there was a door in the backstage wall that had the lock the wrong way round, such that it was possible for students to enter the stage from the rest of the school. The purpose of the lock should have been to keep students off the stage during the school day. We had to make sure to gaff tape the latch open all the time during performances so that actors and crew members could exit the stage. I had a work order submitted for months and months to fix this functionality problem, to no avail. Within that time period, one day the same backstage wall of the theatre was scraped by someone carelessly moving some orchestra shells. The scrape was so deep that it took the black paint off of the wall and exposed the white plaster beneath. I put in a work order. That work order was taken care of within the week! Why?! That wall is *never* seen by the audience - for every single performance in that theatre, either the cyc or the black curtain is down. No one would ever leave the wall exposed (unless it was a very special design choice

9

of the set designer for some reason, and that would be rare), so that work order had a very low priority. Yet, a decision-making administrator only saw the form of one issue, not the priority of malfunction that we were experiencing.

YOUR DESIGN TEAM

If you don't have an experienced and up to date bona fide Theatre Consultant on your design and building team, one good way to find out about the functionality needed is to consult with all the potential users of the theatre. And by this I do not mean the school principal representing these users. Interview each of the performing arts teachers, interview any technicians already working at an existing theatre in the district, especially interview as many tech theatre students are you can – they are probably the largest wealth of knowledge as to how a theatre should function.

Don't have one focus group meeting, keep them on your design team. This design team should be involved in all phases, and should review and approve plans before they become reality. You would be amazed at how much functionality "Theater People" take for granted that needs to be taken into consideration when planning your theatre operations.

I was in on the ground floor (literally) of the planning and construction of one theatre I worked at. Because of this I was able to prevent many problems and issues that I've come across in several high school theatres I had previously worked in, and I was able to correct many of the decisions that were made on paper before they were finalized in concrete and steel. I don't claim to be a theatre designer, but I was able to do this simply because I have a hands-on working knowledge, rather than a theoretical knowledge, of how a high school performing arts center needs to function, and because I also enlisted the technical expertise of my tech crew team.

You will see as you read this book, that there are many functional and operational details to be considered in order to determine your design choices. If you are an Architect who doesn't have the theatre in your blood, this book will help you make decisions that will improve the practical application of your theatre design.

TO ADMINISTRATORS

The trouble is... that while schools manage to raise the money for capital projects to build a theatre facility, once the keys are handed over there is no money budgeted to operate these facilities. This typically leaves the high school with a state-of-the-art theatre facility and no one to properly staff it so that it is appropriate and optimal for educational purposes and suitable for practical and safe operational use.

School district administrators, therefore, typically jump to the conclusion that their Drama teachers can run the facility and that outside events that rent the facility can have full reign of this "classroom" with a custodian site supervising. But Drama teachers and custodians are not theatre technicians and managers, and theatres are not like classrooms. Highly qualified management and staff is needed in order to set up the operating systems, create a safety program, maximize student learning, and determine building performance and academic outcomes. The high school theatre is like no space you've had to manage before.

In addition, when most people think of a theatre at a high school they think "arts". They think about the performance aspects; acting, instrumental music, vocal music, dance, variety shows, and so on. However the performances don't happen in a theatre setting without all the technical factors that go on behind the scenes. Tech theatre is a "Career and Technical Education" (CTE), or vocational, subject. It's also a STEM (science, technology, engineering, mathematics) subject. Or rather, I like to say: "STTEM" – the second "T" being "teamwork"; something inherent in technical theatre. Technical theatre is in fact a situation where STTEM supports the arts. Sadly, many high school theatres do not provide an appropriate education for their tech theatre students, lumping the subject in with the "performing arts", when in fact tech theatre students usually would like to stay as far away from performing as possible. The Education chapter lists the myriad of careers in the Entertainment Industry and in related fields that technical theatre students can go into. As well as being a vocational training ground for STTEM, a lot of high school theatres also operate as rental "road houses", which has its own set of challenges to be aware of.

As you have probably already surmised, it is the ulterior motive of this book to convince you that, after they hand you the keys, it is essential to hire a theatre manager and specialized technicians to run your high school theatre, and a Tech Theatre teacher to teach technical theatre to your students. These people have the technical experience, and the temperament and skillset to oversee the theatre's operations, as well as the knowledge needed for the safety, education and training of the students who work in the theatre. While it is possible to follow a model where a teacher manages the theatre and students staff the shows, it's not ideal.

A theatre in a high school setting without highly qualified management and supervision is akin to students in an art classroom without a highly qualified teacher – they can figure out how to paint a picture or make a sculpture, but they haven't been taught relevance; theory, techniques, tool usage, etc. Or worse yet, it is akin to students in a woodshop or science lab without a highly qualified teacher – an accident waiting to happen. After the capital budget has been spent building your high school a state-of-the art theatre, district money must be found in order to appropriately and safely run your theatre. Districts should *insist* that their theatres be staffed with highly qualified professionals, not *resist* staffing them.

However, if, for whatever reason, you absolutely must manage your high school theatre yourself and staff it with a teacher as manager and students as technicians, and allow outside events full unsupervised reign, then please read this book in its entirety before you open your doors. This book will provide you with a foundation of practical applications and information that will improve the functionality, safety, financial sustainability and student learning capability of your theatre. I'm not presuming to cover all situations in all theatres, however in this book you'll find the most common situations that I've come across in the 20 plus school theatres that I've worked in. This book addresses the basics of what you need to know about making your high school theatre facility functional, operational and safe for all users, as well as an optimal learning environment.

TO ACADEMICS

One subject that is not often taught in university theatre programs is Theatre Management. This differs from Stage Management in that Stage Management is the management of the actual show or event that comes into a theatre, while Theatre Management is the management of the theatre into which the shows and events come. So, most people fall into Theatre Management from one of the other specialties – design, stage management, technical crew, directing, acting or teaching. However with so many high schools building theatres on their campuses these days, I predict that High School Theatre Management is going to become an essential specialty.

That said, one really cannot manage a theatre facility without first having experiences 'in the trenches', so work on as many shows as you can in as many theatres as you can in order to gain the experience and insight needed to manage such a facility. A High School Theatre Manager does not need to be able to run all the aspects of a theatre by themselves, and in fact they should not be running everything themselves – remember, the hospital administrator doesn't perform the surgeries – however a Theatre Manager should have an understanding of the needs of all of the specialties within a theatre facility, without which management decisions cannot be competently made.

The other proficiency a High School Theatre Manager should have is an education background. I highly recommend getting a teaching certificate as well as your degree in Theatre Management. In a high school theatre setting, while you may not be formally teaching a class, you will be working with high school students frequently. A teaching certificate not only makes you more knowledgeable, but also more marketable. In the high school setting you are not just there to manage but also to educate. It also helps that you LOVE working with teens!

The job of a High School Theatre Manager is a rare hybrid job that combines education and management and a theatre background. This book can act as a text book to college students who are interested in preparing for a career as a High School Theatre Manager.

ARCHITECT, ADMINISTRATOR OR ACADEMIC

Without a background in theatre management it is of course impossible to plan for every eventuality and for you to catch everything a theatre person would. (Even with a theatre background there is no way to plan for every eventuality!) However this book will give you a better understanding of the details you should be considering, such as: what consumable equipment to stock, how to create versatile lighting, sound, stage and communication systems; how to develop customized operational policies and procedures that improve personal safety, protect property, and mitigate liability; what systems, forms, scheduling procedures are needed; recommend budgets and fees; plus help with outreach and branding.

This book sets a standard of safety, functions, and education. This book also provides a myriad of stories of faux pas to avoid. You can read this book from cover to cover, use it as a text book, and/or use it as a reference tool as you build and improve your theatre operations know-how. This book also advocates for safe, relevant and empowering learning environments, and will help you design facilities and programs that will maximize student learning – providing real-world experience and transferable personal and career skills for all performing students, and provide vocational training for tech theatre students.

Read on MacDuff!

But, wait, before you go on, you are probably wondering who am I to write such a book. To rephrase a quote from Henry David Thoreau:

"How vain it is to sit down to write when you have not been up a genie lift!"

I am a High School Theatre Operations Consultant. I began my technical theatre career at my own high school theatre in the years of dead-front light boards and manually operated carbon arc followspots. I was lucky enough to go to a high school that had a 950-seat performing arts center that was rented to outside events as well as being used for school productions. Students from the high school were paid to work alongside professional technicians for plays, musicals, operas, movies, lectures and so on.

I have worked in technical theatre on and off for over thirty years now; in educational and professional settings. I have been designing lighting professionally since the early 80's and have designed or mentored student designers in over 100 shows. I have worked in over (I've lost count) 20 theatres, most of them schools. For several years I also worked in construction management and as an architectural lighting designer. I have consulted on the construction and/or equipment upgrades of several school theatres. For five years I worked on a Special Projects assignment as a Theatre Manager for two high schools, where I lead a professional crew of nine theatre technicians, who worked over 200 events a year, and mentored and supported the high school student crews.

My undergraduate degree is in Drama; emphasis Stage Lighting, and my master's degree is in Entertainment Business Management. I also hold a Theatre Arts teacher certification. I was the Lighting Designer and Stage Manager for a production that won the "Rookie Event of the Year Award" at the Key Arena in Seattle, Washington, and I have been nominated three times for Best Lighting Design at Seattle's 5th Avenue Theatre's High School Musical Theatre Awards. My website address is:

www.RCDTheatreOps.com

PART 1 - SYSTEMS

CHAPTER 1

THEATRE BASICS

WHO'S WHO BEHIND THE SCENES

If you are a high school administrator who is not familiar with the world of the theatre and you find that one has suddenly appeared in your high school, you will need to know who are all the players you will be working with and/or needing to hire. Below is a list of Who's Who Behind the Scenes in high school theatre. Not every production or event will need every person on this list, and large productions will need all of them and more.

DIRECTOR - directs the actors in the show – in a high school this is usually the Drama teacher or a guest director, sometimes students assistant-direct full length shows or direct One Act plays.

CHOREOGRAPHER - choreographs any dance pieces in the show – this can be a teacher within the school (some sports teachers also know dance), a hired choreographer from a local dance company, or a particularly talented student.

MUSICAL DIRECTOR - works with the actors on any vocal pieces in the show, and/or rehearses and conducts the orchestra or band that plays with the show. There can be a vocal director and an instrumental director, or one person who does both. Again, a teacher (sometimes the school's choir and/ or band teacher), a hired musician from the community, or a particularly talented student.

STAGE MANAGER (SM) - assists the director at rehearsals, runs the show every night, calls all the cues, in charge back stage. In high schools, this is usually a student. Once the curtain goes up on opening night the student Stage Manager is fully in charge.

ASSISTANT STAGE MANAGER (ASM) - assists the Stage Manager, sometimes is in charge of props. Sometimes also known as the Deck Manager - if the SM is calling the show from the booth the ASM will be in charge of what goes on on the stage deck.

PROPERTY MASTER/MISTRESS (PROPS) – procures or creates the props (any object used by the actors which is not permanently built into the set), sets out the props used by the actors every night, makes repairs as necessary.

SET DESIGNER - designs the set, oversees the construction of the set. In high school theatre this can often be a well-meaning parent who has usually had some construction experience, or a certificated vocational tech theatre teacher.

SET CREW - builds the set, usually the student and/or parents.

RIGGING/STAGE CREW – usually students, who move the set pieces and scenery during the show.

COSTUME DESIGNER - designs the costumes, oversees the making of the costumes, makes repairs as necessary. In high school theatre this can often be a creative parent who has sewing and design experience, sometimes a professional from the community, or a certificated vocational tech theatre teacher.

COSTUME CREW - sews the costumes, usually the students and/or parents.

DRESSERS - help the actors with any quick or complicated costume changes during the show.

MAKE-UP ARTIST - designs the make-up, may help with application of complicated make-up. Usually students or parent volunteers take on this role for shows with more complicated make-up. If not, each actor is responsible for his or her own make-up.

LIGHTING DESIGNER - designs the light plot, oversees the hang and focus, attends tech rehearsals and decides on light levels to be set throughout the play. This is a specialty area, not usually found from within the school, like construction or sewing, so usually a Lighting Designer is hired from the community, a theatre technician employee who performs this task, or a certificated vocational tech theatre teacher.

LIGHT BOARD OPERATOR - programs the light board for tech rehearsals and runs the light board for the performances. Usually a student with a strong interest in lighting.

MASTER ELECTRICIAN - helps with hang and focus, is the technician or student who is most familiar with the craft. The Master Electrician can also be the Light Board Operator but not always.

ELECTRICIANS or LIGHT TECHNICIANS - help with hang and focus, assists the Master Electrician if needed during the show, such as for gel changes, re-patching, helping execute a particularly difficult manual cue on the light board, etc.

SOUND DESIGNER - designs the sound cues, oversees placement of mics on stage and/or on actors, attends Tech Rehearsals and decides on sound levels to be set. This is a specialty area, not usually found in the outside world like construction or sewing, so usually a Sound Designer/Engineer is hired from the community, or a theatre technician employee who performs this task, or a certificated vocational tech theatre teacher.

SOUND BOARD OPERATOR - programs the sound board for tech rehearsals and runs the sound board for the performances. Usually a student with a strong interest in sound.

MIC WRANGLER – in charge of helping the actors put their headset mics on backstage before and during a performance. Usually a student.

RIGGER – when hanging scenery or drops ALWAYS have the processed supervised by a qualified rigger. Remember that you are hanging hundreds of pounds of weight overhead. The correct hardware and process must be used.

RUNNING CREW – the people who move the sets and fly the scenery, during a show. Usually a team of students supervised by a theatre technician.

High school theatre staffing is addressed in detail in the Staffing chapter.

STAGE DIRECTIONS

As well as knowing who's who backstage you will also need to know what's what. At the end of this book is an extensive glossary of predominantly used theatre terms, but one of the important concepts you will need to know and will use a lot is stage directions. Here's a diagram.

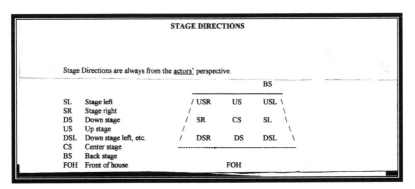

Stage directions are taken from the actor's point of view while standing on the stage. So, if you are sitting in the house - stage left is to your right and stage right is to your left. However, if you are referring to something in the house, then you can refer to house left and house right, which are your left and right. When talking to someone on stage or about something on stage however, we always refer to stage left and stage right, even if you are sitting in the house.

You may understand the importance of always referring to the actor's point of view when giving directions or making reference to their left or their right, however you may be wondering which is down stage and which is up stage. Here is a history lesson that will help you remember.

In our day and age *usually* the stage is a flat horizontal surface and the seats in the house are set on an incline, or "raked". In Shakespearean times this was not the case. There were no seats in the middle of the house and those who could not afford the box/balcony positions that were around the edge of the house would stand on the house floor. However, because they were standing on a level surface it was hard for those in the back to see the actors on the stage. Therefore, stages in Shakespearian times were raked – sloped down towards the audience. So when an actor moved away from the audience he literally walked up hill, hence up stage being at the back of the stage, and when an actor moved towards the audience he literally walked down hill, hence down stage being at the front of the stage.

CHAPTER 2

YOUR STAGE LIGHTING SYSTEM

One discipline the majority of Drama teachers and non-theatre people know the least about is that of Stage Lighting. Most people have had some experience in sound; playing, recording, adjusting the treble and base, etc. Most people have had some experience in construction; for instance, as a child my father helped me build a swing, and in high school I took Art Metal Work. Of course, there's far more to theatrical sound and stagecraft than that, but these topics don't seem to instill the trepidation factor like lighting design does. Short of installing a dimmer switch in their home, most people have little practical experience about the theory and practice of stage lighting.

For this reason I am devoting a chapter to this subject. Following is a very brief overview of stage lighting theory. Reading this won't turn you into a Lighting Designer, but it is important to have some understanding of the complexities in order to make the right decisions about designing and managing your theatre, as well as teaching your students.

This chapter is just a general overview of theatre lighting. If you are an architect or educational facility planner reading this book and you want a more in depth study of stage lighting, please look for my upcoming (or perhaps by the time you're reading this, my already published) book "*Stage Lighting for Architects*". Educators will benefit from this book as well. To be notified when this book comes out, please send your e-mail address to info@RCDTheatreOps.com.

REP PLOT

When I first arrived at one theatre I worked at, one performing arts teacher complained to me that another performing arts teacher was always leaving the lighting system set up one way, and that teacher complained to me that the other teacher was always leaving the lighting system set up another way. The third performing arts teacher stayed out of the fray because she didn't know how to operate the lighting system at all and would rely on the others to set it up and run it for her.

Although every event that comes into a theatre is unique, there are some general systems you can have in place. There is a way to provide a lighting system that can easily be applied to many uses of the space with only small adjustments that need to be made for specific requirements of a show or event. This is called a Rep Plot (short for Repertory Plot).

A Rep Plot is a standardized lighting system, which is versatile for almost all performances, from plays and musicals, to concerts and ballets, to speakers and videos, and allows for show-specific flexibility within a reasonable time frame. If your budget allows, be sure your rep plot is as extensive as possible, if not, choose as best you can from this list:

The Rand Rep Plot Model

Area lights – for 8' acting areas
One back light per area
One top light per area
Down washes – 3 colors
Front washes – 3 colors
Side washes – 3 colors
Break-up gobo patterns – from side and/or front
A center special
Cyc lights
Cyc grazing gobos
Cyc gobos – 3 across

Before you can hang and focus a functional Rep Plot, and provide all users with documents that give them an at-a-glance overview of the Rep Plot for quick reference and easy use, you need to have a basis understanding of stage lighting theory and what all these words mean.

MCCANDLESS

IN 1932 Stanley McCandless published a book titled "A Method of Lighting the Stage". Notice he didn't say "*the*", but just "*a*". However for many decades this has actually been "*the*" standard method taught in schools and used in the industry. These days we also have Broadway Lighting and other methods, but the McCandless Method is still "*the*" best starting point for learning about stage lighting. I recommend getting yourself a copy of this book if you can (it's out of print, but you can still find copies from the link on the Books page at www.RCDTheatreOps.com).

Stanley McCandless taught many of the early greats of stage lighting, including Jean Rosenthal (also recommended reading found on the Books page, her book: "The Magic of Light"). My university stage lighting professor, Tom Ruzika, had the opportunity to meet and be inspired by an encounter with Jean Rosenthal early on in his prolific stage and architectural lighting career (www.ruzika.com). So I consider Stanley McCandless to be my Great-Lighting-Grandfather.

McCandless determined that there are four properties of light that can be manipulated to create mood and location, or to draw the audience's attention. The Four Properties of Light are:

Intensity – how bright the light is.

Color – rudimentary examples include blue or lavender for nighttime, green for a forest.

Distribution – the angle the light comes from, and also whether the focus is diffused or sharp.

Movement – this originally referred to "cuing", which is when the intensity changes either up or down, or the other three properties change from one look to another. This has also begun to refer to actual movement, because "recently" (meaning the past three decades) we now have actual moving lights.

In order to achieve optimal manipulation of these four properties McCandless developed a layout we call the Light Plot. A Light Plot can be designed from scratch for a specific show, or a Rep Plot can be designed to accommodate multiple types of events. A Lighting Plot that is re-designed over and over again is more suited to the university level, where all the students are learning lighting as a vocational choice, and where it is necessary to learn "from scratch". In the high school theatre setting, there is usually very little time - or money - to completely re-design (and re-hang, re-focus, and re-cue) a Light Plot from scratch for each event, so a Rep Plot makes much more sense as it can be easily adjusted to provide lighting for any event from class meetings, speeches, variety shows, band and choir concerts to plays, musicals and dance recitals.

Following is a very basic diagram and explanation of the McCandless layout.

AREA LIGHTING

Stanley McCandless developed a method of evenly lighting the acting area of the stage.

Divide the stage into roughly 8' circular acting areas. Number them from SL to SR, DS to US.

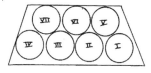

Ideally each area should have two front lights at a 45° angle vertically and in plan. (Not all pipe positions will allow for this precise angle.)

The lights from one side should be a warm colour (pink or amber) and the other a cool color (usually blue), this reproduces the natural effect of sunlight and shadow on the face.

If you are in on the planning stages of a high school theatre, be sure not to layout where circuits go and then hang the lights as the circuits allow – instead layout a light plot and then decide where the circuits need to go based on your light plot, in order to achieve an optimal lighting system. I can't count the number of high school theatres I've been in which don't have enough circuits in the correct positions in order to achieve the versatile rep plot required.

It's very important to have an understanding of a rep plot so that you also know what instruments to provide in your specs. One high school that hired me to design their rep plot in their Black Box theatre had been provided a lighting packet from a local lighting supplier that had no thought as to the functions that the lights would be needed for. For instance, they were supplied with 18 26-degree ellipsoidals. Presumably the designer was thinking that these could be used for the area lights. That would be true in a main stage theatre, but the pipes in a Black Box theatre are comparatively low, so a 26-degree instrument has too narrow a beam spread. It would have been better if they'd provided a combination of 36 and 50-degree instruments. As it was, we had to limit the function of the theatre because there were not enough instruments of the correct beam spread to do anything more than create a proscenium stage in the space.

THE USE OF LIGHTING

So, why do you need to know all this, what is lighting actually used for? Lighting is used for three primary purposes; lighting the actors, lighting the set, and effect (setting mood, location, etc). Following are some tips for each purpose.

LIGHTING THE ACTORS

AREA LIGHTING - Actors or dancers should be lit from two lights from the front at 45 degrees. One side is a cool (bluish) light and the other is a warm (pinkish) light. This mimics the psychological impression of shadow on one side of the face.

DOWN LIGHTING - ideally each acting area should have it's own down light. This provides a 3-D effect to the head.

BACK LIGHTING - ideally each acting area should also have it's own back light. This gives a halo effect, and defines the head and shoulders, making the performer "pop" out from the background..

"SHIN BUSTERS" - mounted on free standing light trees on the sides of the stage deck. Usually for dance lighting. Defines the whole body.

LIGHTING THE SET

When lighting a set, take these items into consideration.

BACKDROPS – give these their own washes to avoid lines from stray instruments.

CURTAINS - usually not lit other than from spill light from area lighting.

CYCLORAMA OR "CYC" - solid flat back drop, can be flat along the back of the stage or encircle the stage, hence the name "cyclorama". Usually white. Lit from the front at a steep angle, from instruments from the pipe above, and/or from floor mounted instruments.

SCRIM – a see-through mesh back drop. Can be white or black. Lit from the same direction as a cyc. If lit from the front appears as solid wall. If lit from the back, it's see through.

SPECIALS - fireplaces, doorways, etc. Usually lit from hidden fixtures in or behind the set, gelled appropriate colors. Eg: a fireplace would be lit from one or more small instruments, gelled with reds and oranges, a doorway would be back lit from above, with the appropriate color gel, depending on whether the door led to another room or to the outside.

VARYING LEVELS - most sets will have different levels that the actors use. In general,
each level should be treated as its own acting area and lit accordingly.

EFFECT LIGHTING

Actors should be enhanced with more than area lights. Ideally two or three color washes should be available, and each area should have a down and/or back light. Other effects are also useful.

FRONT WASH - this is generally from several instruments hung from the house that are aimed from straight on. By itself a wash is very "flat" and does not pick out the features of the face. Best used in conjunction with area lighting for washing the stage with color, for example: for suggesting night time (dark blue). Ideally two or three color washes should be available in your rep plot.

HIGH SIDES - this can be used for molding or color effects. And can, for instance, suggest a sunrise.

GOBOS - Thin metal patterned templates that can be slipped into ellipsoidal instruments. These pattern the stage, such as a dappled leaf effect on the floor and actors, a moon on a back drop or perhaps light coming through a window.

CHANNEL SCHEDULE

In order to keep all of this information straight, Lighting Designers create a Channel Schedule, or as it's more frequently called the Cheat Sheet or Magic Sheet. This is an example of a Cheat Sheet. Note that all of the standard positions are set, and that an area is available in which to record your Specials. Specials customize your Rep Plot into a unique design for each event.

SAMPLE REP PLOT CHEAT SHEET

AREAS

16	17	18	19	20
11	12	13	14	15
6	7	8	9	10
1	2	3	4	5

DOWNS

4TH E WARM		80	81	82
3RD E	WARM	77	78	79
2ND E	COOL	24	25	26
	WARM	74	75	76
1ST E	COOL	21	22	23
	WARM	71	72	73

FRONT WASH

	SR	SL
(W1)BLUE	32	33
(W2)AMBER	30	31

(Amber & Blue = Magenta)

CYC SUBS

(Turn on electric non-dim!)

R	S12
G	S13
B	S14
A	S15

MISC

	SR	SL
FILL WASH	34	35
GOBOS	36	37

LADDERS

		SR		SL	
4					
	TOP	44		49	
	MID	54		59	
	LOW	64		69	
3					
	TOP	43		48	
	MID	53		58	
	LOW	63		68	
2					
	TOP	42		47	
	MID	52		57	
	LOW	62		67	
1					
	TOP	41		46	
	MID	51		56	
	LOW	61		66	
GAL					
	TOP	40	Grn	45	Blu
	MID	50	Mag	55	Pnk
	LOW	60	Lav	65	Amb

SPECIALS

	SR	SL
CURTAIN GOBO		85
CYC GOBO	86	87
BREAK-UPS	36	37

INSTRUMENTS

There are many types of instruments that are used in stage lighting. This is really beyond the scope of this book but I will explain the three most popular types and their uses, as these are handy to have a sense of. They are:

ELLISPOIDAL/LEKO/"SOURCE FOUR"

These terms are used interchangeably. "Source Four" however, is actually a brand name, but these days it has become common for some people use it to describe this specific instrument. You can tell a person's age by whether which term they use.

An ellipsoidal has, as its name suggests, an ellipsoidal shaped reflector with two focal points (yes – tech theatre does use math), plus two plano-convex lenses (flat on one side, rounded on the other side), along with a sliding barrel that allows the light beam to be focused with a hard edge (technically called a 'hard focus') and a soft/diffuse edge (technically called 'fuzzy-wuzzy'). Because this instrument can be focused it can also house a metal or glass pattern that can be projected onto the stage. By substituting different barrels which have their lenses positioned differently, you can also change the angle of the light spread. The most common angles ellipsoidals come in is 19, 26, 36 and 50 degrees. There are wider and narrower available too. Ellipsoidals also have built in shutters that allow you to further control the light – for instance, if you just wanted to light a doorway you could shutter off all four sides so that no light spilled on the surrounding walls. Ellipsoidals are usually used for area lighting, sometimes for washes and for specials.

FRESNEL

Loosely pronounced "fre-nel". You may have heard this term in connection with lighthouses. This instrument has the same fresnel lens that lighthouses do. This lens is 'stepped' and can therefore create an almost parallel beam of light – as used in lighthouses, and also in those annoying traffic lights that you can only see once you pull into that lane. In theatre though the lens is usually formed to create a nice evenly flooded spread of light. By moving the reflector and lamp closer or further away from the lens you can "flood" or "spot" the light spread. Unlike the ellipsoidal where you have to replace the barrel in order to change the beam angle, the fresnel has the capability to change the beam angle within the instrument. However, you give up the hard focus that the ellipsoidal allows. Fresnels are mostly used for washes and specials.

PAR

P.A.R. stands for 'parabolic aluminized reflector'. A PAR has a reflector that is usually made of aluminum and is in the shape of a parabola. A PAR gives a fairly parallel beam, which can be adjusted by the use of different lenses. Also, because of the lens patterns, the light beam of a PAR is oval, not circular. This allows you to better control where the light goes, from an instrument that isn't focusable. PARs are usually used as washes, sides and specials.

There are many other types of instruments including par-nels, cyc lights, scoops, strips, multi-pars, and a variety of LED instruments.

A LAMP, BY ANY OTHER NAME

There is one big faux pas in the theatrical lighting world. And that is: calling a lamp a "light bulb". The correct term – also in the architectural lighting world – is "lamp". The "bulb" is just the glass part. A "lamp" consists of the bulb, the gas, the element and the base.

FIXTURES VS INSTRUMENTS

Another term that is often incorrectly used in the theatre is "fixtures" when intending to refer to "instruments". The term fixtures is commonly used in architectural lighting, whether you are an architect or a homeowner. In the theatre we use the term instruments. Fixtures are *fixed* or installed and usually cannot be moved. Instruments on the other hand can be hung, focused, taken down, moved and hung again. In a theatre the work lights and house lights can be considered fixtures, while the production lights are considered instruments.

THE LIGHT BOARD

If you are considering purchasing a new light board, or if you are designing a theatre, you will be faced with the decision of what board to choose. You don't want to be in a situation such as the example in the introduction where the light board is too high tech to be of any practical use in a high school theatre. For instance, if you don't foresee purchasing $2000.00 moving lights for your high school theatre, and having a professional career training program for a student lighting crew, then there is no need to have a light board sophisticated enough to control moving lights. Leave that for when the vocational student gets to university or starts an apprenticeship.

Another thing to avoid is a small light board has a multitude of functions. Some of these compact boards have so many functions that they've had to get very creative in how to access each function that it makes it too difficult for students to learn and retain how a basic board works. Be careful that the light board that you spec or purchase doesn't have too many steps/modes to go through just to perform simple functions such as patching, recording, play back, etc.

Some light board these days don't have faders for channels and rely only on key pad entry. The choice of whether to go with one of these boards depends on the uses of your theatre and who the users will be. I personally find key pad entry too slow. When I'm designing lights I talk pretty fast and I want my light board operator to keep up. I grit my teeth when I say "Bring channel 46 to 80 percent" and I have to wait to hear tap (Channel), tap (4), tap (6), tap (@), tap (8), tap (0), tap (Enter/*), when the light board op could have just reached over an in one movement moved a fader to 80. Of course, these days kids are so used to completing tasks electronically instead of physically, and there can be reasons why you would want a key pad entry in a more sophisticated situation. Again, it boils down to planning ahead and questioning who are your users and what are the uses of your board. At least with a board with faders the operator has the option to use faders or the key pad, but with a board with only a key pad the operator does not have that option.

In addition, also watch out for light boards that don't use standard industry nomenclature, such as "Cues" and "Subs", for instance. Students don't learn the common terms that are used in the rest of the live theatre industry, and those who already know the common terms will have to re-learn a set of new terms.

Again, state-of-the-art is not always the best choice for a high school theatre. When deciding on a light board remember to ask yourself these questions:

- Will the theatre be primarily used by students who come and go every few years?

- Will there be vocational training for students?

- How many students a year will want to learn to be lighting technicians?

- Will the theatre be staffed by professional technicians?
- Will the technicians run the theatre, and/or work with the students?

- Will the theatre be rented to outside users?

- Who will staff outside events, professional staff or students?

- Will outside users expected to be able to run their own lights?

- Will outside users be permitted to use the theatre's equipment unsupervised?

- Who will restore the equipment each time in preparation for the next user?

There is a school of thought that high school students should have the best technology available because they will soon go to a college or get a job where this technology is used and they will have a head start. However, in a high school setting, usually the need to have an easy to learn light board trumps the need to have the best technology.

This is primarily because most high school theatre departments have students who come and go. If you're lucky you will have a freshman come in with a keen interest in lighting and stay for four years. But what usually happens is that either students come in expressing an interest and soon discover it's not for them, or a student who is passionate has always thought the Drama program was only for actors, and only discovers tech in his/her junior or senior year.

In addition, most typical Drama teachers don't know much tech. They take one look at the light board and leave it up to a student to figure out. Regardless of what light board you have it's best to hire professional technicians who will be there to mentor the students, which allows the Drama teacher to get on and do what they do best which is teaching acting, and directing students.

LIGHT BOARD PLACEMENT

In the Sound chapter I address why you should never put a sound board in the booth, but in the case of a light board, it can go in the booth.

The reason a light board can go in the booth is because typically the Lighting Designer will sit in the house so that she can see what the audience sees when she is choosing light levels and setting cues. She relays the light levels and cue timing over a headset to the light board operator who records them on the board in the booth. Unlike a sound board operator who is constantly having to adjust the sound levels and quality during a production, the light board operator has all the cues pre-programmed and only needs to push the Go button when the Stage Manager says "Go". Since the Stage Manager and light board operator are typically in the booth during shows, the audience doesn't hear them.

During smaller events where the light board operator acts as the Lighting Designer, her line of vision is not interrupted from the booth to the stage, like a sound board operator's hearing is affected, so she can design from the board. However, this isn't the ideal situation because the light board operator isn't seeing what the audience sees, so whenever possible a Lighting Designer and light board operator should work in tandem.

The other solution is to bring the light board into the house. Your theatre should have a second location where the light board can be plugged in at the center of the house. This is so that a light board operator can design and/or operate the lights while seeing what most of the audience sees. It's also convenient and less time consuming when there is both a Lighting Designer and a light board operator, so that the Lighting Designer can just glance at the light board when she needs some information and then can directly give the light board operator her instructions.

CHAPTER 3

WORK LIGHTS

A whole (albeit short) chapter must be devoted to work lights. Work lights are often over used or under used in high school theatres.

There are two basic types of lighting systems in the theatre; production lights and work lights.

Production lights are the ellipsoidals/lekos, fresnels, PARs etc, which are used to light everything from a principal addressing students to a full musical production. This is the light that enables audiences to see performers and presenters. These lights have lamps that have a relatively short lamp life and can cost at least $15 each to replace, some much more. Most of these lamps consume 500 to 1,000 watts of power each, and so are expensive to run. They cause a lot of heat and so increase HVAC costs. In addition these lamps are almost never used without a color filter, or "gel". Gels burn out fairly regularly (meaning their color fades, or a hole is literally burned in the middle of the material), so there is the expense of replacing gels too. For these reasons, production lights must be "saved" (turned off whenever they are not in use) in order to get the best use out of them for the least amount of money. Any person who is in charge of a theatre budget will attest to the importance of "saving the lights" when not in use.

What the audience doesn't see is the times when the work lights are in use. The purpose of work lights, as you can guess, is to light work. Work set building, work hanging production lights, work rehearsing, work doing rigging, work choreographing. These lights, while needing to be bright enough for the work being done, do not need to create mood and location. They are purely for functional reasons.

Work lights usually house one of four main types of light bulbs - called "lamps" in the industry.

> Incandescent – like your standard household lamp. The favorite to our eye, because historically and psychologically we are used to a 'black burning body' as a light source (think cavemen sitting around a fire at night and in the sunshine during the day).

> Fluorescent – better efficacy (more light for the amount of power being used) than incandescents. Awful color, but they last longer than incandescents, and are therefore cheaper to run.

<u>HID</u> – High Intensity Discharge – far better efficacy than either of the above, and they last longer, but they can take ten to twenty minutes to warm up, and hence are not very practical. They also make people look like they're not feeling too well.

<u>LED</u> – Light Emitting Diodes – fast becoming the industry standard for work lights, due to the fact that their efficacy is so good; they don't need replacing very often, and they can instantly be switched on and off.

THE TROUBLE IS...

The trouble is, that many a high school theatre is ill equipped with work lights. In many older theatres they may have been added as an after thought, or sometimes not at all. For this reason, teachers or others working in the theatre will turn on the whole production lighting system in order to light their classes, rehearsals and set building sessions. In one theatre I worked at I figured this amount to equal about 44,000 watts of power being used. In another theatre with a more extensive production lighting system, with no theatre management to stop them from turning on every single production light when working in the theatre, I calculated that they were using about 120,000 watts of power!

In many newer theatres the situation isn't much better. In another theatre I worked at, which had the misfortune to be built in 2008 during the recession, because of budget cuts at the time of installation, work lights were eliminated from the equipment order all together. There were fluorescent overheads installed 40' up at the grid, but these were too far away to be of much use, and no one wanted to use them too much because it would be very difficult to replace the lamps once they burned out. Therefore the classes, rehearsals and set builders turned on most of the production lights in order to be able to see well enough to work in the space. I hate to think how much has been spent in power over the years, just in order to save a bit of money on an initial purchase of necessary equipment.

If you are designing a theatre or managing a theatre that needs to install new work lights you will be able to compare initial costs with running costs and figure out what is the best choice of equipment. I personally prefer LEDs. They can be more expensive per fixture, but the long term financial and functional benefits far outweigh the initial costs.

WHY LED WORK LIGHTS?

Most of the technical theatre people that I've worked with vastly prefer that LED fixtures be used for work lights. The primary reason is that they turn on and off instantly, with no warm up time. Also, if they are installed on the electrics then they are easy to get to should the lamps need replacing. Incandescent and fluorescent fixtures would also be great work lights because they can turn on and off instantly, however they have such a short lamp life that financially they are impractical to use for something that is going to be on most of the time. HID fixtures have a very long lamp life and therefore one would think would be the most practical to use for work lights, but they also have such a long warm up time (and an even longer warm up time if you turn them off and suddenly realize you need to turn them on again) that they are very impractical in a theatre situation. As happened in one theatre I worked at, the warm up time was too long, so people would get impatient and turn on the production lights, which only has the effect of increasing the budget – something one was trying to avoid by installing HIDs in the first place.

WORK LIGHTS POLICY

No matter what situation you have at your high school theatre, you should develop a policy for the use of the work lights and production lights. Here is a sample policy I wrote for a high school that had HID lights on the electrics and above the apron of the stage, fluorescent lights on the grid, and a limited amount of production lights programmed into an auto control to provide a few basic production functions.

SAMPLE PRODUCTION LIGHTS AND WORK LIGHTS USE POLICY

All rehearsals and classes and set building should be conducted with work lights only.

There are work lights on all the electrics and on the apron. These are to be used for anything other than actual tech rehearsals or performances. These have a warm up time, but they are plenty bright once they've warmed up.

The lights marked "Stage Overheads" should be used as little as possible.

These are the fluorescents up above the cables for the fly system. Because these will be difficult to re-lamp, only use these in the case of an emergency when you need light instantly.

For productions requiring only a neutral stage wash and no cuing, use the auto preset faders on the SM Panel.

The preset panel has certain "looks" recorded, and the faders are labeled as such. These are sufficient for school-day assemblies, etc.

If you feel there is a need to turn on the light board for any reason, please contact the Theatre Manager ahead of time, and a lighting technician can be scheduled for your show if it is deemed necessary. Please do not use the light board without a technician supervising. (In the past, light cues for a large production (that took several days to set, involving many people) were almost deleted by two students who were unattended and were trying to re-record cues for a school day event.)

When vacating the theatre, please turn out all lights except for the Night Light.

CHAPTER 4

SOUND AND A/V

Unlike lighting cues that audiences may not always consciously notice, if something goes wrong with the sound it is often very noticeable. It's always preferable to consult professional theatrical sound technicians when designing a high school theatre and it's always preferable to hire professional theatrical sound technicians when managing a high school theatre. In the long run it's the most cost effective decision and it's the best educational decision.

During a school musical at one of the theatres I worked at there were all sorts of issues with the sound for a couple of performances. There was feedback, crackling, and times when you couldn't hear the actors well enough. In addition, at that theatre the headset mics that had been provided when it was built had rather bulbous windscreens (the foam piece that goes over the end of the mic so that the 'wind' from an actor breathing is muted), and the mics were worn at a position on the cheek, such that when an actor turned sideways their noses looked like Pinocchio's! Several of the parents watching the performance those nights were so upset by this visual in general, and with the feedback, static, and intermittent lack of volume that they told the Drama teacher that they wanted to fundraise the money to purchase new headset mics and receivers.

However, it was not the mics that were the problem (other than the 'Pinocchio Effect') – for on those two nights the professional sound technician was unable to be there, so the student sound crew ran the show. While student crews are capable of following their cues in a professional manner (and this particular student sound board operator was particularly good), when something comes along that needs trouble-shooting they don't have the experience and background knowledge to know how to trouble-shoot on the spot. In these situations professional supervision is the fix, not expensive new equipment. It's all about the mix.

Plus, the issue of the bulbous windscreens and the preference to have ones that have a lower profile and are less inconspicuous, is really a visual issue, not one of sound quality, and could be remedied by just purchasing the actual mics, not spending money on new receivers or a whole new sound system.

Because sound issues are something that most audience members are most familiar with and easily recognize, it's important to have good sound equipment in your theatre. It is also important to have a sound technician who is not only knowledgeable about how to run the equipment and how to teach your students how to run it, but is experienced in the theatrical process. Audience members who may not bat an eyelid when watching a show with bad lighting, would not tolerate having to sit through a play with a bad sound system or a good sound system that is badly run. If you are deciding on purchasing sound equipment, consult a sound technician who can help you plan ahead for the variety of events the equipment will need to be used for. It's no good having good sound for a soloist in a jazz band, if the next night the choir can't be heard.

SOUND BOARD

If you are considering purchasing a new sound board, or if you are designing a theatre, you will be faced with the decision of whether to choose an analog board or a digital board. When I said you should supply "good" sound equipment, I don't necessarily mean "high-end state-of-the-art" equipment. In the desire to be as state-of-the-art as possible in high schools these days many people will automatically spec a digital board. However, as with a light board, consider who will be using your equipment before you decide on an analog or digital sound board. State-of-the-art is not always optimal in a high school setting. Apply the same considerations to choosing a sound board as you would to choosing a light board.

- Will the theatre be primarily used by students who come and go every few years?

- Will there be vocational training for students?

- How many students a year will want to learn to be sound technicians?

- Will the theatre be staffed by professional technicians?

- Will the technicians run the theatre, and/or work with the students?

- Will the theatre be rented to outside users?

- Who will staff outside events, professional staff or students?

- Will outside users expected to be able to run their own sound?

- Will outside users be permitted to use the theatre's equipment unsupervised?

- Who will restore the equipment each time in preparation for the next user?

The answers to all of these questions will determine if you want an analog sound board or a digital sound board. I personally consider an analog sound board far better for a high school situation. There is a school of thought that high schoolers should have the best technology available because they will soon go to a college or get a job where this technology is used and they will have a head start. However, in a high school setting, the need to have an easy to learn and use board trumps the need to have the best technology.

Again, you have students who come and go. If you're lucky you will have a freshman come in with a keen interest in sound and stay for four years. But, as with lighting, what usually happens is that either students come in expressing an interest in sound and soon discover it's not for them, or a student who is passionate about sound has always thought the Drama program was only for actors, and only discovers tech in his/her junior or senior year.

If you have a digital board, it's much like using a computer. Consider your Word program. If you want to find a file, you open the program and then open a folder, and perhaps open a folder within that folder, and then open the file. Digital boards are somewhat like that. The process for making adjustments to the sound quality is not all laid out visually in front of you like it is on analog boards. With a digital board, you have to learn and retain in your mind a myriad of sequences. An analog board may appear more complicated to the eye with all those buttons and knobs, but it's actually quicker to learn, and the sound is directly responsive to your actions – you need only turn one knob, not have to go through a multi-step process.

One good feature of digital boards is that a sound technician can create all the settings she prefers and save the settings, then another sound technician can come along and save all his settings. Sort of like saving your settings for a drivers seat in a fancy car. This may sound ideal on the surface, but without collaboration between everyone who uses the board, it's very easy for someone to delete another person's saved settings in favor of their own. This happened all too often in one theatre I worked at, and each technician would arrive expecting to quickly set up for a show, using his saved settings, only to find they had all been deleted. That technician then had to delay the show's set up in order to re-set all their settings.

Again most Drama teachers will take one look at the sound board and leave it up to a student to figure out. A digital board is even harder for a non-tech oriented person to figure out, as it is not visibly obvious what one is meant to do. Regardless of whether you have an analog or digital sound board, it's best to hire professional sound technicians who will be there to mentor the students, and create a set of processes, which allows the Drama teacher to get on and do what they do best which is teaching acting and directing students.

SOUND BOARD LOCATION

I can't count the number of theatres I've worked at where the sound board has been installed in the booth. At one theatre we turned the sound board around on the counter so that the sound technician could sit outside the booth window and reach his arm in to adjust the levels. At three theatres I've worked at we managed to get the sound board moved into the house. Why should the sound board not be in the booth? Because the sound technician needs to hear what the audience hears. They can't set sound levels in they are sitting in a closet. Sound boards in booths are suited to sound recording, but not to a live performance.

There are schools of thought about where the optimal placement is for a sound board in a house. Some sound technicians prefer the sound board to be at top of the house just in front of the booth windows, and some technicians prefer the sound board to be in the center of the house. Regardless, the point is that the sound board should not be in the booth. And, regardless of the placement of the sound board, the space should be calibrated by a theatre sound professional so that all audience members receive the same quality of sound.

MICROPHONES

As with sound boards, consider who will be using the microphones ("mics") and for what purposes, before purchasing new equipment for your existing theatre or spec'ing equipment for a new theatre. Check with the Band teacher – how many solo instrument mics will she want for her jazz band. Check with the Choir teacher – how many vocal mics will he need at maximum. Check with the Drama teacher – what would be the expected amount of actors who will need headset mics in a musical? Check with the school's principal and/or activities director – how many handheld wireless mics would they like to have for assemblies and class meetings? How many wired mics on stands do they think they will need? For what purposes? For the wired mics, where will they plug into and where will the stands be set?

TYPES OF MICS

There are many types of mics, but here's the most common ones found in a high school theatre:

Vocal mics.

Instrument mics.

Choir mics or condenser mics.

Wireless handheld mics.

Headset mics.

Mics are categorized by their "polar pattern". In other words the direction from which they pick up sound.

Some mics, such as a speaking mic are uni-directional and only pick up the sound if you are speaking right down the middle of the mic – they "reject" the sound coming from other directions. You've probably experience this when listing to a speaker who keeps waving their mic around as they talk; their voice cuts in and out. Some mics are bi-directional or omni-directional and pick up the sound coming at it from two or more directions, although they can cause more feedback than uni-directional mics because the sound pattern is not contained.

There are some mics on the market now where you can alter the polar pattern from a control box placed by your sound board. These offer a lot of versatility and are worth considering.

Knowing which mics to choose for your theatre requires an understanding of what mic is needed for what purpose. A lot of sound consultants – particularly those who primarily specialize in places of worship or home theatres – will provide you with a sound package that has a variety of mics. The teachers and theatre technicians are then in the position of trying to make do with what they have. This is backwards. When spec'ing a new mic package for your high school theatre, think ahead to what uses the mics will be needed for and how many people or instruments will need to be mic'd in any given event. Considering the potential purpose for each mic before deciding on the mic package is the right way to go.

MIC CABLES

Likewise, consider ahead of a purchase how many cables and in what lengths you will need. In one new theatre I worked in only 50' and 100' mics cables had been provided. I suppose the sound consultant thought this would be the most versatile mix. But, the stage width was only 40' and there were four sound outlet floor pockets spread across the stage. We vary rarely needed anything longer than a 25', and mostly could have done with 15' mic cables. Providing cables that were too long cost the school district unnecessarily and also created tripping hazards on the stage.

HEADSET MICS VS LAPEL MICS

If you are purchasing headset mics for your actors – typically used in musicals – you may be wondering whether to purchase headset mics or lapel mics.

Lapel mics may seem like a good idea, but consider these drawbacks:

> With lapel mics if you turn your head from side to side it affects the sound volume as you turn away from the mic.

> Some costumes – particularly girls' costumes with thin straps or no straps – don't have anywhere to clip a lapel mic.

I prefer headset mics, but they also have their drawbacks:

> They are delicate and expensive. A headset and receiver can cost about $600.00. A headset can easily be bent and a receiver can easily be dropped. Students must be made aware of the cost and be trained in their proper usage. During a show a 'Mic Wrangler' (usually a student crew member) should be specifically assigned backstage to help actors put on and take off their mics.

> They hook over the ear and everyone has different size ears and heads, so the actual mic at the end of the "boom" – the part of the assembly that looks like a stick – may or may not be in the optimal place for the best sound quality.

> Even if they fit initially, headset mics don't always stay on right. They can get knocked when the actor moves or dances, or when two actors have to hug or kiss. The best solution for this is to purchase "mic tape" to tape the boom to the actor's cheek so that it doesn't move around. The easiest solution for mic tape is to purchase clear medical tape from a pharmacy or grocery store – it comes in a plastic dispenser much like the tape you have on your desk.

> They come with "windshields", which are little foam sleeves that fit over the actual mic part to prevent hearing breathing and movement (think: TV reporter standing in the wind). Windshields are only about 1cm or 2cm long. They fall off and are easily lost. The trouble is that, depending on the size, they cost $8 - $11 each. That can eat into your budget very quickly if you are using 16 headset mics for a musical. Be sure to make your actors aware of the cost of these little pieces of foam.

Boomless headset mics may be your best solution.

> Boomless mics are basically a somewhat stiff cable with a miniature mic on the end. This allows you to drape the mic over an actor's ear and tape it to the cheek in the correct position for that particular actor's head size and shape, and to take into account any head gear they may be wearing.

> Boomless mics can also be draped over the crown of the head and taped to the forehead if that is more functional for the situation.

HEADSET MIC COLORS

If you are spec'ing new equipment for a brand new theatre, or if you are purchasing new equipment for an existing theatre, but sure to specify tan colored headset mics. In one new theatre that I worked at the sound company supplying the mics had spec'd black mics. They'd assumed that because I'd been asking for black everything else in the theatre that we would want black mics.

Think about it what is the most common skin color in your area. Some shade of brown, from light to dark. Unless we are running a pop concert, headset mics should be unobtrusive as possible. Most people don't sit in their living room or walk down the street with a microphone attached to their heads, so it suspends belief for the audience if a Caucasian character's black headset mic is too obvious or the other way around. I of course asked them to change to the tan headset mics. This said, also have some black headset mics available for people with darker skin. Adjust your order for your particular area's demographics.

COMPRESSOR

Experiencing feedback a little too often? Consider adding a compressor if you don't have one. (If you do have one and you are still getting too much feedback, consider adding a professional sound technician.) A compressor keeps all sounds at a given maximum level. For instance if you have 14 actors on headsets and one has a booming voice, the loud voice would never allowed to go over a certain level. Or if a CD has a piece of music that has been recorded louder than the others a compressor regulates the level so that it sounds no louder than the other tracks. It evens out the playing field if you will, and helps prevent feedback caused by a sudden loud noise.

A compressor is particularly helpful when a sound technician is working with students who are just learning about sound and all its nuances. Students don't always know how to listen preventatively, and there's nothing worse than loud feedback ruining the most poignant moment of your musical.

AUTO SYSTEM

Chances are your high school theatre will not only be used for concerts, plays and other shows, but also for class meetings, assemblies and so on. Although I don't advocate anyone using a multi-million dollar state-of-the-art facility without theatre technicians running the equipment or supervising students who are running the equipment, there are times in reality when a high school theatre is treated like a classroom and a teacher or two are supervising a room full of hundreds of students.

In this case, it's best to have installed an "auto system" that can at least perform basic functions without the need to turn on the sound board. Those basic functions are:

Operate one or two wireless handheld mics.
Play a CD.
Show a DVD.
Play a slide presentation or video.

The auto wireless mics, CD, DVD and slide/video presentations are usually operated exactly the same as they are in any home or classroom.

Be sure to think about where you will need to operate these functions from. It's no good having to run up to the top of the house to put in a CD in a console when you are operating it from the stage for instance. At one theatre I worked in the plug-in for a laptop was center stage, upstage of where the projector screen came in. Who would stand behind a projector screen to give a presentation? Who would string a cable across the whole stage to where they wanted to stand? In this theatre we had to have another plug-in installed in the proscenium wall. An unnecessary expense for a school district, had it been thought out upon installation.

SOUND LEVEL SAFETY

A lot of people don't think about sound when they think about theatre safety. However sound safety is very important and because of this it is addressed separately in the Safety chapter.

A/V

Many users will come into a high school theatre for the purposes of showing a slide presentation, a video or movie. Or they may have this feature as a part of their event - for example, some dance companies will show a behind the scenes video during the half hour when the audience is entering the house.

Regardless of the purpose, users often bring their own laptop along with them. And more often than is desired, the picture they see on their laptop screen won't come out of the projector, and thus ensues a scramble to figure out why - a half hour before the house opens. Often times it's just a question of selecting the correct resolution or aspect ratio, but not always.

For this reason I recommend spec'ing or purchasing a dedicated laptop for your high school theatre. A dedicated laptop will always be set at the correct settings and all the user has to do is to supply the CD, DVD or thumb drive. Be sure to purchase a laptop that will play all formats of CD and DVD, because users will bring everything from store bought discs to discs that have been burned in all sorts of formats.

Along with your laptop, also be sure to provide a VGA cable – for the picture – and an 1/8" cable – for the sound. You should also provide a HDMI cable. Some theatres allow for a laptop plug in from the stage, as well as at the sound board. If this is the case, be sure the cables are long enough to reach from where they are plugged in to where a speaker is likely to be standing.

SOUND AND A/V REQUIREMENTS FOR USERS

Because there are a variety of formats that people use to create sound and video files, that may or may not be operational on your sound equipment, I recommend providing users with a requirement guide prior to their event. Following is a sample guide that I had the head sound technician at one theatre create. Depending on your equipment you should create a requirement list too – it saves a lot of hassle and frustration.

SAMPLE SOUND AND A/V REQUIREMENTS

Please provide all A/V files on the following formats:

SOUND

1. Audio CD

2. Data CD or flashdrive containing .wav files

3. Mp3 files, AAC files (These files are compressed and the sound quality may be compromised).

PLEASE NOTE:

We cannot convert audio from iPhone, iPod, Youtube or protected files such as m4p and some aac files.

VIDEO

We recommend playing any movie or video from a DVD

1. DVD-ROM

2. DVD-R

3. DVD+R

4. Blu-Ray

COMPUTER

1. Microsoft Office applications (Word, Excel, PowerPoint, etc.)

2. wmv file

3. Quicktime movie

4. PDF

If you provide your own computer, please bring a connector to convert your output to VGA.

PLEASE NOTE: *Our projector is not equipped to accept HDMI, Mini DVI, Composite, Component video.*

CHAPTER 5

HEADSETS

Communication headset systems get their own chapter because they are one of the most important systems in a theatre to make any event or production run smoothly. No matter the size of your theatre, if you don't have a headset system – get one. If you don't have enough - get more. If you only have wired - get some wireless as well.

Headsets are a vital element of a theatre design. Without headsets the crew cannot communicate to each other. For a substantial size show, the Stage Manager calls the show - this means that she tells every crew member when to take every cue. Each crew member knows *what* each of their jobs are at Cue 12, but the Stage Manager keeps an eye on the show and tells a crew on standby *when* Cue 12 happens. Without this system the success, and even the safety, of the show is compromised. During smaller one-time events where there is only one, or even no, prior rehearsal, and often no Stage Manager, it is imperative that the crew be able to communicate to each other in order to stay one step ahead in order to coordinate their jobs.

You will hear of two types of headsets spoken about around a theatre. One type belongs to the theatre's communication system that the crew uses, the other kind are mics that performers wear. Usually if you just hear the term "headset" we are talking about the communication system. Also, you will hear the whole arrangement, which includes the headset, beltpack and cables referred to as "the headset". Technically the beltpack carries the power and the headset itself is plugged into it, but we call the whole thing "the headset". When a Stage Manager tells her crew to "set up the headsets" she means to plug in or put in place the headsets, cables and beltpacks.

Headsets are a priority item. Try to get the best brand money can buy, but if you can't shift the budget to purchase even an inexpensive headset system, at least find some way so that the crew can communicate to each other. I've worked with walkie talkies, lately cell phones, even a baby monitor. Yes, it's true. In one theatre we did not have any headsets for the followspot operators up in the catwalks, so I brought in an old baby monitor that I had a home. We put the receiver (the end parents would have with them) by the followspot operators and I held the transmitter (the end that would go in the baby's room). That way I could talk to the followspot ops and relay cues to them and they could hear me. Of course they couldn't talk to me, but I could tell each time they received my commands by the correct adjustments made to the followspot light. Find something that works; the smooth operation of every show, not matter how small, depends on communication between your crew members.

HOW MANY HEADSETS JACKS AND WHERE?

How many headsets positions should you spec in a new theatre or how many headsets should you purchase for an existing theatre? It never ceases to amaze me that multi-million dollar, state-of-the-art high school theatres are provided with two to four jacks to plug in headsets and that's it, or the theatre is built with enough jacks, but is stocked with just a few headsets.

The very minimum I recommend is 8 jacks. Here are the locations where you should spec a headset jack:

1.   In the booth where the Stage Manager will sit to call a show.

2.   In the booth where the Light Board Operator will sit to run the light board.

3.   At the sound board (which you've put in the house because you've read this book).

4.   At the position where the first followspot is placed.

5.   At the position where the second followspot is placed. (Even if the followspots are together, each operator needs his or her own headset, or else one followspot will lag behind the other if "Go's" have to be relayed.)

6.   Stage right. This headset jack should be near the fly rail if it's on that side of the stage and should not be placed such that the technician wearing it will drape the cable across a doorway or the path of an entering or exiting actor. Plan ahead for where a crew member is likely to be standing, whether it's a rigger operating the fly rail or a Stage Manager who is calling the show from back stage. Or both.

7.   Stage left, or the side of the stage opposite the fly rail. Likewise with stage left, think about what the technician needs access to and whether the cable will be in the way of actors making entrances and exits, and stage crew moving set pieces.

8.   A jack in the floor at the center of the house where the Lighting Designer will sit to design the show. It's actually best to have two jacks at that position because the Stage Manager should be sitting at the tech table for the first few days of tech next to the Lighting Designer so that they can more easily confer on cues during the tech.

OTHER HEADSET POSITIONS TO CONSIDER

ORCHESTRA PIT

Does your theatre have an orchestra pit? If so, the Stage Manger will need to communicate with the Conductor. The Conductor will not wear the headset during the show, because he or she has to hear the music. But it is useful to be able to communicate with the pit in order to let the Conductor know when to start the overture or the entre-acte, when a cue comes up that needs special notification because the Conductor can't see what is going on, or in case of an emergency where the Conductor needs to talk to the Stage Manager or the reverse.

BOX OFFICE

The Stage Manager needs to communicate with the House Manager about when to start the show, because the Stage Manager must be in her place ten minutes before the show starts, making sure that the actors and crew are ready. If the Stage Manager cannot communicate with the House Manager, the Stage Manager may start the show when her crew and the actors are ready, but there may still be a line of audience members in the lobby still waiting to get into the house. It would be inconvenient, if not unsafe, to black out the house before all of the audience is seated. The House Manager needs to be able to inform the Stage Manager to hold the show if there are still audience members arriving.

DRESSING ROOMS/GREEN ROOM/WAITING ROOMS

It's not a good idea to let performers have access to the crew's communication system – too many cooks... But, for a large show, a Stage Manager may need to communicate with a crew member who has been placed backstage (when I say "backstage" in this case, I mean out of the stage space, not in the wings – the term is somewhat interchangeable and depends on the context of the situation).

SCENE SHOP AND COSTUME SHOP

Another reason it might be a good idea to have a headset backstage would be for a costumer to communicate to the Stage Manager in case there was a problem with a costume, which might require delaying the start of a show, or stalling a scene change. If the budget allows, it's also good to have the option for someone to plug in a headset in the scene shop, although that location is primarily used before the show has opened, not during the running of a show. Only in extenuating circumstances would set building – most likely a repair of some sort - be going on during a show. Some scene shops are used for set storage during a show.

EXTRA JACKS IN THE WINGS

Again, if the budget allows, place at least one extra headset jack on stage right and one extra on stage left. If you already have jacks down stage, consider placing extras up stage, or in the middle of the rail. That way two crew members aren't plugged in at the same place and daisy chained (see next section) together, and won't trip over each other's cables.

LOADING BRIDGE

The loading bridge isn't used during a show, but it is used for re-weighting when hanging lights or scenery. Do not install a headset jack up there. Use a wireless headset, and if a wireless headset is not available crew can shout to each other. Better to go hoarse than to trip over a cable and fall to your death.

DAISY-CHAINING

Most wired headset beltpacks have the capacity to plug one headset beltpack into another in a "daisy chain" configuration, sometimes called "piggy-backing". (If not, don't spec or purchase that brand of headsets, because this option offers a lot of versatility.) The beltpack has three holes. One is for the cable that is plugged into the wall jack, which provides the belt pack with its power and sound, and one for the cable that connects to the belt pack to the actual headset. The third hole is the same as a wall jack hole, and this is where you can plug in another cable that would go to yet another headset beltpack.

If your budget is tight, and you can't spec as many wired wall jacks as you would like to, consider situations in which daisy-chaining would work, whereby you could get away with one wall jack, not two. Daisy-chaining works best where the crew members don't have to move around. For instance, the Light Board Operator could daisy-chain off of the Stage Manager's beltpack if they are both sitting stationary, side by side in the booth. Although I don't thoroughly endorse it, one followspot operator could daisy-chain off of the beltpack of the other followspot operator if the followspots were next to each other. The danger of this would be having a cable strung across the catwalks or beams, which would be a tripping hazard. In addition, cues might be badly timed if one followspot operator has to relay a "Go" to the other followspot operator.

One place where daisy-chaining does not work is backstage. Crew members need to move around backstage and if one was daisy chained off even a crew member who was stationary (a Stage Manager for instance), if that mobile crew member were to walk out of cable-length range, or if someone were to trip over their cable, it could painfully yank the headsets off both of the crew members. Not only that, it could be at an inconvenient time – or potentially critical time in terms of safety – just as the Stage Manager was calling a cue or as a stationary crew member was about to execute a cue. Not to mention the cost of damaging any equipment. Plus, it could cause injury to the person tripping over the cable.

WIRED VS. WIRELESS

There are two ways headsets are powered. One way is by DC, which is batteries (rechargeables save a lot of money – you can spend hundreds of dollars a year on headset batteries - so be sure to include rechargables in your spec's or purchases). The other is by AC, which is plugged into the theatre's hardwired system by way of a cable. Both wireless and wired headsets have their benefits and you should spec some of each.

WIRED

Wired headsets don't eat up batteries, and are best for people who don't have to walk around. For instance, the light board and sound board operators don't usually have to leave their positions during a show, nor do the followspot operators, because boards and followspots are not portable. (Although, that said, even board operators occasionally have to get up from their post to attend to something that might be happening ten feet away. With a wired headset they would then would have to temporarily 'go off headset' and might miss a cue being called.)

WIRELESS

Wireless headsets are best for crew who need to move around, such as a fly system operator. They may have to fly out a drop on Lineset 6 and then rush to fly in a drop at Lineset 20. The fly rail area can be a dangerous place (see The Counterweight System chapter), and although there may be policies that any actor waiting in the wings should stay away from the fly rail, it's not always possible because of space considerations. Imagine what would happen if the crew member on a headset attached to the wall with a 20' wire were to have to move between actors and other crew standing in the wings. The cable would be a big tripping hazard.

Another person who has to move around backstage is a Mic Wrangler. This is the person who is in charge of placing mics on actors who might be sharing them, and is in charge of replacing dead batteries if they occur during a show.

Likewise for the House Manager who has to move around the lobby, in and out of audience members, concession sellers, and the box office. A cable would be very impractical.

WHO GETS WHICH

From our original list of positions, here's who should have what headset capability.

Stage Manager
> The Stage Manager should have both options; a wired headset in the booth if they are calling the show from the booth and a wireless headset to wear if they are calling the show from backstage.

Light Board Operator
> The Light Board operator can make do with a wired headset most of the time, but a wireless headset would be optimal.

Sound Board Operator
> The Sound Board operator (located in the house, because you've read this book) can make do with a wired headset most of the time, but a wireless headset would be optimal.

Followspot Operators
> Followspot operators rarely have to move from their positions, because they are usually located in the beams or catwalks or another position away from distractions. So they can have wired headsets. Ideally, though, they should each be able to plug into their own jacks, even if they are standing next to each other. The headset wires should be carefully located and taped down so that there is no tripping hazard.

Flyman/Fly Rail Side of the Stage
> Wireless.

Stage Right or Left – the other side of the stage from the fly rail
> Get out your crystal ball and decide if the person standing back stage will be issuing orders from where they stand, or whether they will need to move around for set changes, etc. A wired headset is better than no headset, but a wireless headset would be the best choice for flexibility in a variety of show situations.

Center of House – tech table position
> These – at least two jacks are optimal – can be wired. If someone needs to go off headset while at the tech table during a rehearsal, that's ok. It's not likely that anyone would be sitting at a tech table in the house during a show, when leaving a headset could jeopardize the show.

This all said, if you have the choice, there's almost no point in the design, labor and material costs involved in installing a wired system, as it's so restrictive. It's optimal for everyone to be able to move around with a wireless headset.

BATTERIES

And, that said, if you do go with wireless, remember to supply rechargeable batteries and chargers, because you can spend a mint on batteries if not. Be sure to purchase the chargers at the same time as you purchase the headsets. At one theatre I worked at wireless headsets were purchased as a part of an upgrade, but chargers were not purchased. When I later inquired about purchasing the chargers, I was informed that the model of headset and their chargers had gone out of production. Hmm. Probably why the school district was able to get a deal? The chargers would have plugged straight into the side of the beltpack. Consequently, every time we had to replace batteries – I did at least purchase some generic chargers and rechargeable batteries – we had to open the back of the beltpack (a fiddly operation at best, which required a paper clip or penny), remove the "sled", remove the six(!) AA batteries, replace the six(!) AA batteries... Well, you get the idea – a multi part operation rather than a one part operation.

SINGLE CHANNEL VS. DOUBLE CHANNEL

One school of thought is to have two channel capacity. The concept is so that the lighting and sound designers and their board operators can talk together in order to set the cues during tech rehearsals on one channel, and so that the set crew can all converse about the set changes on the other channel, without disrupting each other, while the Stage Manager can hear both channels because it's their job to coordinate these two groups of people and write all the cues in their prompt book or script.   On the surface this seems to make sense, until reality hits and what happens is that the lighting and sound people who can't hear what the set crew are saying start talking to the SM at the same time that the set crew who can't hear that the lighting and sound people are talking start talking to the SM. Instead of being in control of the conversation and situation, the SM is hit from both sides. In addition, sometimes something the lighting and sound crew say, affect the decisions of the set crew, and visa versa. Many problems can be nipped in the bud by collaboration over the headset.

I personally prefer just to have one channel in use. If two conversations or commands need to go on at the same time, I've found that experienced crews get used to this, each person just tunes into the voice of the person that they need to be listening too. I've worked like that many a time and it works just fine if everyone cooperates.

SINGLE MUFF VS. DOUBLE MUFF

The muff is the padded ear piece that is attached to the headband that goes over the technician's head.

Always spec single muff headsets. A theatre is not a recording studio. Theatre technicians absolutely must have single muff headsets. It is essential that one ear is uncovered in order for the technicians to be able to hear what is going on around them. Technicians on stage must be aware of their surroundings. This is a huge safety issue. They must be able to hear warning calls in case a set piece falls or a pipe is coming in above their heads.

Safety aside, it is the job of all technicians to pay attention to what is going on on stage, and most importantly the Stage Manager needs to hear each line the actors say in order to call lighting, sound and set/rigging cues at the right time. Plus, an Assistant Stage Manager, Deck Manager or Stage Manager on stage must be available to answer questions from cast and crew, while also hearing what is going on at other areas of the theatre over the headset.

The sound techs need to be able to communicate with the Stage Manager and other technicians, while being able to hear what the audience hears - they cannot have false sound levels being fed into their headsets. That said, the sound technician should also have a double muff headset that is plugged into their sound board, because occasionally she needs to be able to cue up a sound effect or piece of music without the audience hearing it and without them hearing the audience.

Sometimes, when there are not enough headsets provided in a theatre, there are people who can do without. For instance, if the Stage Manager is calling the show from the booth and is sitting right next to the light board operator then there is really no need for the light board operator to have a headset, as the SM is the only person they need to receive instructions from. In this situation it's especially important not to have a double muff headset because the SM needs to have confirmation that the light board operator has received warnings, standbys and/or has completed cues. They cannot be wearing double muff headsets as they must have one ear free in order to have two way communication with the light board operator.

MUFF COMFORT

During tech rehearsals that can last around 5 to 8 hours – or longer, and during days when there are both matinee and evening performances, crew members are wearing their headsets for hours at a time. It is worth it not to scrimp on cheap headsets with uncomfortable muffs. Also keep in mind that some people have to wear eye glasses and they can have the additional discomfort of having the side of their glasses pressed against the side of their head. And, while they're removable, many people wear earrings. I myself have my favorite pair of "headset friendly" earrings (they're even black, because techies were black clothing in order not to be seen!). Regardless of what else you're wearing, I can attest to how uncomfortable, if not painful, it is to have to wear cheap headsets for hours on end.

CALL LIGHT

A call light is a little light that flashes on the beltpack when another crew member pushes their call button on their beltpack. It will flash a light on all the beltpacks, so that those not on headset know to check in.

As some point in time it may be necessary for any technician to go "off headset". Sound technicians in particular are notorious for never wearing their headsets, which bugs the heck out of the rest of the crew because they can never get a hold of them. However, there is a good reason. The sound crew need to hear what the audience hears, so they can't have their ears covered with headset muffs all the time. However, the stage manager and the rest of the technicians do have to communicate with the sound technicians at times, so make sure the headset system that you spec has a call light on the beltpack. Of course that is assuming that the sound techs have placed their beltpack in their field of vision, which is not always possible to do (say the sound board covers the entire desk surface and there is no where to put the belt pack). For this reason if at all possible, it's best to install some sort of call light at the sound board station within visual range.

CHAPTER 6

THE COUNTERWEIGHT SYSTEM

The *Counterweight System* (or *Fly System* or *Rigging System* as it is interchangeably called) is potentially the most dangerous system in the theatre. Although mentioned intermittently in the Safety chapter, it gets its own chapter as well because of the seriousness of operating this system safely.

If you're not a theatre person, the counterweight system is possibly one of the things you think about when you visualize backstage in a theatre - its' often shown in movies and TV shows. It's that row of ropes that are pulled to raise and lower scenery. But there's far more to it than just walking over to a rope and pulling on it to raise ("fly out") or lower ("fly in") a piece of scenery.

For a start, consider that you are flying hundreds of pounds of weight above the heads of people – children, in the high school setting - who have no hardhats on. What construction site allows that? Not only that, but during an actual performance, although the movements of the scenery have been choreographed and practiced, no one calls out any warning before hundreds of pounds of set pieces come flying down to the stage deck at a fast rate. The people (your students) below simply cannot be in the wrong place at the wrong time.

TRAINING

High school students – and anyone who will be operating the counterweight system - must be taught the theory and practices of operating the system safely. The operator is a part of they system. Whether a rope or cable fails or whether the operator fails, the system is compromised as a whole.

The fact that as soon as your student lays hands on a rope s/he becomes a part of the system, is pause for thought. For this reason, you must have a strict protocol about using the fly system, and although teenagers can actually be trusted to use the fly system safely (high school techies do tend to take ownership of the protocol), they must first be trained. Students should also be taught to be aware with their senses (this goes for any component system of a theatre). They should be taught to look, listen, and smell, and to report anything unusual.

You simply cannot send a untrained high school student over to the ropes and ask them to lower a set wall or a drape. This not only includes the actual flying of set pieces, but how to hang things properly from the pipes and how to re-weight appropriately (it's not recommended that students do this, but more on that later).

As the name suggests the whole system relies on counter balancing, or "counterweighting", objects. Every time you change the weight hanging on a pipe by adding scenery or lights, or by taking off scenery or lights, you have to "counter weight" them with something commonly called pig irons or bricks. Pig irons are iron weights that are stacked on the "arbor" which is the structure that holds them in place.

Not only does this counterweighting have to happen, but it has to happen in a specific order. It is very important to keep the majority of the weight on the stage side, so that when you load weight you load the sets or lights first, and when you take away weight you take away from the arbor side first. Each of these procedures is designed to ensure that a heavy weight will not come crashing down onto the stage where people may be standing.

In addition, counterweight systems are generally built such that, while re-weighting, the lock can hold an imbalance of about 50lbs while re-weighting, but there are precautions you must take in order not to rely on the lock.

So serious is this procedure that there is an industry certification available for those doing stage rigging. The Entertainment Technician Certification Program certifies theatre technicians in the use of counterweight systems, and the mechanical and hydraulic systems that are usually permanently installed in theatres. To find out more go to www.etcp.plasa.org.

That said, in practice most high school theatres don't have ETCP certified riggers on staff. Even professional theatre technicians have initially learned at their own high schools, universities and/or on the job over the years. Not all high schools even hire theatre technicians, so that means that the Drama teacher has to be trained in rigging techniques and safety, but even that doesn't usually happen. And when the Drama teacher doesn't understand, or feel comfortable using, the counterweight system s/he will come to rely on students, who self-train themselves. At one high school theatre that I started working at there was a student who had taken an interest in technical theatre, and took charge of all the rigging, but had no formal procedural or safety training on running a fly system. After he graduated I actually hired him as a technician and I made sure that he went through a rigging training program through a local company.

SAFE OPERATIONS

It's not only important to make sure your students go through the correct training, and have their parents sign a waiver form (see the Safety chapter) before they can operate the counterweight system, but it's also very important to supervise them at all times and to make sure they continue to follow the proper procedures. It's my philosophy that shows should be entirely run by students whenever possible, however there should always be a theatre technician present to supervise, even if it looks like on the surface that they aren't doing anything. As I often say, you don't send the babysitter home after the children are in bed.

But, how do the scenery and lights get on the pipes in the first place? There are specific techniques for attaching scenery to pipes with cables, which are beyond the scope of this book, however you should never have your students do this without supervision from a trained professional technician.

Hundreds of pounds of weight is being hung above people's heads, so the proper procedures must be followed. In the process of hanging lights, safety cables must always be secured first when hanging and last when striking. (If your theatre does not have safety cables on your lighting instruments, stop reading right now and go and purchase one per instrument.) In the process of hanging scenery, rigging hardware has to be correctly installed and utilized. I have always required that a rigging technician be present and in charge of weighting the fly system during set load-ins in high school theatres. I can't recommend strongly enough that you do the same.

There is a proper technique and procedure for flying, and the following is a sample of a written procedure you should have in your theatre.

SAMPLE COUNTERWEIGHT SYSTEM OPERATIONS GUIDELINES

A student crew member may operate the fly system for the purposes of rehearsals and/or performances <u>after turning in the signed permission form</u> and <u>only after receiving training</u> from a theatre technician. (Only theatre technicians are authorized to lead the re-weighting of the battens.)

THE FOLLOWING PROCEDURES MUST BE FOLLOWED:
Operator must have a direct visual line to the area of the stage below the pipe (batten) that is flying in or out. If it is not possible to have a direct visual line, the operator must assign a second person to spot and relay information.

<u>During set-up, initial rehearsals, and strikes.</u>
Stand by the rail and look on the stage to confirm that the area is clear.
Release the safety ring around the handle and lower the handle.
Keeping both hands on the rope, turn body and head around to face stage.
Call in a LOUD voice "_____ (pipe) coming in/going out."
Wait for someone to respond "Clear" or "Thank you". This must be someone who is on stage and has actually looked to see if it is clear. If you do not hear a "Clear", call your warning again. Under no circumstances start to lower the batten if you have not received a "Clear" even if you can see the stage yourself.

Begin to pull the rope in order to lower or raise the batten. Keep both hands on the rope at all times and continually look on the stage. If it is necessary to stop at a spike tape mark, glance occasionally at the rope, but only take your attention off the stage when close to spike.

Stop when the batten is all the way in, all the way out, or on spike. Slow down when approaching the end. Do not let the arbor crash at the stop.

Push the handle up and secure the ring around it.

During final tech rehearsals and performances.

During final tech rehearsals and performances you can't be yelling out commands. By this time performers and other crew members should know when and where scenery, drapes, etc. will be flying in and out. Therefore you do not have to call out, but, *even if you are familiar with the show by this time*, you may not move the batten until told to do so by the lead rigger or by the Stage Manager (SM) – this is called 'taking your cue'. If you have a headset, the SM will be able to talk to you directly. If not, the SM or lead rigger will signal you with a pre-determined hand movement – in this case, when your cue is coming up, you must keep your attention on whomever will be signaling you.

The SM will call, or signal, "Standby rail" or "Standby _____(batten name)".

Respond (by voice or signal) "Rail **standing by**" or "_____ standing by".

Release the ring and the handle and **place both hands on the correct side of the rope.**

IMPORTANT: **DO NOT DO ANYTHING UNTIL YOU HAVE BEEN GIVEN THE "GO".**

The SM will call, or signal "Go".

Unless otherwise told to do so, **pull the rope in a quick, yet controlled manner.**

Watch the stage if it is in your visual line.

Stop when the batten is all the way in/out, or on spike. Slow down when approaching the end. Do not let the arbor crash at the stop.

Push the handle up and secure the ring around it.

Respond to the SM "Rail **complete**" or "_____ complete".

50

Following is a sample of a basic loading policy.

SAMPLE COUNTERWEIGHT LOADING AND UNLOADING PROCEDURES

Only theatre technicians are authorized to lead the re-weighting of the battens. A student or outside event crew member may assist under the direct supervision of a theatre technician, if they have submitted a signed liability waiver form.
Counterweight loading and unloading
TO LOAD A BATTEN SAFELY:
WITH FLYMAN AT THE LOCKING RAIL AND LOADERS ON THE LOADING GALLERY:
Flyman calls in a LOUD voice "_____ (pipe) coming in/going out" and lowers batten to the deck.
Flyman gives clearance to deck crew to place the load on batten.
AFTER load is on batten Flyman calls "Clear the stage, loading in process." All people on the stage must be at least past the center line of the stage and any doors on the working side of the stage should be locked to prevent people walking in during loading.
Flyman estimates weight and directs loaders to load the arbor with appropriate weights equal to the load.
Main loader calls "Clear the deck". The Flyman calls "Deck Clear" when everyone is on the far side of the stage and entry doors are locked.
Loaders raise keeper nuts and spreader plates, leaving one on top of batten weight. Main loader calls "Loading weights".
Loaders place required counterweights on arbor. If many "bricks" are needed, a spreader plate should be inserted between weights every two feet.
When finished, Loaders slide down remaining plates and keeper nuts, locking them in place with thumb screws. Only then do they call down: "Locked and Secured."
Flyman calls to Deck crew to "Clear the Batten."
Flyman removes keeper ring and opens lock handle, and tests load for balance. (There are procedures for securing the ropes before this step that are outside the scope of this book. Always use a trained rigging professional.)
If load is out of balance, repeat above procedure to adjust.
Once weight is correct, Flyman calls "Clear the Batten" and flies the load to trim, locking rope lock and securing with Keeper Ring.

TO UNLOAD, REVERSE THE PROCEEDURE.

WEIGHTS

It's also a good idea to keep a list of the weights of common items you hang on pipes, so that you don't have to weigh things or look up their weights over and over again. For items you do have to weigh, buy your theatre a good bathroom scale. It's also useful to know the maximum weight each batten can take, although in high school theatre this is rarely exceeded. Following is a list I kept in one theatre, but please keep in mind that the weights stated are specific to the brands of instruments in that particular theatre and should only be used as estimates.

SAMPLE LIGHTING INSTRUMENT AND DROP WEIGHTS FOR COUNTERWEIGHT SYSTEM

(Please note: only theatre technicians may supervise re-weighting of pipes.)

Weight limits on battens
(Arbor lengths for each batten can be found on the theatre website under: Stage and Rigging; Linesets.)

5' arbor:	1044 lbs
6' arbor:	1300 lbs
7' arbor:	1567 lbs

Approximate weights of some lighting instruments

6" fresnel	14lbs
10" fresnel	15lbs
Ellipsoidal (not including zooms.)	19lbs
Zoom	21lbs
PARs	12lbs
3-cell LED cycs	41lbs
Single cycs	10lbs
Triple cycs	28lbs
Hid works	25lbs

Weights of some sample drops:

Cardboard added to arches to create barn	120lbs
S of M - Maria's bedroom	150lbs
S of M - french windows	300lbs

LOCKOUT TAGOUT TAGS

Although you may have trained your student crew to use the counterweight system, and although your policy may be that they may only do so under supervision of yourself or a technician, this doesn't not always happen in the high school setting. In one high school theatre that I worked at, one particular teacher would allow students to go into the theatre on their own to set up for a class or rehearsal, or he himself would sometimes fly in drapes etc. The trouble was, besides the obvious safety issues, that sometimes he or his students would grab the wrong rope and move the electrics, which are the pipes on which your lights are hung, or the "borders" (sometimes called "teasers") which are black curtain strips that hide your lights from the site line of your audience. The trouble with this is that the electrics are set at a specific trim height and then the lights are focused to specific areas or set pieces. Once they are focused, moving the electric that they are hung on up or down changes where they are focused. If the border is accidentally moved, it may expose the sight of the lighting instruments to the audience.

In order to prevent people from moving any lines that shouldn't be moved I recommend using what are called "lockout tagout" tags. There are different brands and styles you can get, but I recommend ones that are specifically designed to go in the holes that fixes the rope lock handle in the locked position

Another purpose for a lockout tagout tag is in case a line is deemed too dangerous to move for some reason, or because for some reason it has to be left temporarily out of weight (although in theory this should never happen). In this case, do not use the same lockout tagout tag that you use for your electrics and borders, because someone used to that system would not realize that in this case a real danger was present. They're not cheap, but they are a great value when you consider their purpose.

COUNTERWEIGHT SYSTEM VS. ELECTRIC WINCH SYSTEM

Most high schools these days have a counterweight system where the weight of the scenery or lights is counter-weighted with weights, which are moved by pulling on ropes. As you have read if this is not done correctly this can cause a very unsafe condition. For this reason some districts are persuaded by their insurance companies to install electric winch systems instead. Electric winch systems allow the user to move the pipes with the scenery and lights on up and down with the push of a button. They winch system is strong enough to hold huge amounts of weight, thereby eliminating the need to re-weight every time you add or take off another light or piece of scenery (although the winch can be "taught" what weight it is moving). More sophisticated systems come with a computer, whereby you can program "cues". For instance, if you need to prep for a show, you enter a cue number and all of the legs and the cyc come down in place at once. If you are doing a scene change, you enter a cue number and three pieces of scenery fly out and two fly in. Presto change-o.

On the surface, this may sound far preferable in the high school theatre setting. But I haven't met a high school theatre technician yet who thinks so. There are several negatives about an automated winch system. They include:

> To program in, and execute, a cue needs only one person. In a high school setting where there are usually several students wanting to work backstage, this denies jobs to too many students.

Career and Technical Educational value is lost. The high school students haven't been taught and therefore don't learn about counterweighting protocol and rigging procedures and if they go on to work in another theatre – community, college or professional, most of which have counterweight systems - they could be put themselves and others in danger with a presumed level of training that they don't have.

Most older winch systems have a button that you must actively hold down in order for the pipe to move, however because it's so 'simple' to use, safety training is not adhered to.

In the newer winch systems with computers there is an auto stop built into the system, so that if a drape or pipe hits an object it automatically stops moving. The trouble is, it has to hit the object first. That object could be a student's head.

Electric winches don't know to stop when someone yells "Stop!". When a student is actively lowering a piece of scenery with a counterweighted rope system and a student on stage sees that it is *about* to hit something that was not meant to be there, the student on stage can yell "Stop!" and the student on the fly system can stop lowering the ropes in order to avoid an accident, or worse. If a student pushes a button on the computer screen of an electric winch system that student knows that the system will do what it's programmed to do. So even if that student has been trained to stand by the screen, they are not actively doing anything, or do not appear to be doing anything to other students. If that student is distracted (say by another student – like that would happen!), when the student on stage yells "Stop!" the student operating the screen may not be able to get to the control in time to avert the disaster.

One perceived positive feature about an automated winch system is the ability to create "cues", where several pieces of scenery and/or drapery can fly in and/or out at the push of the button. However, consider a situation where a show is in progress and a crew member leaves a piece of scenery, say a desk, in the wrong place during the previous set change. The next set change comes along. The operator pushes the button and several pieces of scenery fly out while a some fly in. Suddenly a crew member realizes that a wall that is flying in is going to hit the desk. He yells "Stop!" over his headset to the winch operator. The winch operator quickly pushes the stop button. In a situation where a counterweight system is in use, the crew member flying in that particular wall can stop, while the remaining crew members can keep flying their set pieces and drapes. The desk is moved, and that wall continues to fly in. The audience notices nothing amiss. The show goes on. In the same scenario using an automated winch system, when the stop button is pushed all pieces of scenery stop flying in and out. The whole set change is put at a halt. This disrupts the flow of the play. A crew member manages to move the desk and the winch operator can continue the set change cue, but by this time the audience is now drawn into the situation and drawn away from the 'magic' of theatre.

System failure. One high school I'm associated with had a full winch system installed in their new theatre. Within the first two years of its operation the computer system failed several times requiring service. A well maintained counterweight system can last decades.

Again, even though the counterweight system may be perceived as more dangerous to an insurance company, I've never met a theatre technician who is in agreement with that perception. Occasionally more convenient, perhaps. But safer? No.

The system I like the best is a combination, where the light pipes are on a winch system and the scenery pipes are on a counterweight system. One theatre I worked in had a combination system like this and it seemed to work very well. It allows the lighting technicians and student crew to move instruments around quickly without having to close the stage in order to re-weight every single time. Also, during a show, it's very rare that a light pipe has to be brought down to the stage deck. Hanging scenery usually takes up the whole stage during the process regardless, and scenery is being moved in and out during the course of a show. So the counterweight system employs more students and, with a properly trained crew, is actually safer than a winch system.

Again, a student crew member actively working the ropes on a counterweight system can see a hazard about to happen – say an actor walks under a piece of scenery that is being flown in – the student crew member operating a counterweight system would see the actor moving and stop the scenery before it hit the actor on the head. A winch system would only stop itself once it sensed it had already hit something.

INSPECTION

One of the two best ways to optimize safety is to make sure that anyone operating the fly system is properly trained and/or supervised, has turned in a signed liability waiver form, and follows the proper procedures. The other is to make sure that your fly system itself is inspected at least every couple of years, whether you have a counterweight system or a winch system.

A fly system inspection includes a visual inspection of the accessible components of the system (although some parts may be virtually impossible to view if they are above a grid that is close to the ceiling of the fly tower). The inspector will do a physical check of the system to assess if there are any hazardous conditions that might compromise the safety of those operating the system and those on stage while it is being operated. They should fully raise and lower each line (rope) to determine the condition of its functionality, and to look for things such as whether the ropes are frayed, determine the condition of the blocks, cables and other parts, and determine if any lines are out of weight. The inspector should then present your theatre with a full written report, which will recommend any repairs or replacements, and also recommend any preventative maintenance.

I am not a theatre safety expert, and this book can only recommend, not replace safety training in a high school theatre. If you want some specific hard-core information about rigging safety you should contact a professional company such as Stagecraft Industries on the west coast (www.stagecraftindustries.com) to come out to do a safety inspection, or check out websites such as www.plasa.org.

For more in depth information about codes and accepted standards in the rigging industry as a whole – such as ANSI 1.4 2014 about manual counterweight rigging systems – check out http://tsp.plasa.org/tsp/documents/published_docs.php.

CHAPTER 7

SPACE; BUILD, STORAGE, PEOPLE

One common complication that educational theatre people (teachers, theatre staff volunteers and students) have is that there is not enough storage space, build space and people space built into their multi-million dollar high school theatre facilities. Understandably space is expensive to provide and maintain, and the theatre is not the only part of a high school, however if it is your plan to create a theatre program ample space must be provided in order to do so. This chapter is directed primarily to architects, although it's important for administrators and academics understand these issues.

BUILD SPACE

High school theatre can't happen without sets, props and costumes (not to mention lights and sound). Gone are the days of performing in school cafeterias with cardboard scenery and parent-made costumes. If you are providing your theatre department with a theatre with a 20' x 40' proscenium opening, that stage space needs to be filled with something. Whether you have a vocational tech theatre class (see the Education chapter), professional theatre staff, and/or volunteer parents, high school theatre sets and costumes must be quite elaborate to fill up the space and to do justice to the level of today's productions. A 'professional' production also projects a favorable impression of your high school (see the Outreach chapter). If you have any doubt about the professional level of high school theatre today, check out Seattle's 5th Avenue Theatre's annual High School Musical Theatre Awards (https://www.5thavenue.org/education/student-programs#5th-avenue-awards), where over 120 high school theatre productions in the state of Washington contend for nominations and awards announced in a Academy Awards-like ceremony each year.

Sets, props and costumes all need sufficient space to be built. When designing a build space, consider the equipment and activities that need to go in there, including the sheer size and complication of what's being built these days.

A scene shop can have a lot of power tools and will need a lot of floor space and bench space. In addition, also consider the number of people who may be working in there at one time building sets and props, this can be five to ten people – or more if you have a vocational class. Some of the power tools needing space in a scene shop include:

> Band Saw
> Belt Finishing Sander
> Portable Circular Saw
> Disc Sander
> Jig/Bayonet Saw
> Jointer
> Motorized Miter Box
> Planer/Surfacer
> Portable Belt Sander
> Portable Drill
> Portable Finishing Sander
> Portable Router
> Mitre/Radial Arm Saw
> Scroll Saw Notes
> Table Saw
> Wood Lathe
> Uniplane
> Portable Electric Plane
> Wood Shaper

Consider also how much space it takes to sew a costume. Some costumes – think: Cinderella's ball gown – can be quite elaborate and take up yards of material. Most of the high school's I've worked in have teeny costume shops and the costumers usually end up having to set up tables in a backstage hallway or in a classroom. Not only do the costumes themselves take up a lot of space when being constructed, but there can be several sewing machines going at once and several people, each working on a different costume. A costume room should be as big as a classroom, not a closet.

Also take into account how much these spaces will be in use throughout the school year. Even if your high school only puts on two major productions a year, it actually takes most of each semester to build the sets and construct the costumes. There can be several set changes in a play or musical and there can be dozens and dozens of costumes to make. One high school play I worked on had 300 costume pieces. These will not be wasted spaces that are empty most of the year, these spaces are beehives of activity throughout most of the year.

STORAGE SPACE

Once the sets, props and costumes for a show are finished with, the question is what to do with them. Plus spare lights and sound equipment need storage space. Most high schools build up a large inventory that they can use or adapt for more shows down the road. I've seen set pieces and costumes come and go many a time. Some set pieces are taken apart to their component parts, but even then the component parts – or simply the wood used to build them – have to be stored somewhere. Period costumes can be reused the next time a play from that period is produced, but until then they have to be stored somewhere. The costumes for "My Fair Lady" can't be adapted for "West Side Story", so there has to be enough storage to accommodate quite a selection of costumes.

Cost saving is always a consideration when building a high school, but economizing on storage space when you have the capital budget to build later perpetually seeps into the operations budget for the life of the school (see the Financials chapter). All of the high schools I've worked at struggle with space for storage to the point that there is a lot of expensive waste. Some schools theatre departments decide to rent storage units. Some simply end up throwing away valuable supplies and stock. Some end up giving away expensive costumes. For instance, the above-mentioned Cinderella ballgown cost $600 to make. Wood is none to cheap either, and high school theatres must purchase quality wood when you consider that students will be standing on the platforms and stair units that are built.

In addition, plan for high school theatre set, prop and costume storage space to be exclusively for the purpose of storing sets, props and costumes. One school I worked at stored their band costumes in the sewing room, another stored custodial supplies in their scene shop. This caused no end of problems for the theatre department that had storage space issues enough as it was.

PEOPLE SPACE

As well as object storage you also have to have somewhere to put people. Most high school theatres that I've worked in have one or two make-up rooms that can accommodate about 20 actors, and perhaps one or two closet-sized dressing rooms. When you are designing a high school theatre, consider that a school production can have 40 or so actors, in addition to a 20 piece orchestra for a musical, and 10 or 15 student crew members. There can be 70 students working on a production that need to fit somewhere.

In addition, most high schools rent out their theatres to help pay for costs (see the Road House chapter). One of the main staples of income for most of the high school theatres that I've worked at are dance schools. Dance schools can come with 100 to 150 dancers, aged 2 to 18. In order to accommodate this number of people a lot of high school theatres also rent out their performing arts classrooms. Much to the chagrin of the teachers, who have to put away equipment and supplies – particularly the performing arts teachers (think of a band room). One choir teacher I worked with insisted that the sound technician come in a half hour early in order to put away her piano and sound equipment before outside events used her room, and stay a half an hour after the event in order to set the equipment back up again. Because outside events expect to have rental-ready spaces, the technician's time became a school expense.

Most high schools can't afford to have a space be empty during the school, so it may seem impractical to build a 'green room' for performers to only use in non-school hours, but consider the alternate costs that will plague you for the life of the high school theatre. As a compromise, perhaps a room such as that could be booked for testing during the school day, or other miscellaneous school-day activities, which could be scheduled on an as-needed basis around production schedules.

PART 2 - OPERATIONS

CHAPTER 8

STAFFING

To staff or not to staff, that is the question that many school districts that have new or remodeled theatres on their high school campuses ask themselves today. Whether 'tis nobler to hire a Theatre Manager and technicians, or whether the Drama teacher can just run the theatre, the student crew can just work the school shows, and the outside events can just use the theatre on their own – that is the question. This chapter is mostly for administrators, however architects and academics will benefit from the knowledge that will help them in their own planning and decision process.

Many school districts only consider the financial aspects regarding the decision of whether to hire professional theatre staff. But there are some other important things to consider when deciding whether to hire a professional Theatre Manager and technicians or whether to run your theatre with existing district personnel. Before you make that decision a careful assessment must be made. Some questions to ask are:

Is your school staff comfortable with and knowledgeable about your theatre's functional operation?

Is your school staff highly qualified to teach technical theatre?

Is your school staff familiar enough with the theatrical process to make scheduling decisions?

Is there a vocational training program for technical students?

Is your theatre ergonomically functional?

Are operational policies and procedures in place that are strictly enforced?

Is your theatre being used to its full potential?

Is your theatre self-sustaining?

Is learning enhanced through your theatre operations?

Are there safety policies and procedures in place that are strictly enforced?

Is your theatre protected from liabilities and lawsuits?

If you can answer yes to all of the above, then you don't need to hire a Theatre Manager/TD and technicians, and your Drama teacher can just run your high school theatre.

But, before you decide not to hire a Theatre Manager and have a teacher run your theatre for a while to 'see how it goes', let me share with you my experience of working in one high school theatre that had no management for the first two years of operation – it was not pretty. I hope you will find it a compelling testimony as to why you must hire a Theatre Manager and technicians right from the start - even before construction is completed if possible (so that they can prevent costly mistakes) – more on that later.

I have worked as a Theatre Manager and I have worked in the capacity of Lighting Designer in countless schools. I have experienced a lot of staffing arrangements and their consequences. This is one of those times.

One of the high school theatres that I worked at had been built two years before I came on board. Things had not been going so smoothly. And this is where I believe you will be able to avoid easily-preventable liability and cost problems down the road - if a Theatre Manager and professional technicians are hired to run your theatre from the start. Following are some illustrations of the safety, financial and operational issues faced by a theatre that had not had professional staff for the first two years of its operation.

One of the first things I noticed when I arrived at the theatre was, up in the catwalks at the point where there are stairs that go down to the followspot platform, there were no cables across the opening under the lighting pipe, leaving a gap about 3' wide and 4' high – just at the point where someone is most likely to trip or fall in the dark! Plenty of room for a person to fall through; 30 feet above the audience seats. This was one of the first work orders I submitted. The theatre also had off-stage work lights positioned such that they were scorching the backs of the side drapes. There were many other safety breaches, including a hole in the floor of the house by the seats nearest the main entrance – a nice ankle twister - that had never been addressed in two years.

Another scary situation I encountered was the lack of concern for student safety. Not all teachers or custodians were diligent about locking up the theatre after use, despite frequent missives to the contrary. Many teachers also got into the habit of sending students alone into the theatre to obtain equipment, practice, or to get something set up prior to a class. Students, not seeming to understand that an unlocked door was not an open invitation to walk into the theatre, would also sneak in at odd times. It seemed to be common knowledge (and there was evidence) that the students would sneak up to the catwalks (the ones with the gap in the safety cabling about 30 feet above the floor below) in the dark - and eat their lunches up there. Plus, when we (the theatre staff) went into the pit to remove the pit cover for the first time, we found a pair of boy's underwear and a certain latex object down there. During performances, student photographers had full (unattended) run of the galleries and catwalks simply because they preferred to take their photos from up on high. Students were allowed to use the fire exit hallway that runs backstage, where set pieces and other theatrical equipment were often stored, as a convenient way to get to their buses after school. The orchestra pit had neither barrier rope nor safety net until I had them ordered. In addition, without a Theatre Manager to oversee the theatre, community events were allowed unsupervised use of the theatre, usually providing their own – often inexperienced – technical help.

I hope just these few examples from just one theatre will demonstrate the benefits of, and help avoid the pitfalls that could be avoided by, having a Theatre Manager at your high school theatre from the get go. A Theatre Manager can mitigate potentially costly liability issues. Without a Theatre Manager, every user of your high school theatre assumes that these types of things are not their responsibility and that someone else will take care of safety issues and operational functionality. Without someone who has had experience in working in a high school theatre to manage its operation the liability risks cannot be mitigated.

Furthermore, as recommended in the book "Practical Health and Safety Guidelines for School Theater Operations" by Dr. Randall W. A. Davidson, district administration needs to have the knowledge in order to assess what is a good theatre employee, be it Theatre Manager, technician or teacher. Mr. Davidson states "Human relations and personnel directors may not have the professional performing arts background or experience to perform this duty of evaluation…" The content of his book and this book can help provide a better understanding of what one is looking for when staffing your high school theatre.

In this chapter I will address why you should hire professionals and what to look for, however if that really is impossible in your situation, I will also give you some tips on how to manage your theatre yourself. I don't condone that approach, but it's better than no one overseeing your high school theatre.

TEACHERS AS THEATRE MANAGERS

But first, my scary story continues. In addition to student safety, allowing teachers have full access to the theatre and being in charge of their own technical needs, caused many other problems, the least of which was infighting between the teachers because of their different needs for use of the theatre.

When I first arrived on the scene of the aforementioned theatre, one performing arts teacher complained to me that another performing arts teacher was always leaving the equipment set up one way, and the other teacher complained to me that that teacher was always leaving the equipment set up the other way. These two teachers were changing the light focuses, re-recording settings on the light board, and patching the sound board for their own shows and leaving it that way when they were done, so that when the other teacher came in they had to change it all back again to suit their requirements. The third performing arts teacher stayed out of the fray because she didn't know how to operate the equipment at all and would rely on others to set it up and run it for her. In addition, other non-performing arts teachers in the school would also use the theatre during the school day and also make unilateral decisions about the equipment and its usage. For instance, one teacher would send students – unattended - up to the catwalks whenever she needed to use the followspot for a function in another part of the school, and not let anyone know (not that there was a central person to inform), so when the followspot was needed in the theatre they had to go searching for it. If this all sounds hectic and chaotic, it was.

There are ways to provide a lighting plot that can easily be adapted to suit many uses of the theatre with only small adjustments, and the sound system can easily be set up to be automatically accessed for many different activities without the need for teachers to inadvertently change all the settings. (See the Lighting and Sound chapters.) But, what the district administration didn't realize is that

TEACHERS ARE NOT TECHNICIANS.

Like sports teachers who are not usually also proficient in sports medicine, for example, most performing arts teachers are not proficient in technical theatre. In fact, the Department of Labor and Industries requires that all instructors in a career and technical education subject be vocationally certified. (More about this in the Safety chapter.) Performing arts teachers have likely taken college classes in technical theatre in order to fulfill graduation requirements for their degrees, but they are not professionally trained or certificated in vocational technical theatre or theatre management and they are usually nowhere near highly qualified in correctly and safely operating the equipment in a theatre.

Nor are teachers usually paper-pushing people – particularly the creative types. Managing a theatre and all the events that come into it – school events and outside events – requires a surprising amount of desk work; scheduling the theatre, scheduling the staff required for each event, re-scheduling everything every time a change is made, filing, maintaining documents, create forms, file administrative reports, processing user applications, budget tracking, processing timesheets, ordering equipment and parts, writing work orders for maintenance and repairs, and e-mails, e-mails, e-mails. If you are a performing arts teacher, or if you know one, you know that this sort of extensive paperwork is not a performing arts teacher's strong suit.

Nor do overworked performing arts teachers, who also work evening and weekend rehearsals, performances, manage procurements, meetings with parents, and other preparations, have sufficient time to completely oversee all the technical aspects needed for their own performances let alone potentially dozens of others throughout the school year. Some performances such as orchestra or band need very little tech (lights on and off, one hand held mic perhaps), however most performances, such as plays, musicals, jazz concerts, a talent or variety show, a dance recital, etc. need more tech support than is apparent from the end result that the audience sees. But all need scheduling and planning.

In addition, a Drama teacher with little tech knowledge working on a show is very rarely paid an actual salary for their time. Usually they have a stipend of around a couple of thousand dollars for what can be hundreds of hours of work throughout the school year. This is very unfair when you consider that any technicians working the show are being paid hourly, and any Career and Technical Education teachers who have students build sets during the school day are salaried.

Supervision is another issue. During an event (from variety shows to full length plays to concerts) there can simultaneously be students in the booth, students in the house, students on stage, students in the galleries, students in the catwalks, students back stage right, students back stage left, students in the scene shop, students in the back (storage) hallway, students in the costume shop, students in the dressing rooms, students in the classroom and students in the lobby. For a straight play the average amount of cast and crew is 25 students, for a musical the average amount of cast and crew is 55 students, for a choir or band there are 30 to 40 (to 60 in some schools), and larger numbers can certainly apply to variety shows. Officially one teacher is not allowed to have more than about 30 (depending on your state) students sitting in seats in a contained classroom. How is it that one person (even one who has volunteers – usually unskilled) can be allowed to supervise several rooms with over 30 students, where physical and hazardous activities are taking place?

Stagecraft Industries had this to say: *"For one person to be able to be every where all the time is not feasible. This is how soda's get spilled into control boards, circuits get overloaded, cooling fans get blocked, fire doors tied open, cables get strewn in pathways and a long list of horrors that we've both seen. I might compare this to the* school's football coach: can they do the practices and games all by themselves without any assistant coaches? Usually not, it's too much to cover all the various disciplines of football- same as inside a theater. Can users or volunteers be trained, you-bet, but they still need to be monitored since they are 'apprentices' most of the time, lacking formal training and documents to prove it."

CASE STUDIES

A lot of school administrators don't realize that their scene shop is essentially a woodshop and therefore the districts don't require the same level of safety and education as provided for woodshops in a school by the Department of Labor and Industries. And so unfortunately not all high schools provide vocational, or career and technical education (CTE), certified teachers, let alone a Theatre Manager and technicians in their scene shops. So, the Drama teacher takes charge. At a few schools I worked at, the Drama Departments was separate from the job of the theatre staff and so set building for the school plays was not under our jurisdiction (although at times I was able to advocate for safer and more educational situations). Following are a variety of situations for set building in seven of schools of I have worked in, none of which are ideal for student learning, safety and mitigating liability.

School #1

This high school would allow (and still does to my knowledge) their theatre to be rented out to outside groups who had to run their own tech. The same is true of another high school in their district. There were two "Site Supervisors" on the premises at all times, but these Site Supervisors were in name only (I believe they were district office employees earning a few extra bucks). Neither of them had any knowledge of how any of the technical equipment works. When I was using the theatre as the Lighting Designer for an outside event, there were several safety violations, including one person getting hurt by a folding scissor lift because the site managers were unable to tell us how it operated. There were also several technical issues that caused long delays, including a light board that would not record. After several phone calls, we eventually were able to reach a student(!) from the school who then informed us that several of the controls on the light board were non-functional. Had the site supervisors known how to use the equipment, or better yet had the school provided technical support, it would have saved a lot of hassle which put the show in jeopardy. This school would rent their theatre to anyone. We knew what we were doing and had all this trouble, but a user who does not know theatre safety and protocols, and how to look after equipment, is an actual risk to the school district.

School #2

This high school had always had a stage in their cafeteria and the Drama teacher, parents and students would build the set. They eventually had a new theatre built, but during the two years that they were displaced they performed at a neighboring high school in the district. That high school did have a Technical Theatre CTE certified teacher. He would have his students build the sets for the visiting school. Now that this high school's theatre has opened, it is being managed part time by the Drama teacher, who, wisely is obtaining her CTE certification.

School #3

For several years at this high school the teacher who taught the one acting class did most of the set design and building, which he actually enjoyed more than directing. However his duties in his other classes became too much, so he eventually quit directing plays and working on the sets. The school hired a "Drama Advisor" who apparently had no experience what-so-ever in set building and decided not to use too many sets and to have the students build what sets the shows would have. The tech students worked unsupervised in the shop while he was in rehearsal with the cast on stage. For one play there were two parents volunteers, whose children were involved in the show. They both had construction experience, but not stagecraft knowledge. A stage and rigging technician was brought in to review their set design and teach them some stage construction techniques, but there was no formal set construction workshop. After a couple of years that teacher quit, and a teacher from another school, with no experience in directing – although high in enthusiasm and motivational skills - was hired. She brought on board a parent who had a construction background, who designed and built one of the most awesome sets I have ever seen. She had enthusiastic students who would come in and help her after school hours, along with a couple very dedicated parents, however she still ended up doing a lot of the building herself. To her credit though, she did spend a lot of time consulting with the stage and rigging technician. However, she was still a parent volunteer supervising students in a situation that should be reserved for vocationally certificated teachers.

School #4

The Drama teacher at this high school did not have set building experience. Most don't, but the difference about this Drama teacher was that she admitted it. She would always have parent volunteers (and one parent who was also a teacher at the school) who had experience in construction build the set with interested students. For the most part though, the parents would build the set themselves, as there were no requirements for student cast and crew to help build sets. These parents with construction backgrounds were always enthusiastic and put in a lot of their time, however the sets were solid, heavy, all in one unit and immovable. They were not modular, and when moved gouged the stage floor. The set certainly was not build to stagecraft standards. They basically built a house on the stage. For a couple of years a parent who had film experience designed and built the set and would show the kids how to use power tools. He was not CTE certified, let alone a teacher, however he probably had the closest related experience. Because of the situation, a stage and rigging technician would hold a set design, construction and rigging workshop at the start of each year (for several years before he too moved on) intended for any parents and students who would be set building that year. Unfortunately it was not mandatory and was ill attended.

School #5

For many, many years (2 decades?) the Drama teacher of this high school, who had set construction and design knowledge (although was not CTE certified) would supervise his own set construction students. There was a tech theatre class each year, and the students in that class built the majority of the sets (mandatory Saturday work parties for cast and crew were also a practice at this school). The students in the tech theatre class also had to design a set for the play and build models – then one design was chosen. Parents helped out at the Saturday work parties, and built sets alongside the students, supervised by the Drama teacher. That Drama teacher eventually retired and the new Drama teacher did not know how to build sets. For a couple of years, the sets were sparse. Then one of the theatre technicians from another school in the district was sent over to this high school to train students during the tech theatre class time. She was very experienced in set design, construction and decoration but was not a certificated teacher. This arrangement went on for a year or two before she left for another job. That Drama teacher also eventually retired, and there is now a new young Drama teacher who seems to have some experience in set building, but, again, is not CTE certified.

School #6

A requirement of being in a production at this high school was to attend a certain amount of Saturday set building Work Parties. The Drama teacher was somewhat knowledgeable about set building and was present at all times. In some years (decided by the school administration) there was also a tech theatre class and the sets for the plays were at least partially built during that class period. For a few years the Auto Shop teacher (CTE certified in the Automotive field, so at least knew about processes and safety) developed an interest in set design and set construction and self-taught himself techniques while supervising the students and volunteer parents.

School #7

This high school's Drama teacher at the time I worked there was also CTE certificated in tech theatre. He taught and supervised all set building. The current Drama teacher has no experience in set building and is not CTE certificated.

These are just a few examples only of the set building situations in high school theatres. They do not include lights, sound and rigging education and supervision. But as you can see, in most high school theatres, it seems to be a 'crap shoot', dependent on the experience of the Drama teacher and their volunteers at any one given time.

STUDENTS AS STAFF

It's been my experience throughout more than thirty years that performing arts teachers are not usually technically savvy, and that they rely heavily upon their students. Without someone with technical theatre knowledge in your high school it's likely that a lot of the technical duties will be taken over by students and some of the students appear quite competent at this. So the argument I hear a lot from administrators, is why can't students run our theatre?

And so I continue with my scary story of the theatre that had no management for the first two years before I worked there. Because none of the district administration, teachers or community members using the theatre had any technical theatre knowledge, one student in particular developed an aptitude for and interest in technical theatre. This one student was self-taught and pretty much ran the theatre single-handedly for two years, for district users and community users alike. He learned so much about the functions of the theatre that he became the 'go-to' person any time a teacher needed any help during the school day - to the point that he felt compelled to skip classes during the day in order to set up for band and choir concerts or get the stage ready for school meetings, plays, etc. This of course began affecting his grades. The performing arts teachers condoned this because he was needed. He was also in charge of, and learned by trial and error, procedures such as re-weighting the counter-weight system and operating the genie lift in order to focus the lights – procedures that in actual fact require formal safety training and in some cases certification. Often times he would perform these functions in the theatre alone (not even professional theatre technicians are meant to work in a theatre alone). On top of having this knowledge, he was also required to train and lead other students in these procedures, which he was ill equipped to do, having had no leadership training. The district seemed blissfully ignorant of this huge safety and liability faux pas going on under their noses.

It's always been my standpoint that the students should learn the proper operation of the equipment and systems of their theatre, and that they should crew their own shows as much as possible. But, not without highly qualified supervision, and not at the expense of their safety. While tech theatre students are some of the most dedicated, highly motivated, energetic, team-oriented, thick-skinned, professional-acting and technically-proficient people I know, I don't advise having them as your sole technical crew for your theatre. It's simply not safe and there are missed educational opportunities in a variety of specialties.

SPECIALTY KNOWLEDGE

In the specialty area of Lighting the students can turn on the board and bring the lights up and down, they can even be taught to record cues. However, they don't know McCandless theory, they don't know dance lighting techniques, they don't know how to patch a light plot and they therefore often run on a one-to-one patch. They don't know color theory, they don't know cuing and design techniques, and so on. When I started working at the theatre that had not had a manager for the first two years of its operation, the light board had been run with a one-to-one patch for the whole two years! There was no Rep Plot, so every time a show went in there groups had to completely re-configure the lights. The students were also working with electricity. When a plug needed wiring or repairing eager students would take it upon themselves to do that without any supervision whatsoever.

It is standard procedure that once the lighting is designed and programmed during the tech rehearsal process that the lighting technician/designer does not need to attend every show. In the case of lighting a student light board operator can run the equipment for a show without a technician watching over them because they need only push the go button when the stage manager calls "Go" for the cue to happen. There aren't any safety issues about pushing a button. Plus it is not likely that there will be any technical difficulties, but if there are, a technician needs to be on call. During the run of one show I worked on several cues were erased on the light board by another teacher using the theatre between shows (even though there was no reason for him to use the light board). This of course was only discovered an hour before curtain of the next performance, when the student light board operator turned the board on to get ready to run the show. The student light board operator was not able to fix the problem, and I was called in to rectify it. Had a technician – or in this case the Theatre Manager – not been available, this would have greatly compromised the whole show.

The specialty area of sound is a different kettle of fish. The students can turn on the board and plug in the mics, but the sound must be adjusted in real time continually throughout the show. Most students only know how to adjust volume levels. They don't know how, or why, to adjust for the myriad of sound quality, nor for balance. The only way they know how to correct for feedback is to lower the volume.

For one show in one of the theatres I worked at the district sound technician was not able to be at two performances due to an unexpected issue. Problems arose, as they do, but the student sound board operator was not able to fix them. There were noticeable sound issues throughout the two performances, such as mics not working at all, feedback in the house and bad mic quality. Because the sound technician had not been at the performances the whole show was compromised for the 60 or so students involved and the hundreds of audience members paying to see the performance.

The specialty area of Stage and Rigging is not only a procedural knowledge issue but also a safety issue, and while the students are operating the rigging, they must be supervised. Even un-trained students can fly in drapes and drops. But without the proper protocol and if they are unsupervised, the risk of someone being hit on the head with a metal pipe or hundreds of pounds of scenery or lighting equipment is very real. Plus, without training and supervision students are left in charge of re-weighting hundreds of pounds without the correct procedures, which could cause a very bad accident.

One year at one theatre we had a student crew member, who had been trained, but who would fly in set pieces in an unsafe manner, not calling out beforehand, plus kept bouncing the set pieces off the deck. The theatre technician in charge on stage had to assign her to a different position because she was causing a serious safety hazard to the actors on stage. Without a theatre technician mentoring and supervising, this student would have continued to operate in a very unsafe manner. The theatre technician was not running the show for the students, but this is a very good example of why you don't send the babysitter home once the children are in bed. It's also a very good example of why we have professionals supervising students and not parent or teacher volunteers who don't know operational and/or safety procedures. It's also a good example of what could happen if only one teacher were supervising a show – that teacher would most likely be in the house directing, and would not have known about this student's unsafe conduct.

VOLUNTEER COORDINATOR

One school where I worked decided to move to a student and teacher volunteer model for their school events. Each school event coming into the high school theatre would bring its own teachers and students to crew the show. Each school year the participants would be different. The Theatre Manager was expected to train a new batch of teachers and students each time a new event came in. Besides the obvious safety and operational issues, this essentially turned the Theatre Manager into a Volunteer Coordinator and Trainer.

DISTRICT LIABILITY

I think I speak for us all when we say that we are proud of the fact that once the curtain opens, that the shows are entirely run by students. But so is a football game entirely played by students. It doesn't mean that we stop supervising them once the game begins. It doesn't mean that safety professionals don't need to be standing by in the sidelines, just in case something happens.

Safety-wise, without highly qualified management and technical support – I can't say it enough - it's akin to allowing students into a wood shop or metal shop class without a teacher present – they can figure out how to use the equipment and come up with ideas of things to build, but they haven't been taught the safety procedures and aren't supervised. Students running a show without technicians overseeing them, is like allowing them to swim at a pool without lifeguards, or play football without officials on the sidelines. Other than these obvious, and serious, safety and liability concerns, by running tech themselves the students do not learn the curriculum of the subject.

Curriculum-wise it's like allowing students into an art classroom without a teacher present – they can figure out how to paint a picture or make a sculpture, but they haven't been taught theory, techniques, tool usage, etc. I use art, woodshop and sports analogies because that is what most people are most familiar with. Again, when most people go to see a play, they only see the finished product, not what goes on behind the scenes.

Another area that districts are familiar with is the area of employee safety. Usually for safety and liability reasons district employees are required to complete safety training on health topics such as blood-borne pathogens, and allergies and asthma. Yet they allow students to go up into the catwalks 30 feet in the air, to re-weight and operate hundreds of pounds of overhead scenery, work with electricity, and so on, without any, or very little, training, and with little or under-qualified supervision – certainly not in compliance with the Department of Labor and Industry regulations regarding the work minors can and cannot do without proper supervision.

STUDENT RELIABILTY

Another reason not to staff your theatre with students is their reliability level. No matter how dedicated and passionate students may be about tech theatre and no matter their competence level, their commitment can waiver depending on what else is going on in their lives. Even the most dedicated students who eat, live and breathe theatre are not 100% reliable. Here's just a few examples from my experience.

- The week before a school play's tech rehearsals started, a group (read: "clique") of student crew members suddenly quit.

- On the Monday of one tech week the student light board operator announced he'll have to leave at 6p on Wednesday to go to a concert that he'd had tickets to for a couple of months. He had neglected to let anyone know this prior to agreeing to do the show.

- One light board operator asked if he could skip the last show of a run because the opportunity had just come up for him to go to a concert.

- A student backstage crew member left before the end of a matinee show to attend a family event - without letting anyone know.

- A sound crew student was called for 6:30am to help set up for a school day production. She decided to sleep in and get a ride to school with a friend. She arrived at 7:30 without letting anyone know she was planning to be late.

- For a show that rehearsed on the 22nd of one month and performed on the 23rd one stage crew student simply e-mailed: "I just found out that I cannot make it to the event on the 23rd of this month." There was no explanation.

Since she couldn't be there for the performance, she couldn't be a part of the rehearsal either, because she wouldn't be there to do the job assigned to her at the rehearsal for the performance, and a person taking over wouldn't have been at the rehearsal in order to know what to do.

- A student who had volunteered to work two outside events texted at last minute and said his parents wanted him to go to a family function with them during the first event and he was afraid if he didn't go, that they wouldn't let him work the second event, which was the one he preferred.

- A scheduled student sound board operator turned up on Monday of a tech week and announced she had some test studying she had to do in the evenings and her parents wouldn't let her work on the show those nights.

- One student had an aptitude for running sound (in fact I later hired him), but he was also an award winning student musician, so often was not available to run a full show.

In addition, I've had students whom I believe come from dysfunctional family situations, and the theatre program is literally their salvation. But no matter how much they want to be there and promise to be there, circumstances beyond their control often prevent them from being there.

In the theatre each person is given a very specific job to do, and they are the only one who knows how to do that job and is available to do that job. If they don't turn up it can jeopardize the whole event or production for all of the other students, and it can jeopardize safety if others were relying on someone to be somewhere at a certain point.

PARENTS

As you can surmise from some of the examples above, another problem with having students run your shows (school events and/or outside events) is not so much the students themselves, but their parents. Parents don't understand the level of commitment, such as the need to be there for both the rehearsal and the performance. Once you are involved in a rehearsal, you are then the only person who knows how to do your job and when to do your job. So, you can't not turn up for the performance, because curtains won't get flown, lights won't get turned on and so on. Conversely, if you haven't been at the rehearsal you won't know what to do during the performance.

I can't count the number of times during the tech week for a school play that parents have informed me that their student must be home by 8:00pm or 9:00pm, when the rehearsals are usually expected to go until 10:00pm. Rehearsals are not only expected to go until 10:00pm (in every high school theatre I've ever been involved with), but parents are informed about this ahead of time in the information packet that they are given when their child is cast or put on the crew. Nonetheless, the reasons that parents want their children home are because of homework, a test the next day, or just a general curfew. Unfortunately, parents don't have the big picture.

What parents don't realize is that inevitably during tech week there is some big exam scheduled. This is a very common 'Murphy's Law" phenomenon – it happened when I was in high school and it happens every time I work on a high school production now. Some parents simply worry about how tired their child will get, staying up until past 10:00 at night for a week and having to get up to be at school the next morning. But, what parents also don't see is that there are 40 to 80 other students in the same boat – they think it is just their child who is affected. What they also don't see is the educational and real life experience their children are having. I don't know of any good high school theatre that doesn't run their productions without professional expectations. Parents also don't realize that once the curtain goes up on opening night that it is primarily teenagers who run the show in its entirety. Parents also don't look at the big picture and see that tech week happens just once or twice a year (sometimes three) – they are fretting about one or two weeks out of 52.

There are some ways around this – and you have to approach it on a case-by-case basis with each parent. During one high school show that I worked on I had one mother who wanted her Stage Manager daughter to leave by 9:00pm every night. Never mind that this student was in charge of running the entire show and that rehearsals went on until 10:00pm. This mother came in one day early on in tech week and was helping serve dinner during the break. So I brought her into the theatre and put her on headset. She listened for about 45 minutes entranced. She had had no idea the level of 'grown up' responsibility that her daughter had, nor her level of competence and confidence. I never heard a peep out of that parent for the rest of the run of the show. Another set of parents in another high school theatre were concerned about the hours that their son would have to commit to in order to run the followspot for a show. So we invited them into the theatre and gave them the 'grand tour' and their son demonstrated to them, and his younger brother, how he was up in the catwalks running the followspot. That young boy has now graduated from college with a degree in theatre production and has gone on to get his masters and is now gainfully employed in the industry. Also his younger brother participated in every school production thereafter.

Another way to gain student and parent commitment is if your district can pay your students. This not only makes the students even more committed to their calls, but perhaps more importantly validates their time spent not doing homework, or getting less sleep, to their parents. However some school districts don't want to deal with hiring people under 18, because of the added expenses and paperwork and additional insurance required to hire minors, so this may be a moot point in your school district. (However, you can – and I have – hire a student the day he or she turns 18.)

McDONALDS

If you're still not convinced that students should not staff a high school theatre, consider my McDonalds/*theatre* analogy:

Why can't teenagers run McDonalds/*theatres*, they seem to do fine on their own, why do we need management and supervisors?

So that there is <u>one central figure</u>, the store manager – *theatre manager* – who employees – *student stage crew*, shift managers – *theatre technicians*, suppliers – *theatrical supply stores*, customers - *audience*, corporate management – *district administration*, know who to go to with questions, requests, problems, collaboration with other entities and people, and other information.

So that the store manager can <u>oversee</u> that one shift manager - *teacher, or other user of the theatre* - leaves things <u>tidy and in working order</u> for the next shift manager, and so that there is no in fighting between the shift managers – *teachers* – about how things should be run and who is leaving lose ends for the other to pick up after.

So that there is <u>continuity and conformity in the operations</u>; one shift manager doesn't turn the ovens to one temperature, while the next shift manager turns it to another temperature – *so that the lighting rep plot on the board doesn't get recorded over, so that the sound board isn't reconfigured for a show and not returned to a standard set up; you have to be able to walk into your space and know that everything is good to go and that you don't have to scramble to restore changes you didn't expect.*

So that the employees – *student tech crew* – each know how to do their <u>specialty job</u> (cook, front counter, etc.) efficiently and safely; the management doesn't do their jobs for them, but oversees them – *a play can take up to 15 or so tech crew to run the show, lights, sound, rigging, costumers, props, and people tend to gravitate towards one specialty.*

So that no one injures themselves because of a lack of <u>policies and procedures for the safe and appropriate use of equipment,</u> for instance burns themselves on the fries oil fryer – *injures themselves on the counterweight system, moving the pit cover, so that procedures are followed about being up on the beams and use of the Genie.*

So that needed food and packaging <u>supplies</u> – *lamps, mic batteries,* are <u>ordered in a timely manner and in the correct amounts</u>.

So that the shift managers – *theatre technicians* - the employees – *student stage crews,* and customers – *audience,* know<u> who to report problems, broken items, running out of items, or safety problems </u>that need addressing and so that one central figure can be relied upon to follow through on the repair and or replacement.

So that the store manager – *theatre manager* - can <u>schedule the management staff</u> – *the theatre technicians,* employees - *student crew if applicable* - in appropriate amounts according to the needs of the schedule - *show,* such as lunch time is busier than 9pm at night – *once the Theatre Manager holds a Production Meeting with a user, then the amount and type of crew needed for the show can be determined and scheduled.*

So that the store manager – *theatre manager* – can <u>schedule cleaning</u> – custodial hours – based on the scheduled needs of the store; a dinner time is messier than mid-morning, for instance – *the event schedule in the theatre requiring custodial services.*

So that food, packaging, and other supplier and contractors – *theatre repair and supply stores* - have a <u>central figure to go to in order to schedule</u> deliveries, repairs, and confirm/adjust orders.

So that there is an <u>ongoing and standardized training system</u> for new employees – *students* - because of inherent turnover - *students come and go all the time, they* find they don't like tech, they're just doing tech because the didn't get cast in that particular show, they graduate.

So that the customers – *audience* – can expect to receive <u>a standard level of service</u> and the <u>expected quality of product</u> – *the audience has a right to expect the show to run smoothly with no unreasonably long pauses for technical difficulties.*

So that the store manager – *theatre manager,* or appointed shift managers – *theatre technicians,* can <u>oversee and control the security</u> of the restaurant when it is not in use, such as making sure that doors are locked, and equipment and lights are turned off, so that employees – *students* – aren't able to gain unauthorized access and so that power is not wasted on an empty building.

So that the corporate administration – *theatre manager* – can provide <u>outreach, marketing, customer service, branding</u>, etc. in order to get the customers – *in this case; outside users* - to come in and provide revenue – *outside bookings in order to financially support the theatre for district use.*

So that the store manager – *theatre manager* – can assure that all <u>safety policies are posted</u>, and a <u>safety manual is maintained</u>, and a <u>log</u> is kept of injuries and breakages.

So that the administration – *theatre manager* – can assure that <u>information about the store</u> – *the theatre* – is supplied to the public – *outside users, district users, audience, employees, suppliers* - for instance, nutritional information of foods offered employment, locations and hours of operation, etc. – *technical information and specs of the features available at the theatre — the theatre manager maintains a website to provide all this information.*

So that the store manager – *theatre manager* – can <u>keep track of safety regulations that require periodic equipment inspections, fire proofing tests</u>, etc.

So that the store manager – *theatre manager* – is a central person who can <u>maintain a supplies and maintenance budget</u> in order of priority.

Yes, McDonalds is run by teenagers, and probably could be run by teenagers without supervision - but at what cost?

PARENT VOLUNTEERS AS STAFF

Parents seem to be the most widely practiced system of designing and constructing sets in high schools. However they come and go, and their experience varies widely. Plus, very few parents have any lighting or sound expertise.

Compensation for parents range from undying gratitude to stipends of up to around $1000, for what can be tens, if not hundreds, of hours of work. Stipended parents usually end up earning a dollar an hour, if they're lucky. The low pay directly corresponds to the turn over, and to technical knowledge and experience/expertise level, which in turn directly corresponds to the education level and safety level of the students.

As stated before, a parent, no matter their background, is not considered appropriate supervision for minors performing vocational activities. Regardless of their background the parent volunteer is then taking on a teaching and supervisory role, which requires a certificated teacher. Even if the proper safety procedures and training were applied, if an accident or injury happened the school district would still be liable.

THEATRE MANAGER OR TECHNICAL DIRECTOR (TD)

Whether you decide to have your Drama teacher and students run your theatre or whether you decide to hire qualified professionals, there are some things you should be aware of before you make your plans. One of the first things to take into account is the interchange of the job titles Theatre Manager and Technical Director. In actual fact these are two different positions and ideally it's best to have both.

A Theatre Manager, or the person running your theatre, does not necessarily have to be a specialist in every technical aspect of the theatre, but they do have to know enough in order to hire and manage people who do. They have to be organized and self-motivated. They have to be good at maintaining stacks of paperwork. They also have to have a good grasp of how a theater operates and what policies and procedures will make it operate more smoothly. This can come through a degree related to theatre business management, and/or through years of experience of working in a theatre in some capacity or another – preferably both. A Theatre Manager does not always actually run tech for the shows - just as in a hospital, the administrator does not perform the surgeries - but she must have enough specialized knowledge to manage the facility.

A Technical Director (TD) is more of a hands-on position. A TD usually has the technical knowledge of how to program and run lighting and sound computer boards, knows how to hang and focus lights, set up a sound system, and knows the correct rigging hardware and techniques needed to hang scenery. A TD usually has a more general, but hands-on technical knowledge of how the equipment in the theatre works. Sometimes they have a design background or a related degree, but not always.

Which begs the questions, if we have a Theatre Manager and we hire professional crew in each area of tech (lights, sound, and stage and rigging) do we need to also hire a TD? If we don't hire a TD, how many technicians do we need to hire? It would not be practically possible to have one TD in place of technicians. One TD cannot physically be at the light board, the sound board and backstage at the same time. Therefore you still need technicians at each show who can operate in each of those areas. Ideally it would be best to have a Theatre Manager to run the theatre, and a TD to supervise the technicians, who in turn mentor the students. But, usually in high school theatres, regardless of whether the job title is Theatre Manager or Technical Director, one person does both those jobs with the help of the technicians. As their job is so multi-faceted, your Theatre Manager/TD, or the person you choose to run your theatre, has to be that rare person who is as happy sitting at a desk as they are up a ladder.

THE HIGH SCHOOL THEATRE MANAGER'S MISSION STATEMENT

When I started working as a Theatre Manager I suggested that the theatre I worked at have a specialized Mission Statement of its own. Although the district had its own mission statement, and in fact the athletic department had their own specific mission statement, the idea of the theatre having its own specific mission statement was pooh-poohed as unnecessary. However, I adopted the Mission Statement as my own personal creed. I'd like to leave you with my Mission Statement, because a Mission Statement – whatever wording you choose to use - will help guide the management and staff of your high school theatre in it's future operations.

Under the umbrella of

personal safety, student-focused learning, and facility conservation,

I endeavor to

provide real-world experience for all performing students, and vocational training for Tech Theatre students,

in order to

maximize the success of students' school events, develop students' characters, provide students with transferable personal and career skills , and to allow teachers the freedom to do their jobs,

as well as

provide technical supervision and assistance to outside events, so that funds acquired can directly support the operation and maintenance of the theatre for educational use.

JOB DUTIES OF A HIGH SCHOOL THEATRE MANAGER/TD

Following is a list of duties you can expect at Theatre Manager/TD, or the person assigned to manage your high school theatre, to do.

SCHEDULING

Schedule the theatre rentals according to their unique needs.
Optimize the use schedule in order to best provide for the needs of the variety of groups that use the theatre.
Schedule the right number and right specialties of technicians for each event.
Schedule student crew.

MEETINGS

Hold a Production Meeting with each event in order to ascertain prospective users' specific time needs and space requirements, and how to best support them.
Technician and student crew (as appropriate) staff meetings and trainings.
Meet with school district staff as needed to alert them or educate them to issues needing attention in the theatre.

SAFETY

Develop customized operational safety policies and procedures that improve personal safety, protect property, and mitigate liability.
Create customized signs, notices and handouts to enhance safety knowledge.
Enforce all safety and facility use rule and regulations.
Ensure that technicians are trained in safety procedures.
Train student crew in safety procedures.
Train teachers and administration in safety procedures, especially if they will be supervising students in the theatre with no manager or technicians present.
Train all users of the theatre in safety procedures for each event.
Create, compile and maintain a safety manual.
Generate a safety inspection roster and timeline.
Coordinate periodically safety inspections and repairs as indicated.
Engage professional independent theatre technicians, inspectors, suppliers and/or subcontractors as applicable. Recommend changes or improvements to enhance safety.
Create policies and procedures to control security and access of the theatre.

EMPLOYEE MANAGEMENT

Interview technician applicants.
Hire technicians who will provide technical support to increase the efficacy and safe operations of the theatre in the areas of lighting, sound and stage/rigging.
Supervise technicians and evaluate progress.
Make sure employees are trained in the policies and procedures of the theatre so that they may appropriately represent the theatre.
Create a crew schedule to satisfy appropriate technical needs for events.

EDUCATION

Train student stage crew on the proper procedures and protocol of running a show and working together as an efficient technical team.
Develop a Tech Theatre Club or class. Hold technical workshops for students and/or staff.
Provide information on educational standards, learning goals and career development.

ADMINISTRATION AND RECORD KEEPING

Technician timesheets.
Technician training and certification.
Event schedules for billing.
Keep on file student safety waiver forms.
Maintain an incident and accident log book.
Create user application forms covering areas such as technical equipment requirements, production schedules, crewing, and various specialized issues such as food in the space, appropriate footwear, use of fog machines, etc.
Create forms for users to fill out for the theatre management, and for the theatre management to impart essential information to the user.

Create systems for correspondence and collaboration with employees, theatre users, and administration.

Develop a system to track prospective users, the year's users, the current month's users, upcoming month's users, past month's users; noting the production schedule, running order of each day, the technical needs and tracking production meetings and their outcomes.

Other administrative reports.

POLICIES AND PROCEDURES

Create and maintain all theatre use and safety policies and procedures. Post signs and notices as needed to inform staff and users of policies and procedures.

BUDGETING AND FINANCES

Track the annual budget for expenses.

Make suggestions for essential expenses. Verify delivery and payments. Ensure the expenditures are within budget.

Review existing budgets and suggest areas for cost savings.

Research and recommend a competitive fee schedule for renters.

Other financial analysis based on production needs and requirements.

TECHNICAL SUPPORT (whether with or without technicians and/or student crew)

Provide technical support to increase the efficacy and safe operations of the theatres.

Design, hang and focus a functional "Rep Plot" (a standardized lighting system which is versatile for performances from plays and musicals, to concerts, to speakers, which allows for show-specific flexibility within a reasonable time frame).

Maintain up to date documents ("cheat sheets" - sometimes called "magic sheets"), which give event users an at-a-glance overview of the Rep Plot for quick reference and easy use.

Provide the labor to hang and focus, and operate the lights as needed for each given production.

Provide the labor to set up and operate mics, sound system and audio visual for each given production.

Provide the labor to load-in equipment, sets and paraphernalia for each given production.

Provide the labor to hang scenery and drops for each given production.

Organize technical equipment, recommend specific and secure functional equipment storage locations.

EQUIPMENT AND SUPPLY ORDERING AND MAINTANANCE

Another issue confronting a theatre with no management, is who orders and maintains the supplies and equipment? Your theatre may be amply stocked with equipment and supplies, or you may be stocking it for the first time or restocking with up to date equipment. Regardless, purchasing and maintaining equipment is a never ending responsibility for the person managing the theatre. When a user comes into a space, they expect a certain level of availability of supplies to use, from tapes, to tools to rechargeable mic batteries. It causes no end of frustration if a teacher has to delay things because of lack of supplies, and it causes no end of conflicts between teachers who are using other teachers' supplies that had to come out of their budget.

It is up to the person managing your high school theatre to organize the technical equipment, recommend specific and secure functional equipment storage locations. They must also recommend and maintain a list of consumable equipment stock in anticipation of the needs of the users of the space.

A few examples of ordering duties include:
> Maintain expendable supplies such as lamps, gels, batteries, etc. in anticipation of the needs of the users of the space.
> Maintain inventory of tools and equipment needed for a variety of productions.
> Order repairs and parts.
> Order new equipment.

A few examples of maintenance duties include:
> Maintain backstage, the booth, catwalks, backstage areas and so on in a clean and orderly condition.
> Conduct quarterly maintenance "work parties".
> Conduct annual equipment cleanings.

SCHEDULING

Scheduling duties seem to vary between school districts. In some districts the person who schedules all of the facilities in the district also schedules the theatres. However, theatres have more specialized requirements than just scheduling a classroom or gym, which basically need the lights and heat turned on. In one school that I worked at one person scheduled all of the school and outside rentals of the facilities in the whole district, and so once the theatre was built, she took on the scheduling of that building, too. She would quote to the user the insurance requirements and costs and the rental rates, and arranged payment, and then schedule heat, building lights and custodial. However, after that initial contact, the prospective theatre user was referred to the on-site Theatre Manager. This is an inefficient system, as the district facilities' scheduler does not have the theatrical knowledge to be able to advise the theatre users about how much time is needed for their rehearsals and performances. So after the user had spoken to the Theatre Manager about their needs, they were inconveniently shunted back to the district scheduler to change the rental period. Because of the nature of the theatrical process it makes more sense to have the Theatre Manager maintain the schedule for the theatre, do all the scheduling, and then inform the district (who then schedules building lights, heat, custodial, etc.) not the other way around. This is the way it worked at another school that I worked in and it ran very smoothly, with very little 'run around' for the school and outside users.

MARKETING AND OUTREACH

Even a high school theatre needs to develop an image (brand) in the community. Familiarity breeds ownership, pride and a sense of belonging within the community. Increase branding that will stand for professional, state-of-the-art facilities, which will be an integral part of the community.

The Theatre Manager/TD should develop a "sub-website" within the district's website, which will provide information about the theatre such as: technical specifications and inventory, rental rates, availability at-a-glance, application information, policies and procedures, and other information that is often requested by users and/or often needs to be conveyed to users. The Theatre Manager should also conduct site visits for prospective users, and assist with other marketing of the facility and proactive encouragement of groups to rent the theatre as per school district guidelines.

INNOVATION/LOOKING TO THE FUTURE/PLANNING

A high school Theatre Manager and or TD, besides managing systems, should also be a leader and innovator, and should support you in the on-going functionality of your theatre. Your Theatre Manager should proactively make recommendations to improve the practical application of the physical space, such as what consumable equipment to stock, how to create versatile lighting, sound, stage and communication systems; how to develop customized operational policies and procedures that improve personal safety, protect property, and mitigate liability; what systems, forms, scheduling procedures are needed; recommend budgets and fees; plus help with outreach and branding.

In the educational setting, he can help set up programs which will maximize student learning, assist with providing real-world experience and transferable personal and career skills for all performing students, and vocational training for tech students.

DURING CONSTRUCTION OR REMODEL

If you are fortunate enough to be able to hire a Theatre Manager during construction, or before a remodel or up grade, the Theatre Manager can review construction documents and make recommendations to improve the functionality of the physical space in the areas of:

- Building layout

- Lighting System

- Sound System

- Rigging System

- Communication Systems

- Furnishings

- Consumable supplies

- Traffic patters, doors, locks, room configurations.

- Efficiency and practicality of the equipment package - is the equipment obsolete, overkill or just right?

- Enhance the functional placement of equipment.

- Optimal amount and quality of equipment to efficiently run a production

- Reconfiguring the layout of the backstage area for optimal functionality

- Optimize the communication system to fulfill the needs for the operation of a production.

PROFESSIONAL TECHNICIANS

If you decide - and I can't strongly endorse it enough - to hire professional technicians, one question is how many people do you need to keep on the books? I've found that the magic number seems to be three in each area: lighting, sound and stage/rigging. Be aware that you are not increasing the amount of hours you have to pay for when you increase the number of techs you have, you are just increasing your options. The reason for keeping so many people on your crew and not hiring a single person to do the job is because usually a high school theatre cannot provide enough hours for one single person to earn a living working solely for the school district. Therefore most technicians have other jobs. I've had technicians that work in pizza restaurants, technicians who DJ, technicians who also work as technicians in other local theatres, technicians who work for local theatrical suppliers, technicians who freelance as commercial project installers and much more. While it would be nice to just have one person in each area to rely on, for scheduling purposes you need to have at least two or three people to choose from in each tech area, because you are also juggling around your technician's other work schedules, so you need a pool from which to choose. It's for this reason I also recommend that your Theatre Manager schedules technicians two to three months in advance, so that you know ahead of time that you have committed technicians for your events.

TECHNICIANS AS MENTORS

All your technicians have to not only be self sufficient in their jobs, but also comfortable in mentoring students. Many high schools don't have a dedicated Tech Theatre class, so the only way students are exposed to tech theatre is during the two weeks (one week of tech rehearsals, two weekends of performances) a show is in the theatre, or if they work other events that come into the theatre. "On-the-job" is a valuable way to learn, however it is a limited way to learn. So, consider your technicians as your "guest teachers" – usually at a lower cost than the hourly rate of a teacher. The technicians have the education and real world knowledge of the subject. They are also your "life guards" who watch over the students, yell at them to 'stop running', and are ready to dive in if there's trouble.

QUALIFICATIONS

All tech areas have creative and technical aspects about them. For instance, in lighting you can have people who specialize in design and people who specialize in programming. For the purposes of high school theatre (mostly due to budget) your lighting techs in particular must know design lights as well as how to program a board. Likewise with your sound technicians, they should have experience in sound design and running sound boards. And if your stage and rigging technician will actually be helping the school production with set building, they also need to have knowledge of set design and decorating.

Regardless of their specialty technicians in your high school theatre should have the following qualifications:

- Demonstrate an ability to develop and maintain effective leadership skills in people and production management.
- Specialized experience in, and knowledge of, one of the following technical theatre areas of expertise: Lighting. Sound and audio/visual. Scenery and rigging.

- General experience in, and knowledge of, all areas of expertise, including lighting, sound, scenery and rigging, and audio/visual.
- Ability to set up and operate theater equipment with a high level of safety, following and enforcing all safety rules and guidelines.
- Current on industry standards and systems through training.
- Ability to quickly, but calmly, resolve technical difficulties.
  Ability to follow directions of the Theatre Manager or person in charge, work cooperatively as a part of team, and supervise Theatre Technician IIs.
- Ability to work in a positive mentorship role to the school's student crew members and production student crew members.
- Ability to maintain positive public relations with a variety of personalities and a diverse event schedule.
- Flexible with last minute changes with on-the-job requirements; schedule, responsibilities, locations, etc.
- Maintains the stage, backstage areas, scene shop, assigned classrooms, catwalk, booth and other related areas in the performing arts centers, in a clean and orderly condition.
- Maintains equipment and tools in a safe and clean condition.
- Knowledge of building and fire code regulations.
- Ability to communicate effectively both orally and in writing, and to maintain records and reports.
- Ability to work with a diverse group of co-workers, supervisors, subordinates, students, teachers, school administrators, commercial clients, vendors and the public.
- Ability to problem solve and think creatively.
- Ability to remain calm and keep a professional demeanor in stressful situations.
- Ability to be flexible, organized and manage time effectively.
- Ability to function as part of a team.
- Ability to maintain confidentiality.
- Ability to exercise sensitivity in dealing with individuals of diverse socio-economic backgrounds, cognitive and physical abilities as well as with individuals of diverse cultural and ethnic backgrounds.
- Ability to work positively with teenagers.
- Ability to safely lift and carry equipment weighing 40+ pounds.
- Ability to climb ladders while carrying equipment, operate a Genie lift, and work at heights.
- Must be able to work with power, computerized and hand tools specific to the craft.
- Must be able to perform routine repairs or replace equipment as needed.

RANKS

Commonly in many theatres there are two ranks of employees: the Theatre Manager and "Everyone Else". Many school district administrators perceive only that they are operating a building that has one manager and a staff. In reality however, there are technicians with a wide variety of education and training, prior experience in the field, skill levels, and job responsibilities. Within the walls of the theatre, this model causes conflict and confusion. Those with less experience and skill don't feel, or act, as if they are subordinates, because they see themselves as equal because they all have equal pay and rank. I have seen this cause many a conflict between technicians. In one theatre I worked in there were about ten or so technicians and they all had the same job description and salary level. When the Theatre Manager was not present at a show there was a lot of infighting as to who was in charge.

I highly recommend having at least two tiers of technicians, if not three, so that it is clear who has authority. In addition to having tiers, the Theatre Manager should also make it clear who is "Acting Site Manager" in their absence. There should also be a policy set up something like the following:

SAMPLE TECHNICIAN HEIRARCHY POLICY

Theatre Technician I will work under the direction of the Theatre Manager as applicable and may be required to supervise Theatre Technician II and/or student crew members. Theatre Technician I has decision-making authority over a Theatre Technician II in the same specialty area, and over all Theatre Technician IIs regarding general operation of a production, but should take into account the advice of a Theatre Technician II in a specialty area other than their own for the good of the production.

MORE THAN ONE THEATRE IN A SCHOOL DISTRICT

If your school district has more than one theatre, there are pros and cons of hiring one Theatre Manager for the whole district versus having a Theatre Manager on site at each theatre.

There are a lot of positives to having one Theatre Manager in charge overseeing all of the theatres in your district. For instance, if you have more than one theatre in your district it's more feasible to staff both/all theatres with the same technicians, therefore it's best to have one person overseeing all of the scheduling of the theatres and the staffing, so that two Theatre Managers aren't competing over the Technicians' time. One Theatre Manager would also have knowledge of the events in each theatre, so that if one theatre needed some equipment they could possibly borrow it from the other theatre if it was not in use.

The main drawback to having one Theatre Manager or other person in charge is that they can't be in two (or more) places at once. In reality it is best to have someone on site at all times for safety, security, assistance and knowledge.

The ideal situation would be to have one Theatre Manager for the district and then each theatre has its own TD on site with specialized Technicians reporting to the TD. Another solution would be to have one Theatre Manager who is on site at one theatre, and an Assistant Theatre Manager who is on site at the other theatre(s). But, budget doesn't always allow for that level of professionalism, so each district has to decide for themselves which situation best suits their needs.

STAFFING

In an ideal world, where education and safety was paramount in the high school theatre setting, would be as follows:

THE RAND STAFFING MODEL

Drama Teacher
Instrumental Music Teacher
Vocal Music Teacher
Dance Teacher
CTE Tech Theatre Teacher
Theatre Manager
TD (Lead Technician)
One dedicated Lighting Technician and one sub
One dedicated Sound Technician and one sub
One dedicated Stage/Rigging Technician and one sub
Paid Student Crew

All theatre staff would be salaried professionals, and students would be paid for their hours. I realize that this is a high "gold standard", but when you consider the staffing model of an entire sports program in a high school you find that it's not unreasonable.

THE EXCEPTION TO THE RULE

There is always an exception to the rule. While I don't advocate running a high school event or show without professional technicians present for many reasons, there are some events that teachers and administrators can run by themselves if budgets are tight. These are events such as school-day assemblies, lectures, demonstrations, and so on. But they don't always require technicians only if they don't require the full use of the sound and lighting equipment, and use of the rigging system, and all the students are contained in the seats in the house. In this case the theatre becomes like a large lecture hall. These days most new theatres are fitted with a auto system for lights and sound as well as a manual system. The auto system is preset with straightforward options, such as lights on, lights off, plug in iPod or CD, connect a laptop to the projector, and turn on one or two wireless mics. Most teachers and administrators are used to using this level of technology in their classrooms, offices and meeting rooms, so they can run similar equipment in your theatre.

But that said, although teachers and administrators may know how to turn on a few lights and operate a mic and a projector, there remains the issue of the safety/security of the students (can one teacher keep any eye on a theatre full of potentially hundreds of students while having to run the equipment at the same time), and preservation of the equipment (will a teacher, administrator, assigned students use the equipment properly, maintain it in good condition and restore it to its original settings once finished). The theatre is not a safe place and it's recommended that no one should be given full reign of the space without site supervision by qualified professionals to maintain functionality, preserve the equipment, and supervise safety.

If events do not need special lighting, sound and rigging that the theatre provides, then really they should be conducted in the gym or commons. However, in reality the theatre is used during the school day and technicians are not always present. If you choose to permit this in your school you should come up with a policy regarding what sort of events need technicians, based on their level of technical difficultly, preservation of your multi-million dollar facility, quality of the event, and student safety.

UNSUPERVISED

If your district or school administration does choose to allow people to use your high school theatre without professionals present, make sure that all users are provided with safety information, which is announced to all students and staff who will be using the theatre. Some suggested rules to be announced follow.

SAMPLE RULES FOR UNSUPERVISED USE OF THEATRE

No food or drinks in the theatre.

Do not put your feet on the seats, the arms of the seats, or on the back of the seats in front of you.

Do not jump up on, or off of, the edge of the stage.

No bare feet, socks, flip-flops or slippers in any area of the facility. Plan to wear closed-toed shoes.

No running on the stage, in the house or backstage area.

In case of fire, notify as many people in the vicinity as it is safe for you to do so and evacuate the building immediately. Pull the fire alarm if you can reach one safely. Do not attempt to extinguish the fire yourself.

Avoid rolling heavy set pieces or pianos over floor pockets, they cannot take the weight.

Keep a 4' distance from the locking rail on stage left. Under no circumstances should you attempt to operate the ropes of the counterweight system.

Do not touch or play with the drapes.

No one may go up to the galleries or catwalks.

IF THE ORCHESTRA PIT IS OPEN: do not lean over the orchestra pit from the house, or walk within 6' of the pit on the stage side.

Only tapes approved by the theatre staff may be used on walls, floors or other surfaces.

When leaving the theatre:
Turn off all lights. Turn on "Night Light". Lock all doors.
If the pit is open, please check with the Theatre Manager about procedures.

Assuming people other than technicians will be using the equipment, following is a suggested checklist in order to determine under what conditions technicians would be needed in your high school theatre.

SAMPLE TECHNICAL SUPERVISION POLICY

A TEACHER OR ADMINISTRATOR MAY SUPERVISE A MEETING, ASSEMBLY OR CLASSES IN THE THEATRE IN SITUATIONS WHEN THE EVENT:

☐ is on the apron, requiring only the main curtain to be traveled only (not flown),

☐ is on the full stage but does not need any drapes flow in, requiring use of fly system, unless an adult or student, who has a signed liability waiver on file and has completed the safety training, is operating the fly system, under the supervision of the teacher or administrator,

☐ only needs one or two handheld mics for the speaker(s) on stage,

☐ shows a movie/video using the house projector 'auto' system,

☐ uses sound (music or special effects sound) from an iPod or CD or cassette tape, which requires hook up to, and control from, the 'auto' system,

☐ only needs a general stage wash of lights, and house lights, that can be turned on from the preset on the stage manager's panel, (please note: if the houselights are dimmed or out for any part of the event, the aisle safety lights must be turned on from the stage manager's panel),

☐ otherwise does not require: access to the booth, use of the sound board, use of the light board, any draperies to be flown in (other than the main curtain to be traveled close).

Please note: the supervisor is responsible for clearing the stage deck, turning off all the lights, with the exception of turning on the Night Light, and locking all the interior & exterior doors at the end of the event.

A LIGHTING TECHNICIAN MUST BE PRESENT FOR MEETINGS, ASSEMBLIES OR CLASSES IN THE THEATRE WHEN THE EVENT:

☐ has light cues (blackouts, different "looks") that require access to the light board, and/or needs the houselights to be dimmed and raised at any time before, during or after the event,

☐ needs lighting instruments to be re-hung, refocused, patched or gelled for a specific function,

- □ requires the use of one or more followspots (this would require one or two more lighting technicians in addition to the light board operator, or trained student crew members with signed waivers),
- □ requires access to the galleries or catwalks in order to access lighting instruments and/or equipment,
- □ otherwise requires use of the house lighting system,
- □ will be bringing in an independent lighting system for use during the event.

A SOUND TECHNICIAN MUST BE PRESENT FOR MEETINGS, ASSEMBLIES OR CLASSES IN THE THEATRE WHEN THE EVENT:
- □ shows a movie/video from the house projector or supplied projector, which requires entry into the booth and hook up to the sound board,
- □ uses sound (music or special effects sound) from an iPod or CD or cassette tape, which requires hook up to, and control from, the sound board,
- □ has the band and/or choir (or other group of more than one person and/or instrument) performing, which needs more than the hand-held mic(s) set up and access to the sound board,
- □ has a full stage performance requiring the overhead mics, access to sound board and/or headset mics,
- □ otherwise requires use of the house sound system,
- □ will be bringing in an independent sound system for use during the event,
- □ a second technician may need to be present backstage if the event requires use of wireless mics.

A STAGE/RIGGING TECHNICIAN MUST BE PRESENT FOR MEETINGS, ASSEMBLIES OR CLASSES IN THE THEATRE WHEN THE EVENT:
- □ uses the full stage, and therefore needs to utilize the counterweight system in order to lower stage drapes to set for masking, drops or decorative pieces (exception: if the user has been trained to do this by the theatre staff, and/or if there is a sound and/or lighting technician present, they can take care of setting the drapes at the beginning of the event and striking the drapes at the end of the event),
- □ uses the full stage, and requires drops or drapes to be moved during the event,
- □ requires the main curtain to be flown, not traveled,
- □ needs to have any special drops or decorative pieces to be hung from pipes that require re-weighting and/or use of the counterweight system during the event,
- □ otherwise requires use of the house rigging system,
- □ requires access to and/or use of the scene shop,
- □ will be bringing in large set pieces for use during the event.

TO HIRE OR NOT TO HIRE

If you do make the choice not to hire qualified professionals for your high school theatre, this chapter has at least given you some ideas of the operations that have to go on behind the scenes in order for your theatres to be safe, functional, educational, and for the multi-million dollar space to be preserved. Whether you hire a Theatre Manager/TD and technicians, or whether you have teachers and students run your theatre and/or allow outside users to use the facility unsupervised, will be an individual choice for each school district. In the closing of this chapter I have only one word to offer you to help you make your comfort-level decision, and that word is:

liability.

CHAPTER 9

ROAD HOUSE

It is likely that your new high school's performing arts department and other school groups are not going to be the only users of your theatre. So many high school theatres operate as "road houses" these days to help cover educational operational costs.

This is a good idea, but because of this an architect must plan for, and an administrator must be prepared for, a variety of transient users (school, district and outside events) that need constant monitoring and supervision for safety, building preservation, operational functionality and educational training.

I've seen so many high schools assume that the Drama teacher can take care of managing a theatre and that the students can crew the events. It then comes as a surprise when they later discover that the Drama teacher is not a manager and the students are unreliable, and only then do they come to the conclusion that they must hire a Theatre Manager and professional theatre technicians.

There are some important things to consider when deciding whether to hire a professional Theatre Manager and technicians or whether your existing teaching staff and students can run outside events. These are the same questions to ask when deciding if your outside events need highly qualified professionals. Again, they are:

> Is your school staff comfortable with and knowledgeable about your theatre's functional operation?

> Is your school staff familiar enough with the theatrical process to make scheduling decisions?

> Is there a vocational training program for technical students?

> Is your theatre ergonomically functional?

> Are operational policies and procedures in place that are strictly enforced?

> Is your theatre being used to its full potential?

> Is your theatre self-sustaining?

> Is learning enhanced through your theatre operations?

Are there safety policies and procedures in place that are strictly enforced?

Is your theatre protected from liabilities and lawsuits?

I can't recommend strongly enough that you hire a Theatre Manager and technicians. This isn't to say that students can't work outside events, in fact I strongly advocate for that (and if you can pay them, that's even better), but not without the supervision of professionals. Outside users are paying to use your facility and they are required to pay to use your technicians, so they expect a professional experience.

In addition, it's essential to have certain technicians (depending on the specific needs of each event) to be present for safety and liability reasons, as well as for the success of the event or show. I would encourage hiring professionals for any high school theatre that also acts as a "road house".

HOW MANY TECHNICIANS

Again, I recommend a crew of at least 9 technicians who work the outside events (between 1 to 3 technicians work any given event). The Theatre Manager should be at as many events as possible for a couple of reasons.

One reason is to oversee the event. Your lighting technician is running the light board, your sound technician is running the sound board, and your stage technician is calling cues backstage. If something happens during the rehearsal or show – say a followspot lamps blows or a headset mic's battery runs out) the technicians are unable to leave their posts in order to do anything about it without stopping the whole rehearsal or compromising the show. Another reason the Theatre Manager should be present is in case a technician doesn't show up, is taken ill or has an emergency. The show must go on so the Theatre Manager can fill in and do their job. Yet another reason is good old customer service. Events perceive the Theatre Manager as the person who is going to hold everything together and make their event successful. Even though in reality for most events I've supervised as a Theatre Manager my technicians have "got this", I can't count the number of times during Production Meetings with school groups and outside events when the person in charge looks at me with a worried look on their face an says "You'll be there, won't you?".

The good news about outside events is that you can require that they have the appropriate amount of technicians on staff and you can directly charge the event for the technician's time. So, the staffing of technicians is at no cost to the district and the Theatre Manager's time can be built into the rental rates.

BOOKING PRIORITIES

Of course, the primary purpose of a high school theatre is for the students' education, so school events should have first priority, followed by district (other schools) events, and finally outside events. In my experience the school events calendar is often not finalized until September, and at the same time you've got dance schools and other events that need to settle their dates in order to inform their parents and start their marketing.

A system that seems to work well is for your Theatre Manager to inform your outside events that while he can't release their dates until September, that he can prioritize the outside events between themselves, so that once a date becomes available the Theatre Manager can release it to the outside event who turned in their required paperwork first. At one theatre I had dance companies who were booking two years in advance in order to beat out the other dance companies for dates. Of course, the Theatre Manager comes to know your theatre's rhythm, and she'll know, for instance, that it's likely that an outside event can get dates in September (before school events have had time to rehearse) and in late December (when school events are wrapping up, no teacher wanting to produce a show right before the winter holiday) and in late June (once school is out, but before summer school begins). Your Theatre Manager will know when your school usually puts on their plays and musical, so she will come to know the times of year when your theatre is not likely to be available to outside events, and can plan accordingly.

NOT A PROFIT

And, while school districts are not technically allowed to make a "profit", some do charge a "mark-up" if you will, on their technician's time. This "mark-up" and the "proceeds" for the facility rental go towards running the theatre for the students' use. So that, for instance, the technicians can then be provided for the education and safety of the students and for the preservation of the theatre at no, or little cost to the school district.

Outside events can be the bread and butter of a high school theatre, so you want their repeat business. Most high school theatres that I've worked in have at least five to ten dance schools and several other groups who rent out their theatre two or three times a year, or more. These events aren't going to keep coming back if the theatre staff isn't professional and dedicated to the success of their event. A professional theatre staff is essential to the endurance of your high school theatre.

CHAPTER 10

FINANCIALS

This chapter is primarily directed to district administrators, however, everyone involved with planning and operating a high school theatre should be aware of the financials.

THE BOSS

A Theatre Manager's job has certain financial skill requirements. These are the facets of the job that we don't think about when we think of a Theatre Manager overseeing technicians and working with student crews backstage during a show. However, there is a lot of behind the scenes paper work that the Theatre Manager does and some of it is financial. For instance, once she receives an outside event production company's rider, or a schools "wish list" for a production, she must price out an accurate cost of production. These costs include the hourly rental of the facility, the hourly fees for each technician, custodial services and rental of any equipment. Often times, the user has costs that they haven't considered that need to be explained. This is where your Theatre Manager's background knowledge of theatre assists her in the financial aspects of her job. For instance, the production company might want several backdrops flown in and out during their show, and while they have considered the cost of a flyman to do that during the performances, they may not have considered the cost of the labor required for the time it takes to hang and weight the drops in preparation for a show, and the time it takes to take it all down again. The person managing your theatre will be able to look beyond the obvious. Whenever possible she will have a pre-production meeting with the person in charge of the incoming production (school, or outside events) to discuss specific costs of the whole process. A large chunk of your Theatre Manager's job is her daytime management and financial responsibilities, which can only be effectual through her understanding of the theatrical process.

THE BOSS OF THE BOSS

The Theatre Manager's direct supervisor is usually someone in district management. It could be the Business Director, the Facility Director, or another Director, depending on how the responsibility of district upper management is laid out. Regardless of who is the direct supervisor of your Theatre Manager, the complexity of the financial responsibilities of this position cannot be underestimated.

As well as a Theatre Manager, a high school theatre needs a district level Facilities or Business Director who can manage that facility from a financial business standpoint. Too often a new theatre is thought of as just another "facility" of the district, so it falls under the jurisdiction of the district's Financial Business Director or a Facilities Management Director (sometimes the same person depending on the size of the district). As this person typically has no or little experience in theatre, other than the few plays she may been in as a student, she subsequently experiences a huge learning curve over the first few years of the high school theatre's operation. It can feel like she is eating and breathing theatre – this learning curve is likely greater than in any other aspect of district management. In order to skillfully ride this learning curve, the Business Director must work closely with the Theatre Manager.

There are a lot of unique financial restrictions, and therefore financial challenges, of running a theatre in a high school setting, because of the fact that a school district is not a private business. For instance, because the theatre is a public entity, it is not allowed to make a profit. Therefore, when outside events rent out your theatre their riders have to be very specifically priced. In addition, the Business Director has to practice "public" not "private" accounting, which means, in the case of a high school theatre facility, that she is more concerned about the Operation Fund accounting aspects than the Capital Fund accounting aspects.

One of your Financial Director's tools is a Break Even Analysis, which allows her to estimate the operation costs your theatre each year. A graph can be created that shows the variable costs of operation on one line, the fixed costs of operation on another line and a third for a combination. Two additional lines can be used to further analyze break even marks; one which indicates the "revenue" if only the schools used the space (some school districts actually charge school groups a fee to use their own facility) and one which indicates the revenue if the theatre was booked out only to private outside events (who pay a higher fee). The Financial Director can then assess the break-even points of the two circumstances separately or in combination. In reality, each year is a different combination of the two, so the break-even point would be somewhere in the middle. Using the information in the graph, the financial director can then produce a Basic Costs Estimate.

SAMPLE BREAK EVEN ANALYSIS CHART

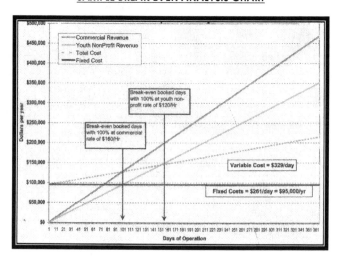

But you didn't mention his consideration of cost of capital in the graph, I hear you say. This is because high school theatres are typically financed by a bond or levy, which is a fixed cost from another budget – some which are financed over a period of time, in some cases thirty years. Consequently, when your Financial Director looks at the break-even points of the theatre's operations, she does not take capital into consideration. The fixed costs therefore comprise mostly of electricity to light and heat the building and the salary of the Theatre Manager, both of which have to be paid every day, whether or not the building is in use. The variable costs mostly include the labor of the technicians and janitors needed for each show that comes in to use the space and any supplies purchased. In addition, the asset is not depreciated and the district doesn't pay taxes. As you can see the financial job functions of a school district Finance Director who oversees the financial side of theatre operations are sometimes different than Finance Directors who are working in the private sector.

THE BUSINESS OF HIGH SCHOOL SHOW BUSINESS

In some aspects, though, from a business perspective, a high school theatre is essentially a "company". Although a school district is a non-profit organization and does not have "revenue" per se, the high school theatre is renting out their space to outside users and is scheduling in school and district users as well. Although they cannot make a "profit", there are expenses to be covered and for that reason most school districts must bring in some form of "revenue".

As mentioned above, while many businesses are initially capital intensive, in the educational world the finances for building the facilities can come from a different levy or bond than the finances for staffing the facility. So that means that once the theatre is built or remodeled, there is no "mortgage". But, too often in my experience, there has been no money budgeted to staff the facility. It takes a school district by surprise after their high school theatre is built that it is not the same type of facility as a classroom or gym, and that there are special operational and safety factors that can't be handled by a teacher, and must be handled by theatre professionals.

So, after the construction is complete the school district is caught having to find a way to quickly increase "revenue" in order to be able to meet unforeseen expenses. The durable source of a high school's operating income is through "revenues" from their "services" (building rental and technical staffing). For a period of time after construction is complete the "revenue" has to catch up to the operating expenses. Like any business, this could take a few years. This often comes as a surprise to school district administration. In one theatre that I worked in, it took two years of advocacy and research before the administration could be convinced that it must budget for a Theatre Manager and technicians. In other theatres I've worked at they still don't have official Theatre Manager and technician positions. Those theatres are not only now in poor shape, but are not safe for students to work in. I suspect that had many district administrators been educated prior to construction about just what it takes to run a high school theatre facility that a lot of districts would have chosen not to include a theatre in their high school plans.

The primary source of "revenue" for a high school theatre, which is a performance-based business, is building rental fees and technician fees. And a dominant factor is "repeat business". Do the dance companies and variety shows that rent your high school theatre feel that the rental rates are reasonable and do they feel that the "service" provide by the technicians is professional? If both of these factors aspects are in play, they will keep coming back.

The high school theatre is a "company" that offers a service as their product, not tangible assets. They do not have a tangible inventory that they are selling. Yes, they have to keep an "inventory" of equipment and supplies that the users consume, but they are not in the business of selling these items for the most part (some equipment is rented out in some high school theatres). In other words, they are not directly involved in inventory turnover. They are primarily "selling" use time or intangible services. For this reason, the high school theatre's "revenues" depend primarily on services to determine its efficiency ratios. These are ratios that are used to analyze how well the theatre balances its assets and liabilities.

It's been my experience that most school districts look at the short term, in a sort of panicked way, when it comes to efficiency ratios. For instance, in the Headset chapter I discuss the pros and cons of purchasing a battery charger and rechargeable batteries. This is a large expense in the short term, but will save a lot of money in the long run. Unfortunately, I've seen districts balk at the larger short-term expense too often, jeopardizing their long term "revenue" success.

In order for a school district to monitor their expenditures in the short and long terms, some of the ratios it is important to consider would be Gross and Net Profit Margin Ratios, Operating Return on Assets Ratio at the time of building or remodeling, and then monitored after that, and of course Free Cash Flow is important for monitoring and sustaining growth.

Balance sheet benchmarks compare how much short-term assets the "company" holds versus its assets held in physical buildings and equipment. Because of the cost of buildings and equipment, the nature of the ratios must include a higher concentration of long-term debt. Paying for a building and the installed equipment, and then waiting to make a long term profit from the user rental fees affects the levels of performance compared to a company that purchases rubber ducks and turns around and sells them at a profit the next day.

It's important to know what expenditure on equipment and wages brings in (and brings back) the most users, so it is important to monitor that ratio in order to gauge how effective the high school theatre's operation is over periods of time. It could also be assumed that this ratio is the only factor to consider, but this cannot be taken for granted and would be a weak assumption, as other factors might determine the use of the space, so this should also be monitored and the reasons for any fluctuations analyzed, and then acted upon. As you can see, finances are tightly tied to staffing, safety, equipment quality, and operating policies and procedures.

School district administration has to take into account this web when considering who should be running their high school theatres. The person managing your theatre must responsible for accounts payable (expense budget) and accounts receivable (rental rates). They must review existing budgets and suggest areas for cost savings, make suggestions for essential expenses, research and recommend a competitive fee schedule for renters, and conduct other financial analysis based on production needs and requirements. The person running your theatre must work closely with the school district's Business/Finance Director in order to monitor efficiency ratios in the context of the theatre operations.

Part of the job of the person managing your theatre is to manage the finances. There will be perpetual financial waste if your theatre is not managed properly by someone who does not understand the theatrical process. So your Theatre Manager should not only have a theatre background, but also some financial savvy as well in order to make wise decisions. For instance, at one theatre I worked at I discovered an

$11,000.00 error in the annual lamp budget. In another instance, I saved a district that was painting their stage deck about $4000 from the previous time they'd had it painted, simply by making more informed choices about the process. Yet another time, which I describe below, I was able to swap out, at no cost, some lighting equipment that required $360 replacement lamps for equipment that required $15 replacement lamps.

FINANCIAL KNOW-HOW

A conversation with the Business Director at one school district I had worked in provided insight into the financial realities of what really goes on "behind the scenes" of running a publicly funded theatre, and the expectations of the financial qualifications of its Theatre Manager.

In this district the existing Theatre Manager had been hired right out of the teaching profession. The Business Director told me that while the Theatre Manager was strong in the mentoring and educational aspects of the job he had no management and financial background expected of a Theatre Manager who is in charge of hiring, maintenance and scheduling of personnel, managing the budget of the day-to-day operations, advising on rates, salaries and rentals. While I maintain that the Theatre Manager must have some background not only in theatre but also in working with students (it is after all a high school theatre), I agree that management and financial skills are a very important aptitude for a high school Theatre Manager to have. And conversely, if a financier does not have a theatre background, expensive operations mistakes can occur. This Business Manager recognized that these days high school theatres are essentially run like road-houses and he ruminated, at the end of the day, he is running a business, and a Theatre Manager must have business qualities as well as theatrical and educational experience.

On the other end of the spectrum I had a conversation with another Business Manger at another district that I worked in a few years later. I asked him about the "revenue" and "expenses" of the theatre I was managing at the time. His response was that he'd never looked at those figures and he did not know how much gross "revenue" the high school theatres were creating. The "revenue" from the theatre had not been separated and just went into the district facility revenue pot, and all district expenses were budgeted from that pot. Four years into the theatre's operation, he had never done a cash flow analysis in order to determine the theatre facility's break even points.

I recommend choosing the person who will be running your high school theatre very carefully, and I maintain that trying to "save money" and having your Drama teacher (who has a completely different skill set) or a technician (yet another specialized skill set) manage your theatre, is not the best financial choice in the long term. Right now there are very few degrees available in actual Theatre Management, so many people come to the position from a wide variety of backgrounds. For this reason, people who have previously worked as Stage Managers make good candidates for Theatre Managers. They have been in charge of all of the aspects of technical production, and may also have a specialty in a certain area, but they are also good 'paperwork people'. They are typically organized and usually good with numbers.

OPERATING BUDGET

It's important to come up with a reasonable annual budget for your Theatre Manager, or whoever is running your theatre, to make purchases. There are obviously going to be expenses that come up. Supplies and equipment will be needed, repairs and maintenance will be needed. I also recommend you build in some funds for at least one major purchase each year. It doesn't have to be a big purchase, but something over and above the basic supplies you might need that will give your theatre the edge for outside events and educational experiences for your students. It can be a gobo rotator, a few LED instruments, a moving light, a sound compressor, or a mic where you can remotely control the polar pattern.

Following are some expenses you can expect your theatre to have each year.

Consumable supplies

Lamps
Gels
Batteries
Tapes
Rigging equipment

Non-consumable supplies

Gobos
Gobo holders
Mics

Big ticket items

More headsets
A followspot
LED lights
Gobo rotator
Moving light
Mics
Speakers
Monitors
Compressor
Projector Screen

ADMINISTRATIVE EXPENSES

The above are the expenses the person running your theatre would have a budget to cover each year. As a school district, there are more encompassing expenses in running your theatre that need to be taken into consideration. There are fixed expenses and variable expenses.

Fixed Expenses would include:

> Building lease
> Utilities
> Stage/rigging equipment, sound and lighting systems, house expenses, etc.
> Office furniture and supplies, phones, computer systems, etc.
> Liability insurance
> Salaries, wages and employee benefits

Variable Expenses (although more in the Drama teacher's realm, not the Theatre Manager's) would include:

> Set building for each new show.
> Lighting/sound equipment leased or purchased for each new show
> Outsourced production and manufacturing of merchandise as applicable
> Salaries, wages and employee benefits

FINANCIAL WASTE

With no central experienced person in a management position, expensive theatre equipment is not maintained and repaired as needed, and is usually left in disarray - whatever was most convenient for the previous user. Without a manager and technicians equipment is used improperly, is not stored safely and there is the risk of expensive losses. At one theatre I worked at, it was the custom to store a $500 wireless handheld microphone in an unlocked drawer on stage in a theatre that often times was left unsecured, just for the ease of obtaining it when needed without having to walk up to the booth. Another theatre stored their wireless handheld mic in an unlocked drawer by the sound board in the middle of the house for the same reason.

There is some equipment should never be ordered for a high school theatre in the first place. For instance, in one theatre I worked in we had followspots that required a cool down time for the lamp, before turning off the fan (much like a projector). However the students would just turn off the lamp and fan at the same time despite training to the contrary. This significantly shortens the lamp-life. In one year I had to replace the followspot lamps twice (they should have lasted years). Those lamps cost $360 each. There are other brands of followspots that do a sufficient job, and the lamps are such that they don't need a cool down time. These lamps cost about $15 each. They have a shorter rated lamp life, but they can last up to a year or more. At that cost, the students could burn out one a month (not that they do) and still not approach anywhere near the cost of one of the aforementioned lamps. I was able to arrange for a trade and an upgrade order, at no cost, in order to rectify this problem. This is just one example, but without someone running your theatre with knowledge of theatrical equipment and what is appropriate for high school theatre usage, money is being thrown away. If you are an architect spec'ing equipment, take into consideration the operating budget of the equipment you are spec'ing and see if there is a good alternative with a lower operating budget.

In addition it's been my experience in more than one high school theatre without management, that teachers using the theatres turn on the whole production lighting system in order to light their classes, rehearsals and set building sessions. At one theatre I figured this to amount to equal about 44,000 watts of power being used. At another theatre with a more extensive lighting system, I estimated they were using about 120,000 watts of power for classes and rehearsals. In fact, at one theatre, because of budget cuts at the time of installation, work lights were eliminated from the equipment order all together. I hate to think how much was spent in power over the years in order to save a bit of money on a necessary equipment purchase. If you don't have work lights at your theatre take the time to compare initial costs with running costs and find out what is the best choice of equipment.

Additionally, if the people running your theatre have little to no technical theatre experience in lighting, sound and rigging and are not able to efficiently and correctly use the state of the art equipment it's a waste of money in installing state-of-the-art equipment in the first place if it's not used to its full professional and educational potential, as in the example I gave in the Introduction chapter regarding the programmable LED lighting system in the junior high school.

RENTAL RATES

A public school cannot make a "profit", however, ideally you want your high school theatre to be self-sustaining – outside events supporting the school's performing arts. In order to offset your expenses, you must set your rental fees/rates high enough to cover your costs, but low enough to be competitive. Remember, other local high school theatres that also act as road-houses are your "competitors", so have a look at their rates and set yours accordingly.

Some things to consider are:

> Will you set different rates for district-sponsored events, non-profits, non-profits serving only youth, and commercial - or will there be just one rate.

> Will you charge a different rate for rehearsals than for performances?
>> Rehearsals may need the same tech support, but don't have a house full of audience members to clean up after.

> Will you charge separately for technicians or will they be include in the rates?
>> Another question to ask yourself is under what conditions will you require lighting, sound and or stage/rigging technicians and how many. This should be up to your discretion, not the event's. How much will you charge for the technicians, a hourly rate or a set fee? Think about how much you pay your technicians. Some high school theatres will charge a bit of a "mark-up" (this is not to make a "profit", as public high schools aren't allowed to do that, but the extra money is plowed back into the upkeep of the theatre, or used to help offset employment costs).

> How much will you charge for custodial?
>> Is this an hourly rate or flat fee? Will there be an hour minimum? Under what conditions will you require custodial – for instance, if a group is rehearsing on Day 1 and performing on Day 2, would you require custodians to come in after Day 1?

> Are there any other rooms that are being used?
>> Most high school theatres aren't built with greenrooms, so often times adjacent classrooms will be rented out. How much will you charge for room rentals?

Will you charge for specific equipment use?

>Most theatres provide chairs, tables, music stands, a podium, etc. It's usually expected that these type of items will be available, the question is do you include them in your rental rate or will you charge for them separately. If you are charging for things like chairs and music stands separately it's a bit hard for the technicians to police whether a group uses 31 or 32 chairs, so be careful not to get too detailed.

Piano tuning

>Assuming your theatre has a piano, will you require it to be tuned before or after each rental? Continually tuning it will become expensive, so you may want to charge for each event that needs it.

Orchestra Pit

>If your theatre has an orchestra pit and it's not on a hydraulic lift, it will be held in place by scaffolding. This can take three or four technicians about three hours to remove and replace. That gets pretty expensive, so you should probably charge for any group that wants to use the pit. After your technicians have removed and replaced your pit cover a couple of times you will have a pretty good idea of how long it takes and how many technicians it takes, so you can figure out a flat fee.

Marley floor

>If you have a lot of dance companies that rent your theatre – the last school district I worked at had ten dance companies that would rent the space at least once or twice every year – you might consider purchasing a Marley floor and then renting it out to them.

Other

>You don't want to nickel and dime everyone who comes into the theatre, because pretty soon they won't be coming back, but you do want to be able to cover the district expenses of running your theatre, and probably charge a bit of a "profit" so that you can continue to support your theatre for your school students too. So, consider if there's anything else you can charge users for, but don't go overboard. Some items are expected to be available in a theatre, such as chairs, tables, music stands, but some theatres charge for them. This can be a logistical nightmare, asking your technicians to become chair police. Some theatres also charge for the orchestra shells to be set up, but this really is reflected in your technician's timesheets, that you use to bill your users.

SALARIES/WAGES

Another aspect of running a high school theatre that falls under your district's Financial Director's umbrella is the consideration of the salary structure of the Theatre Manager and the technicians. Because so many high schools are now building theatres on their campuses, the rate of pay has to be competitive in the "market", or the theatre cannot compete for the professional talent needed to staff the facility.

In the case of a high school theatre the salary of the Theatre Manager, or person managing your theatre should be fixed, just as any other manager in your district. Other salaries – or wages – are usually variable and show-specific, such as technicians and custodians. The variable expense salaries are typically allocated to the operating budget, and usually there is a budget for the variable salaries or wages that are paid by the district when the staff works for a school or district event. In the case of an outside event, typically the Theatre Manager's salary is included in the cost of the facility rental and the variable salaries or wages of the technicians and custodians are billed directly to the event, and so are not included in the district's theatre operating budget.

RATE OF PAY

How do you figure out what to pay a Theatre Manager and technicians if your district has never had a theatre in it before? One school of thought is to see what other districts are paying their theatre staff, but I have found that this is like jumping off the bridge just because your friends all did. Unfortunately, still today, the arts are not valued as much as football or robotics, and other school districts around you may reflect this. If you truly wish your theatre to be run by the most qualified team, just as you wish your school to be staffed by the most highly qualified of teachers, then you need to be ahead of the crowd, not following it. I have seen too many good technicians leave in search of better pay, benefits and working conditions, too many times. High turn over is not good for the facility, not good for the students, and in the long run not good for the district's bottom line.

I recommend the following: Look at the salary levels of your teachers. Your Theatre Manager will be working closely with your students, training them and supervising them. Look as the salary level of other middle managers in your school district. Your Theatre Manager will likely report directly to your district's Business or Facilities Director - who typically directly reports to the superintendent - just as other middle management in your district does. Your theatre manager is two tiers from the top and has a huge responsibility in a position that carries a high liability factor – if you want a good person to stick around, pay them accordingly.

Good technicians are a scarce resource. I have worked with technicians who are brilliant at what they do, but can't work with people very well. For instance I once hired a very good sound technician, however he turned out to be rather ornery and impatient with those who didn't know as much as he did. He would not only yell at students, but also at users who were paying hundreds, if not thousands, of dollars to rent the facility. On the other side there are people that I would have loved to have hired as technicians who were not only self-starters but also truly enjoyed working with high school kids, but did not have enough theatre experience to run a show. There are some technicians that I've worked with who had both these qualities – good technically and good with people, but most of these personalities have higher ambitions than working in a high school theatre. They stick around for a year or two, and then are off on tour or starting their own companies. Not a situation conducive to the educational and financial outcomes you want from your theatres. A person who has the technical experience under their belt, enjoys working with students, and who finds value in working in the high school setting is a rare commodity. For this reason, unless the compensation is competitive, you will have a high turn over in your theatre staff, and/or people who don't like working with your students. The practical implications of financial compensation are a part of the growing pains that you will face, and the Theatre Manager is charged with running the theatre within these financial constraints.

CHAPTER 11

ADMINISTRATIVE SYSTEMS

A Theatre Manager not only has to manage the operations between the walls of the theatre, but he also has to oversee the administrative side of managing a high school theatre. In other words, the paper pushing. When you think of theatre management, you may envision the activities that go on inside the theatre in order to produce a play or an event. But theatre management actually involves a substantial amount of paperwork. A Theatre Manager must be that rare person who is as happy behind a desk as they are up a genie lift.

All sorts of systems need to be put into place and maintained in a high school theatre. Scheduling procedures must be followed, forms need to be generated and maintained, equipment and supplies need to be ordered, production planning needs to happen, and e-mails need to dealt with - it's not unusual for the Theatre Manager to be carrying on several production planning e-mail conversations at the same time.

Plus, one decision can create a domino effect of paperwork. If someone in charge of an event let's your Theatre Manager know that they decided to change the start time by even half an hour, then he must not only respond to that person to confirm, but then he needs to change the schedule on the event calendar and his calendar, e-mail the technicians to let them know of the change, inform any student crew who might be working on the event, reschedule heat and/or lights for the building if it's out of school hours, and inform the custodians. High schools also operate with their own calendar and/or a district calendar, so either the Theatre Manager has to make those changes or inform the person who does. That's a lot of work for one small change in the schedule, but it's essential in order for the theatre to operate effectively.

This chapter will help district administrators understand the extent of the administrative responsibilities of a Theatre Manager, and will also give architects some idea of what to plan for (like an office with a window, please...). What's written here are not the only administrative responsibilities of a Theatre Manager, other things will evolve organically as the needs arise in your theatre. But, it only takes something going wrong once for a good Theatre Manager to realize you need a procedure or policy to stop that from happening again, however it's best if you and your Theatre Manager can anticipate as many situations as possible.

Here are a few of the administrative responsibilities that your Theatre Manager will need to develop when setting up the administration operations of your theatre.

- Create user application forms covering areas such as technical equipment requirements, production schedules, crewing, and various specialized issues such as food in the space, appropriate footwear, use of fog machines, etc.

- Create forms for users to fill out for the theatre management, and for the theatre management to impart essential information to the user.

- Create systems for correspondence and collaboration with employees, theatre users, and administration.

- Create scheduling procedures in order to optimize the use schedule to best provide for the needs of the variety of groups that use the theatre.

- Create policies and procedures to control security and access of the theatre.

- Create a system of mandatory Production Meetings in order to ascertain prospective users' specific time needs and space requirements.

- Create a system to track prospective users, the year's users, the current month's users, upcoming month's users, past month's users; noting the production schedule, running order of each day, the technical needs and tracking production meetings and their outcomes.

All this may seem a bit overwhelming and you may be wondering how to get to the point where all of those systems are in place. It's a question of taking one thing at a time. So let's start at the very beginning - a very fine place to start. Most theatres are not heavily booked out at the beginning of the school year. In September and October a high school theatre can be "dark" (not in use) most of the time, because the band needs time to rehearse their first concert, the drama department has to cast their play and start rehearsals, community dance schools are just getting back into their classes and so on. At most there may be a few class assemblies, parent meetings and so on. This is just as well, because there is a lot of planning that needs to be done by your Theatre Manager when they come back from their summer break. The following sample "To Do" lists will help you decide what needs to be done in your theatre to get it, and keep it, running smoothly.

START OF SCHOOL YEAR TO DO LIST

It's hard to remember what you did a year ago at the start of the previous school year, and you don't want your Theatre Manager to get stuck finding out they forgot to take care of an essential item before your first event. Some of the action items below may not make sense to you, or pertain to you, but the point is that as you have to get revved up again at the start of each school year, so it's a good idea to develop a list. Here's the start of school year to do list that I developed.

SAMPLE START OF SCHOOL YEAR TO DO LIST

CONTACT TECHNICIANS TO COME IN AND SIGN THEIR CONTRACTS.

HIRE MORE TECHNICIANS AS NEEDED.

FINALIZE INPUTTING THEATRE EVENTS INTO ONLINE CALENDAR AND CROSS REFERENCE WITH USE APPLICATIONS FORMS (USE BLANK SHEETS FOR EVENTS WHO HAVEN'T TURNED IN FORMS YET).

DELETE LAST YEAR'S MONTHS FROM THE ONLINE THEATRE CALENDAR (MAKE SURE YOU HAVE A PRINTED HARD COPY FIRST!).

CONTACT BAND AND CHOIR TEACHERS AND ASK THEM TO CONFIRM THEIR EVENT SCHEDULES AND TO FILL OUT BAND AND CHOIR USE FORMS FOR EACH EVENT (THROUGH DECEMBER, AT LEAST).

MEET WITH DISTRICT SCHEDULER SO SHE CAN INPUT THE THEATRE SCHEDULE INTO DISTRICT MASTER SCHEDULE.

SEND E-MAIL TO TECH THEATRE CLUB STUDENTS TO TOUCH BASE, ANNOUNCE FIRST MEETING TIME, ASK THEM TO SIGN UP FOR SHOWS THROUGH DECEMBER.

PREP FOR FIRST TECH THEATRE CLUB MEETING.

SCHEDULE SET BUILDING WORKSHOP. (REPEAT FOR SPRING PLAY.)

PREP HANDOUTS FOR SET BUILDING WORKSHOP. (REPEAT FOR SPRING PLAY.)

CONTACT EVENTS FOR OCTOBER AND SET UP PRODUCTION MEETINGS. (REPEAT MONTHLY.)

SCHEDULE GENIE LIFT FOR OCTOBER, AND POST NOTICE ON GENIE. (REPEAT MONTHLY.)

GIVE DISTRICT SCHEDULER OCTOBER'S SCHEDULE SO SHE CAN SCHEDULE HEAT AND CUSTODIAL. (REPEAT MONTHLY.)

CONTACT TECH THEATRE STUDENTS ABOUT SIGNING UP FOR OCTOBER'S EVENTS. (REPEAT MONTHLY.)

LET PERFORMING ARTS TEACHERS KNOW OF ANY OF THEIR ROOM USAGE FOR ANY OUTSIDE EVENTS IN OCTOBER. (REPEAT MONTHLY.)

SCHEDULE STUDENT THEATRE ETIQUETTE TALK WITH ALL PERFORMING ARTS TEACHERS. TWO OPTIONS (STUDENTS ATTEND ONE).

PREP FOR THEATRE ETIQUETTE TALKS.

SEND "SAFETY ANNOUNCEMENTS FOR TRYOUTS" TO DRAMA TEACHER BEFORE AUDITIONS. (REPEAT FOR SPRING PLAY.)

SCHEDULE FLY SYSTEM/CATWALKS TRAINING/WAIVER SIGNING FOR FALL PLAY CREW. (REPEAT FOR SPRING PLAY AS NEEDED.)

PREP FOR FLYSYSTEM/CATWALKS TRAINING.
ORDER SUPPLIES NEEDED FOR THEATRE FOR NEXT FEW MONTHS.

MAKE UP MORE PRODUCTION MEETING PACKAGES (THEATRE SHOULD HAVE 10 IN THE BOOTH TO START OFF WITH).

ARRANGE FOR OPEN PO FOR THE YEAR AT THEATRICAL SUPPLY STORE.

SET UP NEW PO TRACKING SPREADSHEET FOR THE YEAR.

PRINT OUT MORE "STUDENT CREW APPROVED" FORMS, IN SAFETY FILE, CHANGE YEAR-DATE, POST IN THEATRE AT FLY RAIL (KEEP UP PREVIOUS YEARS). PROBABLY NEED ABOUT 3 SHEETS IN PAC.

SCHEDULE YEAR'S TECH THEATRE CLUB MEETING – ENTER INTO OUTLOOK CALENDAR, ENTER IN TO THEATRE CALENDAR.

A start of year to do list such as this can take several weeks to complete, because as your Theatre Manager is working on these action items, people are contacting him about all sorts of things, and some days they find that all he's done all day is answer a round robin of incoming e-mails, and he's not done a single thing on his to do list.

END OF SCHOOL YEAR TO DO LIST

Then of course, the school year eventually does come to an end, so it's best to have an end of school year check list too. This usually isn't as extensive as the beginning of the year, nor is there as much time for administrative duties as the theatre is usually quite busy with end of year school events and community dance school recitals. However, one of the biggest jobs to take care of at the end of the school year is to create next year's event calendar on the website and enter in all of next year's school events. In most districts each high school's events take precedent over other district events, which takes precedent over community events. The principals start working on the calendar for the whole school for the following year around March and don't usually have it completed until May or early June. Even then it's not set in stone, and is not officially finalized until September. But, knowing that your Theatre Manager will have extensive administrative duties come September, it's preferable to take the time in June to enter all of the school's theatre events into the event calendar. At the top of each month your Theatre Manager should post a "disclaimer" that the schedule will not be finalized until September. That all said, sometimes June gets to be so busy that your Theatre Manager won't get to entering the preliminary theatre calendar on the website in June and will have to do it in September.

Some outside events are very organized and are chomping at the bit to schedule dates, so your Theatre Manager can put them in the calendar, but make sure that they know that the Theatre Manager cannot confirm their reservation until sometime in September. The reason to put them in the calendar is to confirm that they were the first of the outside events to request that date, so they do have precedence over another outside event at least, even if they might be bumped be a school event. It should be noted that once the school calendar if finalized and your Theatre Manager has all of the school events and outside events entered into the calendar, that a new school event cannot bump an already scheduled outside event. Outside events need to do their planning, advertising, etc, and must be able to rely upon their booked dates once finalized. The school teachers had their chance to request a date at the start of the school year, and now must take what left over dates are available. This actually works out fine, and I've never had a school event that couldn't find a date.

SUMMER TO DO LIST

Many high school theatres are "dark" during the summer months. This is a shame because there is a huge multimillion dollar facility sitting there eating up electricity when it could be rented out. However, if your theatre is dark for the summer, this is a good time to get to all of the things you couldn't get to during the school year. Usually these are a lot of maintenance items that couldn't get done because the stage was in use during most of the school year. The Summer To Do List your Theatre Manager should create will be addressed in the Maintenance chapter.

MONTHLY TO DO LIST

As your theatre's operations grow, you'll find your Theatre Manager is doing some repetitive tasks. Each event is different, but there are some common preparations. I found it easiest to make a monthly do to list. Here are a few suggestions for your Theatre Manager.

Schedule production meetings for the upcoming month's events.
Production meetings are addressed in their own chapter. The basic process is to create a form letter, tweak it each month as applicable, and about mid-month have your Theatre Manager sent it out to every event that will be coming into the theatre the following month. Your Theatre Manager should make a note to check the list of events in a week to make sure everyone has responded and has scheduled a Production Meeting with them – some people need more than one reminder, especially those new to the theatre, as they don't yet understand the importance of a Production Meeting.

Schedule the genie and any other equipment you share with your school as a whole.
("Genie" is a brand name, however in the theatre "a genie" has come to be used as a generic term for any sort of lift.) In some high schools I've worked at the theatre had their own genie. However some schools do not have a genie lift dedicated to the theatre. It is very important to have a genie available, not only for planned events such as light hangs and focuses, but also for

emergency situations (say a lamp burns out in a down light essential for musicians to be able to read their music, that is on an electric just above a row of orchestra shells and you can't bring the electric to the stage deck because of the shells and orchestra instruments that are set up below it, but you can manage to get a genie upstage of the shells in order to reach the electric – it's happened). In the schools where the theatre had no dedicated genie I was able to convince the school that the genie should be parked in the theatre hallway when not in use, because we can't spend the time to go looking for it and driving it from wherever it is to the theatre when we've got an audience waiting for a show to begin. Then I would look through the next month's schedule and I write a list of any dates and times that there is any possibility whatsoever that we might need the genie. I would then e-mail the list to all custodian and other staff who might need know each month, and I also print out two copies of the list and tape it (with blue painter's tape of course) to the genie. I'd tape up one copy on either side of the genie, so that the schedule was visible regardless of which way the genie is parked. I found that this system of sharing the genie with the rest of the school worked well.

Schedule custodial.

Again, your Theatre Manager should write out a list of the upcoming month's events and send it to the custodial staff. Sometimes the stage needs mopping with their ride-on mopping machine before an event – this is especially important before dance. Then of course, the house needs cleaning and/or vacuuming after, and sometimes before an event (no matter how many signs you have up saying no food in the house or how many ushers you have posted at the doors, people still manage to bring food in and then leave the wrappers and containers on the floor). The bathrooms of course need to be cleaned, the lobby and hallways vacuumed, or swept and/or mopped, and so on. Find out how much notice your custodial staff will need and be sure to honor that. Most school custodial staff are initially taken by surprise when they find out just what it takes to maintain a theatre, it's so much more than cleaning classrooms and hallways.

Schedule heat or air-conditioning and lights.

These days with the economy being so bad, and even when it's not, one way a school district tries to save money is to turn off heat or air-conditioning to the buildings, and lights to buildings and exterior areas after school or during weekends and holidays. These periods of course are when your theatre is primarily booked for rehearsals and events, and there's nothing more distracting than sitting in a cold or over-heated theatre. Your district maintenance department can't be expected to keep track of your theatre schedule when they have the whole district to be looking after, so also provide them with a monthly list of the specific times you need heat or air-conditioning and lights (such as for hallways and parking lots) for your theatre.

Let teachers know the dates outside groups are renting their rooms.

For whatever reason, high school theatres never seem to have enough room to house all of the participants of events (see the Storage chapter). Performing arts students, such as band, choir and drama can use their own classrooms as a green room, but where do you put the ballet school that comes in with over 100 students, or the church that has three Sunday schools at the time of their service, or the touring show that has 20 performers and 5 technical staff. For this reason some high schools also rent out their classrooms. Much to the chagrin of the teachers. But it seems to be a necessary evil, plus the rooms don't personally "belong" to the teachers. Without these outside rentals many high school theatres could not afford to operate for the students. As a courtesy, once a month, the Theatre Manager should send out a list of room usage to the teachers, so that they know ahead of time if someone will be in their room and can prep it accordingly.

Fill out Tech Cost Estimates.

Groups like to know ahead of time what their rental is likely to cost them. Outside events always have to pay to rent the theatre, but in some districts some student groups also have to pay some associated costs. Again create a generic form (an Excel spreadsheet is best), and once a month – or sooner if they specifically request it – send out a cost estimate to each of the following month's events. A little tip – keep the costs as reasonable as you can, but send out your first estimate as 'ideal' as you can too. For instance, ideally it's best to allow twice the length of a production for the tech rehearsal. However, in reality, especially if it's a one night event, a rehearsal has to be rushed through in an hour or so. If you know this is likely to be the case, if you quote them accordingly they're still going to see it as too expensive – remember, they're trying to make money too – and want to cut it back. Giving them the ideal situation quote will allow them to do this. There are groups who understand the value of a tech rehearsal and how long they really take, so this group will then have realistic expectations of the budget. You never know the first time you work with a group whether they're professionals or penny pinchers, so quote them the ideal time initially, and if they do want to cut down on costs they will be glad that you are able to work with them on that.

Send school and/or district administration a list of events in the upcoming months so they can publicize them to parents and/or the community.

Most districts and schools have a newsletter that goes out to parents and sometimes to the community at large listing the events that will be going on at the school; sports, meetings, performing arts, and so on. But, the district and school administration may not know about outside events coming into their own theatres, or possibly the professional level that some school productions and performances can be, so send them a monthly list too for publication.

Schedule student crews for the events.

> Whether you have professional technicians who work your events and students who apprentice under them, or whether you have students who run your theatre events (not advised), the Theatre Manager must get your students scheduled for up coming events. About a month ahead is all that students and their families can commit to, and on the flip side, they appreciate a decent amount of notice.

Schedule technicians quarterly.

> Because of the nature of theatre schedules not being consistent employment, theatre technicians usually also have other jobs and they appreciate knowing their schedule so that they can schedule their other jobs around this one, and also it works in your favor because you can have them committed to your schedule first and you don't have to work around their work schedules. It's a win-win.

Enter all of the theatre events in the upcoming month into your office calendar.

> Your Theatre Manager should do this monthly. You don't want to enter the events into your office calendar too far ahead of time because times and dates change, events get added or canceled. But you need to have them in there early enough so that you don't schedule a meeting or activity when you're meant to be working an event.

Enter all of the theatre events and major office meetings in the upcoming month into your personal calendar.

> Your Theatre Manager should also do this monthly. Because a Theatre Manager has to work evenings and weekends as well as 'office hours' they cannot rely on standard hours like a "9 to 5-er" does. They may not want to enter work meetings into your personal calendar too far ahead of time because times and dates change, events and meetings get added or canceled. And again, you need to have them in there early enough so that you don't schedule a personal commitment when you absolutely must be in the office or in the theatre.

Conversely also enter monthly any important personal events into your office calendar.

> This is so that your Theatre Manager doesn't schedule a meeting when they have a personal commitment. And, if you have the theatre events entered into your office calendar, when you enter your personal commitments, you can see if one coincides with an event and decide what you need to do about that.

> All of this sounds like a lot of cross referencing, but when you have three calendars – the theatre calendar that the public sees that keeps track of all of your events, an office calendar, and a

personal calendar at home - and you are the only person scheduling the theatre and there is no second person to catch any mistakes, then cross referencing is essential in order to avoid the disaster of double booking two important commitments or events. It's also important because of the irregular hours your Theatre Manager keeps.

As you can see, the person managing your theatre must, by the very nature of the job, have an ultra-organized personality, and have their own checks and balances system in place, because no on else is going to be checking up on them, and a mistake can adversely affect a production.

MISCELLANEOUS TO DO LISTS

A Theatre Manager's beginning and end of year checklists and monthly to do checklists are only the tip of the iceberg I'm afraid. Things will crop up all the time throughout the year and it can seem overwhelming, but a little bit of organizing can help. One way of organizing a to do list is to create 4 priority sections. When something that needs doing crops up, put it in the section in order of priority. It's ok that there always seem to be things in the 4th priority section that never get done. These should be things that it would be nice if they could happen, but don't hugely affect the efficient running of the theatre if they don't.

Another thing I do is to carry a pad of stickies around with me. Each time something crops up I "write a stickie". Then when I'm back in the office, I arrange the day's stickies on my desk in order of importance. The stickies closest to my computer are of greater priority than the ones furthest away.

Here is a sample of one of my to do list of items that might crop up during the year (in no particular order):

SAMPLE MISCELLANEOUS TO DO LIST

GET KEYS FOR NEW TECHNICIANS
FOLLOW UP ON SUMMER MAINENTANCE LIST.
INSTALL MISSING SEAT BOLTS.
CHECK UP ON TWO 19deg ELLIPSOIDALS BEING REPAIRED.
FOLLOW UP ON LOCK ON NEW DOOR TO BEAMS.
INVENTORY ORDER:
6 (2,PLUS 4 SPARE) GLAs
MORE GELS AS NEEDED
CREATE LIABILITY WAIVER FOR COUNTERWEIGHT SYSTEM, GALLERIES AND CATWALKS.
REPORT DOOR PROBLEMS TO MAINTENANCE.
WEBSITE: GROUND PLANS.
REQUEST 8' LADDER.
ARRANGE FOR WORK PARTY FOR CREW TO COMPLETE REPAIRS LISTED IN STAGECRAFT SAFETY

```
PLAN SAFETY TRAINING WORKSHOP.
ADJUST SIDE MASKING.
TRAINING SESSION FOR ENGLISH CLASS STUDENT CREW.
HIRE SOUND TECHNICIAN.
CREATE HEADSET DISTRIBUTION FORM.
CHECK AND REVISE LIGHTING INSTRUMENT INVENTORY.
ORDER/PURCHASE:
FEMALE 3-PRONG TWIST TO MALE STAGE PIN ADPATORS.
BROOM FOR DRAPES.
CHECK INTO TECHNOLOGY GRANT INFO.
GET 2ND MONITOR FOR LIGHT BOARD.
RENEW CPR TRAINING
```

Well, you get the idea. The Theatre Manager's to do list is varied and never ending, and they must be on the ball and make sure nothing slips through the cracks because it affects the functioning of the theatre for hundreds of people.

SCHEDULING THE THEATRE

One of the primary management responsibilities of the Theatre Manager is the scheduling of the theatre. It is essential that you have one central person doing this. This person also needs to be

familiar with theatre operations. If a high school theatre is scheduled by someone in the district who has no knowledge of the needs of a staged event, events tend to overlap in the space. For instance, lets say the drama teacher and the band teacher submit the dates of their performance nights. A scheduler with no theatre background might schedule the band concert a week before the show dates, however a theatre person would know that there is a week of tech rehearsals before the show dates and that the set is loaded in and finalized a week before that, so the band cannot use the stage while all of the space is taken up with the show's set. A theatre person has the innate knowledge of how much time a group needs to book the space for, and it eliminates the need to go back and forth between the theater users and a district scheduler who doesn't have the theatrical knowledge and can't initially foresee the needs of an event.

In one district where I worked a person in the district office took all the reservations, even though they had a Theatre Manager. This system gives the users booking the space the run around. The district facilities person would book the theatre, the user would then contact the theatre manager about their needs, only to find that they needed to extend the time for a tech rehearsal, etc., and then they would have to go back to the district facilities person to re-book the time.

With more than one person responsible for scheduling, teachers, staff and the community people don't know who to go to for information and to request scheduling, plus they'll get the run around, which can be very frustrating. At one theatre I managed, before I came on board the booking of the theatre was shared – somehow – by the facilities scheduler whose office was in the district offices, the principal, the school's activities director *and* the drama teacher. You can feel the frustration and subsequent relief in the following written comment from a teacher.

> "I have a very strong preference gained through experience as to how things work best, and that is that one person should be in charge, and that goes for everybody, including administration. From a user standpoint, it works far better that way, trust me. When [the theatre] was in "new" phase, I had to go through four different people to get anything done. All meant well, but it was a constant battle of phone calls, e-mails, and desperation. I was not originally in favor of the creation of the theater manager position because I thought it would add one more layer of red tape. I was wrong. It worked wonders, and under that system I had just one person to call and one person to whom I was accountable for all activities, including plays, tournaments, award ceremonies, and so forth. The theater manager needs to be given the final say on all usage, including that backed by administration."

WEBSITE CALENDAR

One of the first things you should do when you open your theatre to the community, is to have your Theatre Manager create a website - or "sub-website" of your district's website. One reason for this is so that the prospective users can see what events are going on and what dates are available, as well as where the technicians can check their schedules. That said, always inform technicians of their schedules personally and any additional calls, changes in call times or dates and any canceled calls. Don't expect them to constantly be checking the calendar. However, as this is a business and this is their place of employment, do expect them to be responsive to any e-mails or texts you send them within a reasonable amount of time (you set what you consider to be reasonable and inform them – usually within a day), plus they should check their calls on the calendar prior to heading out to work just in case. More information about what to include in your website can be found in the Outreach chapter.

EVENT TRACKING

Since there is – should be – only one person in charge of scheduling, this creates a situation where there is no second person to catch any mistakes. Therefore your Theatre Manager needs to have a checks and balances system. One way is to cross reference the schedule kept on the online calendar (which the users and the technicians can access) with a hard copy filing system for event paperwork and production notes.

The Theatre Manager should create three manila files and label them "Pending Events", "Past Events" and "Inquiries", and get a binder in which to carry around the Rental Applications and production notes of the current month. When these hard copy notes don't match the online calendar, then something is wrong and events can be double checked in order to determine the correct information. Here's how a manila file folder filing system works.

PROCESSING RENTAL APPLICATIONS

Each time a Rental Agreement is received (whether it be a school event or an outside event), the important information should be highlighted, such as date(s) of the event, times, event name, event contact person, and other things one needs to know at a glance. Also, write the date on the top right hand corner, then turn it sideways and write the date on that top right hand corner. That way when it's filed in the manila folders the date can be easily seen, and when it's in the binder the date can easily be seen too.

Next:
- File it in the "Pending Events" file in order of date.
- Enter the event in the online calendar.
- Contact the technicians or student crew needed to work the event to ask it they are available to work.
- When they respond that they can, enter their name in the online calendar *and* on your Rental Agreement.
- If your district or school uses another scheduling system, the event must also be entered in there, or inform the person who does this.
- Certificates of Insurance (most school districts require them) should also be requested and sent to the appropriate person in the district who tracks them.

Once a month – about the middle of the month – the following month's event paperwork should be put into the 'traveling' binder, which the Theatre Manager will carry around with them for easy access and guard with their lives. I always keep my binder with me and never leave it in the office. You never know if something might come up and you are unable to get to your office before an event. And if you are taken suddenly ill or have an accident, someone can come and get the binder from you, because your office may be inaccessible during typical late and weekend theatre hours.

The events for the following month should then be contacted and a time for a Production Meeting set up. (More about Production Meetings in that chapter.) The time of the Production Meeting should be recorded on the Rental Agreement.

After the Production Meeting happens all notes should be stapled to the Rental Agreement.

Once an event has passed, that Rental Agreement and any accompanying documents should be taken out of binder and filed in the "Past Events" file.

It's always good to keep an "Inquiries" file, just in case the event ends up happening later on, or if the event organizer needs to be contacted for any reason in the future.

RENTAL AGREEMENT INFORMATION

What kind of information should your district Theatre Rental Agreement include? Each theatre is different of course, but in general your Rental Agreement should at least include the following information:

- Name of the event.
- Date(s) of the event.
- Contact person's name and contact information.

- The title of the event.
- A brief description of the event – what type of event is it.
- Any other rooms besides the actual theatre and dressing rooms that the event needs to rent.
- Expected number of participants.
- Audience size expected.
- Any specific technical requirements, such as how many mics, do they need followspots, will the have audio/visual.
- Any equipment requirements, do they need a piano, music stands, chairs, etc. How many?
- Do they need use of your ticket booth.
- Time(s) of event.
- The event schedule needs to be spelled out. Many of your renters will be non-theatre people. They don't realize what's involved in preparing for a show. I've had people tell me they will all arrive at 6:30 for a 7:00 show and be out of the theatre by 8:30. I don't think so. So create a schedule for them to fill out that will help them think out their time requirements, such as:
  - Arrive/Set-Up:
  - Start Rehearsal (allow 2x the show's running time):
  - Break/dinner:
  - Prep stage:
  - House opens:
  - Show starts:
  - Show ends:
  - Clean-up ends:

  (During the Production Meeting these times can be adjusted, but these give them some idea of what to start planning for.)

This may be all that is needed for school and district events, but for outside events must have legal policies and procedures spelled out on a second page, which the person in charge of the event must sign. You need information such as:

- Your policies about when applications can be submitted and if priorities are given to school events.
- Your insurance requirements.
- Your changes policy.
- Your cancelation policy.
- Your billing policy.
- Your policy for their promotion of their event and the district's non-involvement.
- Your policy for determining what technicians or student crew you will require to run their event.
- Your custodial procedures.
- Your policies and procedures about what equipment is available for use.
- Your occupancy policy – such as no one will be admitted until a theatre staff member is present.
- Your policy about their supervision of their own participants.
- The school district policy about tobacco, alcohol and drugs on the premises.
- Your policy about bringing prop weapons onto school district premises. (It's a good idea to have prop weapons immediately checked in with you or one of the theatre technicians.)
- Policies about set-up and clean-up.
- Your safety policy. Maybe not the whole thing, but where they can find the information, and that they are responsible for knowing it.

- Your policy about food, drinks and gum in the theatre and the rest of the premises.
- Your policy about live animals on stage. (I've actually had llamas appear on stage without me knowing they had been loaded into the backstage area while I was in the booth!)

Prepare for as many contingencies as you can.

CHECKLISTS

As well as forms to keep track of your own organization, it's handy to have forms to help your technicians keep track of their organization, so that nothing gets left out 'in the trenches'. Pre- and post-show checklists are invaluable tools to ensure that everything that needs to get done for an event does get done for an event. These are for your own technicians, student crew, or other theatre employees to refer to. Here are sample checklists.

SAMPLE PRE-SHOW CHECKLIST

UNLOCK ALL BACKSTAGE DOORS.
UNLOCK ALL THEATRE DOORS.
UNLOCK LOBBY BATHROOM DOORS.
SET BUILDING ENTRY-DOOR CRASH BARS.
GAFF TAPE DOOR LOCKS AS NEEDED.
TURN ON DRESSING ROOM MONITORS (CHANNEL 20).
SET UP HEADSETS BACKSTAGE, SOUND BOARD, BOOTH, CATWALKS.
FLY IN DRAPES AND LADDERS.
STUDENT TECHNICIANS CHECK OUT BADGES.
POST A COPY OF THE "STRIKE CHECKLIST" BACKSTAGE FOR USERS (DISTRICTAND OUTSIDE).
IF SHOW REQUIRES USE OF CATWALKS LOCK OPEN THE CRASH BAR TO THE DOOR.

SAMPLE POST-SHOW CHECKLIST

STRIKE HEADSETS FROM BACKSTAGE, SOUND BOARD, BOOTH, CATWALKS –
STORE IN BOOTH.
FLY OUT ALL DRAPES AND LADDERS.
STORE PROJECTION SCREEN KEY.
STAGE CLEARED OF SET PIECES, CHAIRS, MUSIC STANDS, PIANO ETC.
REMOVE SHOW SPIKE TAPE FROM FLY AND FLOOR.
RETURN ALL EQUIPMENT USED TO BOOTH OR OTHER STORAGE LOCATION.
TURN OFF DRESSING ROOM MONITORS.
REMOVE ALL GAFF TAPE FROM DOORS.
TURN OFF LIGHTBOARD IF USED.
TURN OFF SOUND BOARD OR AUTO SOUND SYSTEM.
CONFIRM FOLLOWSPOTS ARE TURNED OFF.
CHAIRS AND TABLES USED IN LOBBY PUT AWAY.
STUDENT TECHNICIANS SIGN IN BADGES.
LOCK ALL BACKSTAGE DOORS.
LOCK ALL THEATRE DOORS.
LOCK LOBBY BATHROOM DOORS.
RELEASE BUILDING ENTRY-DOOR CRASH BARS.
CLOSE AND FLY MAIN CURTAIN.
TURN OFF ALL LIGHTS, LEAVE ON NIGHT LIGHT.

As you can see, the behind-the-scenes/behind-the-desk dichotomy of managing a theatre can be a full time job, and one that needs to be coordinated by a single person, so that the left hand knows what the right hand is doing at all times.

ORDERING AND MAINTAINING EQUIPMENT AND SUPPLIES

There is no way we can cover all of the equipment needed in a theatre in this book; the areas of tech theatre - lighting, sound and stage/rigging - are so specialized, there are a wide variety of brands available each with their own advantages, plus new equipment and supplies are coming on the market all the time. Regardless, your Theatre Manager should have some sort of spreadsheet in which to keep a running tally of items purchased so that they don't go over budget each year.

It's also important for your Theatre Manager to find a local theatrical supplier and repair shop that is reliable, reputable and knowledgeable. I found that for myself in Pacific Northwest Theatre Associates (www.PNTA.com). Not that there aren't other good suppliers in my area, but I kept an open P.O. at so that when I ran out of gels or forgot to order lamps, or needed a belt pack repaired quickly – or when my student light board op spilled water on the light board during tech week and we had to get it repaired and rent a replacement pronto – I always had somewhere to go in a hurry. Having an established relationship with a theatre supplier is worth its weight in gold. If you don't have such a supplier or repair shop near you, many, such as PNTA can ship orders and repairs fairly quickly. Even though my supplier was only a 40 minute drive away (well, with no traffic...) I would have them ship me supplies and usually received them within the next day or two. A very valuable service for a busy Theatre Manager.

CHAPTER 12

MAINTENANCE

Because a high school theatre acting as a "road house" can be very busy with school and outside events, sometimes it's all the Theatre Manager can do to just get the shows produced, and "things that should be done" get left by the wayside. Sometimes it's because these things take more time than is immediately available, sometimes it's because specialty equipment might need to be ordered, and sometimes it's because the work might take scheduling several technicians at once. There's always something that needs to be done that isn't getting done soon enough.

WORK PARTIES

A Theatre Manager should schedule regular work "parties" (they actually can be fun!) at least twice a year - sometimes three or four times a year if need be – during the theatre's slower months. In educational theatre, I've found that good months to schedule larger maintenance projects are:

- September through early October – school events haven't had time to prepare or practice at the start of the year, so that time is typically slow.

- January through March – this is likely after your school's large fall/winter production and before your school's large spring production while rehearsals are going on.

- July and August – school is out, and many outside events take off for the summer as well.

Following is one of my work party to do lists of 'saved up' jobs that we didn't have time to complete during one school year.

LIGHTING TO DO

Re-record Stage Manager Panel presets.

Re-label 1st cats non-dims and apron floods on SM Panel.

File gels.

Figure out best placement for conductor light.

Gel catwalk safety lights.

Re-gel Rep ladders. Safety cables for each work light.

Light board. Sub- pages: rep plot, rep dance plot.

Cyc lights – park LEDs to free up sub on board.

Cyc lights – switch to "smoothing"(see manual in drawer under SM Panel in booth).

Lower electrics and re-focus areas, lower borders.

Move cyc lights more center stage, move legs in.

Choir/band shell lighting. Add front lights. Focus down lights down, not as backs.

Re-gel yellow in Rep ladders.

3rd LX, two fresnels in circuits #102 and #118 are missing safety cables

3rd LX, fresnel plugged into circuit #114 is missing its strain relief on the cord cap.

Switch gels and channel no.s on cheat sheet for warm and cool downs

Repatch front wash channels so that SR is SR and SL is SL

Add 4th ladders to all dance subs

Focus 4th ladders off cyc as needed

Check saved name of rep/dance plot – re name if necessary

Re-wire cables with plugs (in booth)

'Psych Cyc' Sub 17 – take out all channels but cyc

Check power to gallery Edison outlets – report if not working

Move LEDs to front wash position

Re-patch LEDs and i-Cue to channels with faders

SOUND TO DO

Check patch and labeling of monitors.

Re-install overhead mics.

Revise step-by-step instructions for operating projector

PAC laptop – install BYOD

Reconfigure board, create 'rep plot' for LS-9

Organize/tidy sound cupboard

PAC laptop – install BYOD

Devise step-by-step instructions for operating projector

STAGE/RIGGING TO DO

Replace lock-washers that have split on battens.

Re-tie/stretch cyc.

Move 4th border downstage of cyc.

Label underside of ends of battens.

Adjust side masking sight lines

Rep spikes on ropes – dark green.

Restore SL side masking.

Move 4th border in front of mid-traveler.

3rd legs – reversed left and right. Tension blocks lineset numbers 1, 9, 20, 37 need to be raised and adjusted to take out rope slack.

Move spreader plate on main curtain arbor – currently 4 bricks higher than it should be.

1st border "lift line the top bolt of the batten clamp the lock washer has split open

Address split lock washer on the SR batten splice, which is over tightened.

Label all keys in lock box with sharpie

Run headset cable over SL backstage door – unplug from pit

MISCELLANEOUS TO DO

Take interior photos for website.

Rearrange piano room, fit in shells, risers and piano.

Re-bolt house seats.

Tape walkway on shop floor.

Return equipment transfers.

You may not understand any of these lists of gobble-de-gook, or you may be saying 'been there done that'. Regardless, these are the types of action items the Theatre Manager must keep track of and address within reasonable time frames. Another reason to hold work parties is for liability reasons. It's imperative that your theatre be kept in safe and functional working order for all of the groups that use it.

PREVENTATIVE MAINTENANCE SCHEDULE

There are codes, recommendations, guidelines, and school district policies that your Theatre Manager should follow, so she should also have a pre-programmed preventative maintenance schedule. If a serious incident or injury happens in your theatre, and she can prove that she has been diligent with theatre maintenance (as well as safety – see the Safety chapter), there's less of a chance of the blame falling on her shoulders. And most importantly, there's less of a chance of someone getting hurt if your theatre is kept in the best condition possible.

Some inspections and tests I recommend your Theatre Manager have done periodically include (but are not limited to):

Flame test the drapes – every 2 years.
All drapes have a tab on the side. Cut off a piece of this material from a random drape and send it in to be tested.

Fire Curtain – test annually.
The fire curtain separates the audience from the stage in case of a fire in either area of the theatre. Not all theatres have fire curtains and a high school theatre is least likely to have one because they are very expensive to install and maintain (for this reason, many high schools have ¾ fly towers which do not require a fire curtain). But if you do have a fire curtain, there are NFPA (National Fire Protection Association) code requirements based on square footage. Fire curtains usually reserved for larger prosceniums and are not always found in a high school theatre, however your main – or "grand" - curtain will at least be fire treated and can at least serve as a barrier for a period of time if it is closed at the time of a fire. Both fire curtains and main/grand curtains can at least stop smoke and some heat, and prevent property damage and people injury, such as smoke inhalation.

Smoke vents – test after the first year, then every 2 years.
There are (there should be) large trap doors in the roof of your theatre, above the stage and above the audience, which function as smoke vents in the case of a fire. You want to be sure that they are opening easily.

General fire inspection – annually.
This would include making sure exits aren't blocked, recharging fire extinguishers, etc. Some of this your school is required to do in general and your school custodial staff may take care of some items on your checklist, so be sure to coordinate with them.

Counterweight System
This should be inspected every two to three years by a professional rigging company.

SUMMER MAINTENANCE

Summer is the best time to schedule maintenance. There are some items that your technicians can do (and in fact may be the only people in your district qualified to do), some items can, and should, be done by custodians who have the proper equipment, some items need to be done by your district's maintenance department, and then there are items that need to be taken care of by a professional company, such as rigging. Following is one of my Summer Maintenance lists one year (also repeated in the Safety chapter). Your theatre may not need all of these items done, or not every year, and your theatre may have other items to add.

SAMPLE SUMMER MAINTENANCE TASKS

TECHNICIANS

LIGHTING

Lens and reflector cleaning, re-hang and focus rep plot.

Confirm lighting inventory on website

SOUND

Organize/tidy sound cupboard

Confirm sound inventory on website

STAGE

Check weights on each line, re-weight as needed

Confirm lineset order on website

Paint stage deck

All items that need to go to repair shop for repair or maintenance

CUSTODIAL

Vacuum all drapes

Vacuum out all floor pockets on stage deck

Replace any burned out house lights

DISTRICT MAINTENANCE

Test smoke vents

Operate smoke vents

Fire inspection

Re-charge fire extinguishers

PROFESSIONAL THEATRICAL INSPECTORS

Rigging Safety Inspection

Drapes Flame Testing

PERPETUAL MAINTENANCE

Despite all of these maintenance to do lists, the Theatre Manager, technicians, and even the students, should pay attention to potential maintenance needs every time they are in the theatre and using the equipment. They should be aware with all of their senses. If something doesn't look, sound, smell or feel right (ok, no tasting the fly ropes) they should report it to the Theatre Manager immediately. Maintenance is the responsibility of anyone who uses a high school theatre.

CHAPTER 13

BRANDING AND OUTREACH

Theatres (professional, community and even school theatres) need to develop an identity (brand) in the community. Branding is more than sales and marketing, it is about the psychological and emotional connection people have with your facility. The familiarity that branding creates generates ownership, pride, loyalty and a sense of belonging. You want your high school theatre to be an integral part of your community. Every time someone in your community thinks about live theatre, you want them to think about your high school theatre and you want them to think of it as a credible state-of-the-art facility where they can go and see quality events. My parents who are in their early eighties as of this writing still go to concerts and lectures at my old high school's theatre. If they are looking for an evening out, they will check there.

The history of entertainment media shows us not only a progression of technologies, but also a progression of marketing methods associated with those technologies. Although live performance has been around since the Romans and the Greeks, in Europe it became popular to have traveling troops come to you, rather than have the audience go to them. However, the eventual popularity of live performance in a fixed space brought advantages to the performers in that they no longer had to travel from place to place to perform their shows. With a performance space of their own, the music and the theatre could become more elaborate in terms of sets, costumes, musical instruments, etc. The performers' schedules also became fixed, so that things did not change with each audience. But, the troops still had to market themselves as before. So, the challenge was to find new methods to get the audience to come to them. While some marketing methods that they employed seem rather basic to us these days, it's those basics that are advantageous to apply to the new world of entertainment marketing today. Lessons such as how to draw your audience to you, how to insure that your audience is subjected to your marketing and how to convey product quality, all find their beginnings in our history of media.

BRANDING

Even though you are a school theatre, it's still important to brand your facility. Branding - the personal emotional connection and the reputation in the community - can happen through the name you pick for your theatre, what logo you design, how professional your staff is perceived by the users (school and community alike), the quality of the events at your theatre, the signature at the bottom of every e-mail that you send, and so much more. All you have to do is search "branding" online and you will get more ideas than you know what to do with. Also, don't discount social media as a branding tool. Does your theatre have a facebook page? Branding, unlike marketing, doesn't have to be expensive, but, like marketing, it does need to be consistent.

SOCIAL MEDIA

Consider social media for your facility; Facebook, Twitter, YouTube, blogs, etc. When utilizing these marketing opportunities, remember to actively manage your campaign and keep track of Key Performance Indicators (KPIs).

The following data can be used in a monthly reconciliation of the KPIs to measure the success of your campaign:

- Ratio of Unique Visitors to ticket sales.

- Ratio of number of visitors to the site (site clicker) to ticket sales.

- Ratio of origin of inquiries to ticket sales. (Each ticket purchaser will be asked – online or over the phone – "where did you hear of us"?)

- Ratio of time on site to ticket sales.

- Ratio of new Facebook fans and Twitter followers to ticket sales.

- Ratio of blog participants to ticket sales.

Your district communications department can be a great resource in helping you with branding, outreach and marketing.

WEBSITE

One cheap and easy way to market and enhance branding is to develop a website separate from the school district website. It can be a completely separate website, or a "sub-website" on the district website. Users can go directly to the theatre website using an address or they can quickly access the website by clicking on a tab or link on the school district website. You should make it possible for users to reach your website in a variety of ways.

You need a website that will provide information such as: technical specifications and inventory, rental rates, availability at-a-glance, application information, policies and procedures, technical specs, and other information that is often requested by users and/or often needs to be conveyed to users. There should be no confusion about where to find the information and who to talk to about your specific event needs.

Here's a site map of the type of some of the information you should have on your website; your needs may vary.

Event Calendar
Fee Schedule
Driving Directions
Contact Us
Forms
        Use Application for Outside Event
        Use Application for District Event
Safety Policies and Procedures
Strike checklist
Building Information
        Floor plan of the facility
        Seating chart
Lighting
        Rep Plot
        Channel Schedule
        Light board
        Lighting Equipment Inventory
Sound
        Sound board
        Sound Equipment Inventory
Stage and Rigging
        Stage Specs
        Linesets
Audio/Visual
        Projector and screen information

Every page should have some wording such as: "For further information please contact the Theatre Manager", and this should clearly be a link to the Contact Us page to make it easier for the user to find.

Not only should the Theatre Manager be the sole contact on the website, but the theatre website should be solely managed by the Theatre Manager, who should be the only person who makes changes to the information there and updates the schedule and technician calls for events. If you have more than one person in charge of making changes conflicting information can occur.

OUTSIDE EVENT RENTALS

Your high school theatre is probably used by your high school, other schools in the district, and outside events. Public schools aren't allowed to make a "profit", however the "rent" from outside groups is essential to making your theatre self-sufficient. The "rent" pays for the Theatre Manager to keep the theatre running optimally, technicians to run the building for school and outside events and to mentor students, student crew wages if you go that route, supply replenishment, equipment purchases, repairs, maintenance and all the operations costs. So you want to proactively market to groups to rent your theatre. One good source of revenue are local dance schools.

They usually do a dance recital at the end of the school year and a holiday show in the winter. They also know the value of holding tech rehearsals, and usually will have at least two shows in order to accommodate all of their parents. Aim to have five to ten local dance schools that regularly rent your theatre if you can.

Another way to bring in events is to contact local events planners and let them know that your venue is available for event rentals. Some events that a state-of-the-art theatre are suited to range from bands, to lectures, to stand up comedy. I've even had a wedding held at one of the theatres I worked at. Your brand isn't just important for the community, it's also important for your outside events to have a good feeling about renting your theatre.

Get the word out by sending your school and/or district administration a list of events in the upcoming months so they can publicize them in their news letter or website pages to parents, who are after all, your community. At one theatre I worked at I found a local community website where one could list their venue and events for free. I listed our highs school theatre, and then I also gave URL of the website page to each group who came in to use the theatre, so that they could publicize their event there if they choose. This in turn gives you the added benefit of having the theatre publicized. See if there is such an events website in your community.

Conduct site visits for prospective users. Most people need to physically be in a space before they can decide if it's right for their event. If you can, set up the drapes and a nice light cue, but if not, at least show them some photos of previous shows and events so that they can imagine what their event would look like. You want them to know that you will treat their event as professionally as possible so that they keep coming back year after year.

RATES

<u>OUTSIDE USERS</u>

No matter the economy, people need to escape to entertainment. And while the arts in education are taking a big hit in the economy unfortunately, professional theatre revenues remain (although perpetually "struggling") at a fair constant. For this reason, you need your high school theatre to produce professional quality work from your schools and to bring in professional outside events, all of which boost the venue's branding within the community. In addition, the structure of the performing arts that seems to be changing, as digital technologies allow live performances to be broadcast on cable channels, the internet and recorded onto DVDs, so you are also up against the "couch potato" public.

How much should you charge and what should you charge for? In most of the theatres where I've worked, there is an hourly rate for the rental of the space, and then technicians' hourly time is charged separately. Be sure to stipulate that your Theatre Manager is the one who decides which and how many technicians are needed for a given event, or you will have users trying to avoid hiring technicians in order to keep costs down. This compromises the success of their show as well as safety. Don't forget to charge for custodial hours – cleaning a theatre is not on a high school custodian's usual rounds.

Other items that a user might use are sometimes charged and sometimes not. They include:

> Chairs
> Tables
> Music stands
> Piano tuning
> Choir risers
> Choir shells
> Marley floor
> Orchestra pit removal and restoration

When making your decision what to charge for, keep in mind the practicalities of having to keep track of all of the charges. For instance, do you really want your rigging technician having to keep track of how many chairs a group used, and to admonish them for using more than requested, or do you want her paying attention to her job backstage?

In order to attract more outside events consider lowering your rates during slower months. I used to manage a rental cabin business, which was always slow in March and April. One year I started drastically cutting my rental rates in half – March Madness and Amazing April. By "slashing" my rates my revenues actually nearly doubled for those months because I had more than twice as many bookings.

In educational theatre, I've found that slower months include:

- September through early October – school events haven't had time to prepare or practice at the start of the year, so that time is typically slow.

- January through March – this is likely after your school's large fall/winter production and before your school's large spring production while rehearsals are going on.

- July and August – school is out, and many outside events take off for the summer as well.

There is no point in having your facility sit empty for weeks or months on end, with electricity bills and maintenance costs eating up your district's budget. If you can rent it out for even a fraction of your standard rates, then outside events can help pay more of your bills.

SCHOOL USERS

Some high schools where I've worked charge school clubs to use their theatres. I've seen the whole gamut. In one high school theatre I worked in the school district *insisted* that any school group that used the theatre have technicians present for safety and liability reasons, and the district covered the costs. In another high school theatre I worked in the school district *resisted* providing technicians for school clubs. They would only provide technicians for curricular events, and required that the technicians' time came out of the club budgets for what they called "co-curricular" and "non-curricular" events. This meant that groups of students such as band and choir who practiced during the school day did not have to pay for technicians for their concerts, while groups of students who practiced after school, such as the school play, had to pay for technicians for their plays. Other groups that had to pay were school Variety Shows and the like. For this reason, some school groups were always trying to get around having technicians work their events and shows, to the point that some clubs – such as a group that put on an annual Talent Show – decided to hold their even in the gym each year. A show in a gym, when the school has a multi-million-dollar theatre? I don't believe any less learning was going on after school hours than was going on during school hours. I found this appalling – charging students to use their own facilities, when the theatre was making money from all the outside events that rented it.

I strongly recommend for safety, liability and educational reasons, that you are a high school that *insists* on providing technicians for all of your school events. Your district's "brand" (read: reputation) is always being judged by the decisions you make about your students.

MARKETING PLAN

Consider incorporating all of the above into a marketing plan, just as a business would. Here is a sample high school theatre marketing plan which you can build your own around:

SAMPLE MARKETING PLAN for a HIGH SCHOOL THEATRE

OBJECTIVES
Main objective is to focus on the local market.
Two market categories:
Families
Tourists

GOALS
Main goal is to sell out every performance.
Secondary goals include:
Repeat customers
Customers do our marketing for us – word of mouth

TYPES OF TARGET MEDIA OUTLETS
Family publications
Local broadcasting
Public transit
Tourists
Travel publications

BUILDING BRAND VALUE
All marketing must generate the professional image through:
Visuals and artwork
Facebook page
Choice of still photography, film clips

SPECIFIC MEDIA VEHICLES TO BUILD BRAND VALUE
PUBLICATIONS: Local newspapers, parent newsletters
BROADCASTING: local radio station
SIGNS: signage outside of high school
INTERNET: Website, Facebook page, blog
MERCHANDISING: school apparel – theatre specific logos
GUERILLA MARKETING: 'teaser' performances within the school, the district, the community.

PROMOTION TO MEDIA
Press releases
Host business breakfast or lunch at local chambers of commerce
Promotional gifts and give-aways
Promotional tours of the theatre

BUILDING COMMUNITY INTERACTIVITY (Marketing doesn't have to be expensive)
Website
Feedback page on website
Inviting feedback and suggestions from our audiences
Kids coloring page on website that changes weekly/monthly
A downloadable page that changes monthly
Contests to win backstage passes
Winners will receive a backstage tour and premier seating
Audience involvement
Contests on radio stations for show tickets

BRAND STORY
Develop a new marketing message based on our specific target audience that builds on their knowledge of story telling using video or writing as it would appear on your website, in a press release, in an ad, or as our school's publications to parents and the community.

MEASURING MARKETING EFFECTIVENESS
Track dates of ticket sales and dates of marketing.
On-the-street surveys of brand familiarity, brand imagery and purchase intent, in relation to demographics.

PART 3- FUNCTIONALITY

130

CHAPTER 14

EDUCATION

"So much has changed technically and yet in other ways I'm sure little has. The stuff actually happening on the stage is probably not different at all...and its got me thinking back on those years and everything I learned. Yes, about how to run a dinosaur of a light board and an arc follow spot, but really how to be part of a team and work with people and be a leader. I've learned a lot in my adult career but the things that helped me have some measure of success were the group and people skills I learned when I was 16. Plus just how to work. It's something that some people never quite learn."

- Roy Kienitz
Former Under Secretary of Transportation,
Obama Administration – First Term

Obviously it is important to address education in a book about high school theatres - let's not forget the ultimate reason that a high school theatre exists – education. But what isn't as obvious to architects, administrators and academics, who haven't experienced the behind-the-scenes operations of their high school theatre, is the educational value. Most tech theatre students who work in your high school theatre will probably not go on to work in the entertainment industry – but then most students in a math class will probably not go on to be mathematicians – however the career skills and life skills they gain are invaluable.

In my experience over the years of working in educational technical theatre, I have found that students who work in technical theatre - from 5th graders to 12th graders - are some of the most highly motivated, dedicated, energetic, team-oriented, thick-skinned, professional-acting and technically-proficient students you can hope to work with. And if they're not, they don't last long and they quickly find that tech theatre is not for them.

When I am working with technical theatre students, I am always pleased to see that, as well as increasing their proficiency in the curriculum content, the students have further developed a broad range of skills that will benefit them throughout their lives, such as:

creative thinking,
teamwork,
decision making,
problem solving,
perseverance,
working with different personalities and standards,
analytical thinking,
self-responsibility and
responsibility to others.

These aren't skills you learn just by sitting in a classroom.
I am also a firm believer of providing students with as professional experience as possible. Teach your student crew professional protocols, and provide school groups who perform in events in your theatres with a professional experience. There is a school of thought that putting on a school show should be just for fun and it's not important to be all professional about it. I thoroughly disagree. Why are FBLA (Future Business Leaders of America) students required to dress in office attire when attending their conferences – couldn't they attend in jeans? Why do sports teams wear expensive uniforms – couldn't they play just as well in t-shirts and shorts? Why do robotics clubs, such as the renown FIRST Robotics (www.usfirst.org), expect students to have "gracious professionalism"? For the same reasons that your events in your high school theatres should be run as professionally as possible. To teach students the professional standards and expectations that they will encounter in the 'real world'.

REAL WORLD APPLICATIONS

Only a small percentage of the students in your high school tech theatre program will actually go on to make some aspect of technical theatre their career, but the skills all students learn in tech theatre are transferable to a wide variety of jobs. I have a favorite quote that I always hang on the tech booth wall of any theatre that I work in and it reads:

"An actor without techies is a naked person standing in the dark trying to emote. A techie without actors is a person with marketable skills."

High school technical theatre students who do go on to work in the Entertainment Industry are not just "skilled labor" but leaders, innovators, collaborators. Designers, managers and technicians in the Entertainment industry are the backbone of every event our society. We often think of them in live theatre, sitcoms and movies, but they also work for:

political rallies,
sporting events,
concerts,
documentaries,
radio programs,
Olympic games,

amusement parks,
conferences,
tradeshows,
press conferences,
circuses,
museums…

For students who may not go on to pursue a degree or career in the entertainment industry, the transferable skills and knowledge learned in technical theatre are relevant to a wide variety of careers that have similar knowledge bases and practices as technical theatre such as:

architecture,
construction,
engineering,
science,
people management,
project management,
art,
technology,
computer drafting and design,
computer programming,
robotics…

Here are some related areas of interest that my tech theatre students have been interested in or have gone on to work in:

physics,
photography,
engineering,
construction,
computer programming,
CAD,
art,
graphic design,
website design.

Those that have chosen to work in the theatre industry have got themselves jobs as

professional lighting technicians,
technical directors,
lighting designers,
stage managers,
teachers
and more.

IN DEMAND JOB SKILLS

Working on a stage crew helps prepare students with 8 of the most In-Demand Job Skills in today's world. The following list is from an article on the Monster website, by James C. Gonyea, which lists skills that the US Department of Labor says are on employers' wish lists.. The underlined words indicate a job skill that is used when working on a stage crew.

133

Problem-Solving Skills

"Many of the tasks we face each day in our personal and business lives are complex in nature. People who can identify problems, research solutions and make effective decisions are increasingly desired in such fields as business administration, management consulting, public administration, science, medicine and engineering."

If you ever have the opportunity, sit in on a Production Meeting between student set crew members and their set designer. It is the embodiment of problem solving. The director wants this and that for their set and the designer and crew have to figure out how to build the set within budget, within time, within ease of set changes, with a restriction on space in the scene shop and back stage, within safety requirements and within the director's vision of how the play should look. This is one big problem solving festival!

Vocational-Technical Skills

"Today, technology is advanced in all areas of human endeavor. Installation, testing and repair of most electrical, electronic and mechanical equipment in fields such as engineering, telecommunications, automotive, transportation and aerospace requires people with advanced vocational-technical skills."

These skills are practiced in the theatre time and time again. Plays are temporary things. The set design and the lighting and sound has to be installed, tested, repaired, taken down, and done all over again for the next play. Students receive continuous hands-on experience.

Human Relations Skills

"All companies with more than one employee face inevitable problems dealing with how people interact with each other. Often, the success of a company depends upon how well people can work together. It is the job of human resource managers, personnel officers, department managers and administrators to understand the needs of workers and how best to meet those needs within the confines of the employment environment."

Human relations skills are inherent in the theatre. There are so many specialties, each with their own knowledge and temperaments, and they all have to work together to create an end product. If they can't work well together then the end result – the play – wouldn't happen.

Computer Programming Skills

"Understanding how to harness a computer's power and program it to meet the specific needs of a particular company can dramatically increase your

employment opportunities. Specific languages most in demand today include C++, Java, HTML, Visual Basic, Unix and SQL Server."

Set builders and lighting technicians use CAD (Computer Aided Drafting). Lighting technicians and sound technicians have boards they have to 'harness' and program for each show.

Teaching-Training Skill

"Our modern society develops and collects more new data in a day than our ancestors did in a year. As a result, there will continue to be a demand for <u>people with teaching and training skills</u> in the fields of education, social services, management consulting and commerce."

Students may not go on to be teachers, but in the business world training happens all the time. It can be a formal training session, or integrated on the job training. Students only stay in a high school for four years. Those with more experience in technical theatre take new students under their wing and teach them the trade. Those students then 'raise up the ranks' and in turn teach the next lot of students. This skill develops naturally in tech theatre.

Science and Math Skills

"Great advances are being made daily in the fields of science, medicine and engineering. <u>Bright minds skilled in the sciences and math</u> are needed to meet the challenges of these fields."

Bright minds indeed. Try figuring out the dimensions of set pieces, how long to cut a board of wood for a set or a piece of material for a costume, the angles of light, the physical properties of light and sound – where is science and math not used in some form in technical theatre.

Information Management Skills

"In the Age of Information, America now produces information as the basis of its economic system, and <u>individuals who possess the ability to manage information</u> are critical to most businesses. Systems analysts, information technologists, database administrators and telecommunication engineers are examples of people with highly developed information management skills."

Information management is also inherent in the tech theatre setting. Students must manage information, analyze systems, create databases just in order to create sets, lights, sound and costumes. You can't do your job without information management.

Business Management Skills

"The business of America is business! Understanding of how to run a successful company is highly in demand. At the core of these skills is the ability to manage people, systems, resources and finances; to understand the needs of consumers and how to translate those needs into business opportunities."

A play is essentially a company, with people, systems, resources and finances that are working towards creating a business opportunity – the play – in order to fulfill the needs of their consumers – the audience. It's not called Show *Business* for nothing.

STTEM

What a lot of people also don't realize is that Tech Theatre is a STEM subject – or as I prefer a STTEM subject. Most people think only of the performing "arts" when they think of a high school theatre. In actuality, tech theatre is...

where
Science
Technology
Teamwork
Engineering
Mathematics
support the Arts.

"As a CEO of a science center – one of my goals is to expose kids to the idea of careers that use STEM education – i.e. stage designers and technicians being one of them. Using theatrical tech as a way of teaching science and engineering is a good way for us to get to the kids."

- Phil Lindsey
CEO Mobius Children's Museum & Mobius Science Center, Spokane, WA

LEARNING GOALS

Participation on a technical theatre crew incorporates many of the learning goals that states require in order for students to be prepared for the in-demand job skills in today's STTEM-oriented work world. Following is a study I once did on the Learning Goals specifically for students on a stage lighting crew. These learning goals can be applied to all aspects of technical theatre.

Students on the Stage Lighting Crew will learn how to:

think creatively
use technology
work as a team
make decisions
be responsible
problem solve
think analytically
be leaders

Stage lighting is a discipline that utilizes a blend of artistry, technical knowledge, physical effort and life skills. Lighting is a very specialized field which incorporates a broad range of skills such as: creative thinking, use of technology, use of mathematics, team work, decision making, problem solving, perseverance, working with different personalities and standards, analytical thinking, and responsibility. The learning objective is that students will be able to demonstrate artistic design theory and techniques such as color theory, use the four properties of light for mood manipulation and perform drafting basics, and demonstrate the above range of skills. Not only will students gain knowledge about a unique subject, but the skills students learn and use while working on a lighting crew will benefit them throughout their lives.

GOAL: reading, comprehension, communication

Students must be able to read and quickly comprehend scripts, instructions, cue sheets and technical data. They must be able to clearly and effectively, through written and verbal means, communicate to other members of the production team, through the use of cue sheets, script cues and other written information pertinent to the production.

GOAL: mathematics, science, arts, fitness

Stage Lighting utilizes a blend of technical knowledge, artistry and physical effort.

Students will apply the concepts and principals of math and science in their work. They must be able to do basic algebra and will apply this computational knowledge to the study of electricity. Light itself is a radiant energy in one octave of the electromagnetic spectrum, identified by frequency of wavelength. The color of light is a fascinating scientific phenomenon to study in and of itself. The use of technology is also incorporated into Stage Lighting, as students learn how to use a light board. Students also have to opportunity to take apart lighting instruments, to see how they are designed, how they work and for what applications they are used. Historically lighting was an engineering discipline, and it is only in recent decades that those with a knowledge of the science of lighting have combined it with their artistic talents to become Lighting Designers.

To some extent artistry may be an inborn trait, however art techniques can be taught, and the artistic talent, which I believe is within each of us, can be tapped. The students will learn about color choices, mixing colors, how different light angles affect the viewer's perception of an object, how to enhance an "object" (usually an actor or set piece), and how to create mood using color, angles and intensity of light. These disciplines draw from both scientific fact and artistic talent. Drafting is also an important skill that Lighting Designers must know in order to communicate their design (the Light Plot) to the crew. Being able to draft and read a Light Plot is essential. Student will learn some basics about drafting for Stage Lighting.

Once the lighting plot is drafted, little time is spent sitting at a desk. Hanging and Focusing a production can be quite a rigorous task; ladders to climb, heavy instruments to carry, bolts that won't loosen, a lot of walking around and running here and there! At Bear Creek Elementary, because of liability issues, the children are not permitted to go up on our Genie Lift to hang and focus lights (yours truly will do that!). However, I encourage children to come and help out at a Hang and Focus session, so that they can be a part of the process.

GOAL: think analytically, thinking creatively, problem solving

Analytical thinking, problem solving, and creativity are very important in stagecraft, as every play, show, dance and assembly is different. Students need to draw from what they have learned to integrate their experience and knowledge and apply it to each production. Each design will be different, and the problems that come up will be different for each production. Through their participation in workshop classes, shows and assemblies this year, the students will learn theory and practical lessons, and apply it to their own design at the end of the year.

GOAL: relate school experiences and learning to career

While not everyone will pursue being a Stage Lighting Designer as a career (and there are those who manage to make a living from it), the skills learned from one's experiences in the educational setting can help prepare students for the "outside world". These skills include, but are not limited to: responsibility, dependability, attention focusing, teamwork and problem solving.

In technical theatre (including the educational experience), as in many job situations, you are often the only person who can do your job. You turn up through sickness and in health. While lead actors will often have understudies, this is not the case with the tech crew. If you don't turn up one day it may be quite difficult for someone not familiar with what you were doing to take over. When you are the Light Board Operator, for instance, your job can be quite complicated. It is the Light Board Operator's responsibility to the Lighting Designer to know how to run the board, make accurate records at rehearsals, so that the cues can be duplicated, as designed, at the next rehearsal and at performances. It is also the Light Board Operator's responsibility to the cast to write down cues and notes clearly so that someone could take over in an emergency. The Lighting Designer and his or her crew have a responsibility to the director and the cast to execute appropriate cues at the correct time, with the correct emphasis.

Rehearsals can sometimes be long and tedious. Students must be able to focus their attention for an extended period of time. Rehearsals can also be hectic and frustrating at times. Students must also be able to focus their attention in this sort of environment on the instructions given to them, and to quickly and correctly record and execute the cues each time.

Teamwork involves people of different skills and backgrounds working together to create one end result, in this case, a show. Working on a team can be challenging, because while people with different skills and mind sets are needed to fill each discipline it can also be hard to work with someone who doesn't think quite like you do. The teamwork we experience in the Lighting Crew helps students learn to work with different people, to appreciate these differences, to see how they can be valuable. The students learn how to work as a leader one minute and a follower the next. For example, Lighting Designers are experts at what they do. They are in charge of the crew who is running the show, and have the responsibility of creating the best lighting design, with the artistic and technical knowledge they have acquired. Yet, ultimately, the director is in charge, so the designer must use their skills to make the director's vision come to life. The Lighting Designer simultaneously leads the light crew, and is lead by the director. Teamwork is often like this in the "real" work world. You may be a leader in your field, but at the same time, you can be a subordinate to a "boss" or other company. Learning how to combine these two begins at school, and probably takes a lifetime to master.

How do these goals look like in the real life educational setting?

The learning process for technical theory would start with students demonstrating an understanding of "easy electricity" for stage lighting, by role playing a human model of an electrical circuit. Students will also be able to state electrical calculations (integrating skills and concepts from other disciplines) needed specifically for the application of stage lighting. The learning objective for artistic theory would include students being able to demonstrate the McCandless Method of Lighting the Stage and the four properties of light as applicable to design. Students would demonstrate a working knowledge of color theory, mood and lighting motivation, with a hands-on session on color manipulation and design. This section would incorporate art and design concepts children may already have a previous knowledge of. Students will also be able to define the historical periods of stage lighting (recognizing the arts from a variety of historical periods, and understanding the role of the arts in the historical development of cultures).

The learning process by the end of practical application sessions would include students being able to demonstrate how their school's lighting system works, how to draft a light plot using templates and correct drafting techniques (connecting the concepts and skills from one art form to another), how to run the light board and house lights, and how to hang and focus lights for a physical, hands on understanding of stage lighting artistry and technology (if applicable – some schools do not allow the children to do this, in that case they would have the opportunity to observe a hang and focus session). Students would also have the opportunity to take apart the various light fixtures at their school, and would be able to relate how they are designed and how they work to the design applications they are used for. By the end of the workshop students will also be able to demonstrate how to write and read cues, how to Stage Manage a show and how to call the cues. In addition, throughout the year students could also take it in turns to be supervised in running the light board and stage managing any productions and/or assemblies that the school would put on (demonstrating and responding to proper etiquette in art settings and performances, and applying a performance process in the arts).

Students can create a lighting design of their own (develop, organize, apply and refine a creative process with instructor direction, assistance and independently, also selecting, developing, rehearsing and presenting refined work using a performance process, and evaluating art presentations of self), thus demonstrating that the learning objectives had been met. This could take the form of a composition designed to a piece of music with manikins or models to stand in as dancers, or coincide with a school production such as an assembly, dance workshop, variety show or play (personal feelings and ideas through a variety of forms, using the arts for inspiration and persuasion, and identify how criteria impacts personal decision making).

A field trip could be arranged to a local community theatre, for a tour of their stage and lighting system. This could be timed to coincide with a dress rehearsal, so that the students also have the opportunity to observe and critic someone else's design process and outcome. The learning objective is that students will attempt to analyze evaluate and interpret works of drama using concepts and vocabulary, and analyze theatre and visual arts encountered in daily life.

Additional sessions with the students could address architectural lighting specialties. This would give students an opportunity to relate how an interest in lighting design can be turned into a lucrative career outside of the theatre. Students will also be informed of where to go for further education in this field (connections between the arts and other disciplines, understanding and applying the role of art in the world of work.)

Lighting can also be integrated into curricula in many ways. In an art class students can be taught to see how painters, photographers and other artists use light in their work. In a technical drafting class teachers can incorporate drafting lighting plots for the stage and or lighting plans for buildings. When studying architecture teachers could incorporate architectural lighting as a part of their lesson plans. The history of lighting is quite fascinating and could be incorporated into history or social sciences lessons about how people once lived. Electrical theory will fit in well within a science curriculum. Figuring out lighting needs for the theatre primarily uses the formula W=VA (watts equals volts times amps), which is an exercise in simple algebra and can be incorporated into classroom math problems. Stage lighting is a discipline that draws from many aspects of the standard curriculum.

CTE – VOCATIONAL EDUCATION

The same fulfillment of learning goals would be applicable to any discipline in technical theatre. But who is going to create this class if the drama teacher doesn't know the technical side of the craft? In previous schools I've been in sometimes the drama teacher does teach this class, in other schools I've seen the auto shop teacher, the speech and debate teacher, and the English teacher have an affinity for technical theatre – set building in particular. Sometimes a teacher knows one aspect of technical theatre and has guest professionals come in to teach other specifics. Sometime product reps will come in for free.

Rarely have I seen a dedicated tech theatre teacher teach tech theatre in high schools, despite the fact that most states have some sort of career and technical education (CTE) requirements in their schools, which encompass subjects in highly-skilled, high demand careers, such as auto shop, culinary, media, health industry, information technology, and so on, the primary purpose of which is to provide career and technical education training and employment preparation. These courses connect classroom learning directly to the 'real world', and also offer students opportunities for job shadowing, internships as well as field trips and guest speakers coming into the classroom. And the "three R's" are integrated into the curriculum. Teachers of these programs are highly qualified, and must have had a certain amount of hours (in terms of years) of paid work in the field they are teaching.

Again, rarely have I seen technical theatre given the attention that woodshop, culinary arts and fashion design are given in high schools, despite the fact that the Department of Labor and Industries prohibits children under 18 to be engaged in occupational activities, such as working with power tools, lifting heavy objects and working at heights, except for those enrolled in an educational program with a vocationally certified instructor. Some states even have a Tech Theatre CTE program available, yet not all districts incorporate Tech Theatre into their curriculums, despite having multi-million dollar performing arts facilities on their high school campuses.

Your state may have a similar program. But even if it does not, the point is that only someone with a technical theatre background should be teaching technical theatre – they should be "Highly Qualified", just as math, art and sports teachers are required to be "Highly Qualified". That sentence sounds like a no-brainer, but I've seen so many schools where this is not the case. And not only that, I've seen students who have self-taught themselves more than the teacher knows in some schools. Don't let this be your school. It's not only a huge liability in terms of student safety, but it's an educational disgrace.

In a CTE Tech Theatre class students learn design concepts, use of technology, problem solving and analytical thinking. They also develop self-confidence, leadership skills, creative thinking, teamwork, decision making, and responsibility to self and others – the 'lessons' that cannot be learned from a book. In addition, because not all students will go on to work for Cirque du Soleil or design the Super Bowl Half Time Show, students benefit from a myriad of transferable life skills and competencies that will put them in good stead in many industries.

The objectives of this type of program are as follows:

- Students will demonstrate specific subject knowledge about design concepts, use of technology, problem solving and analytical thinking by following the procedures for running a production.
- Student will demonstrate self-confidence, leadership skills, creative thinking, teamwork, decision making, and responsibility to self and others by their actions in the context of a show setting.
- Students will demonstrate the attainment of transferable life skills and competencies, regardless of whether they pursue a future in the entertainment industry, by documenting these in a variety of college and career applications.
- Students who otherwise are not succeeding in school will demonstrate a sense of value and inspiration to succeed by working with dedication in the theatre discipline.

An educational situation without instructional strategies is akin to students in an art classroom without a teacher present – they can figure out how to paint a picture or make a sculpture, but they haven't been taught relevance; theory, techniques, tool usage, etc. This applies to the three main aspects of technical theatre; lighting, sound and rigging.

Lighting.

Left to their own devices students can turn on the board and bring the lights up and down, they can even figure out how to record and execute cues. However, they don't know McCandless theory, they don't know dance lighting techniques, they don't know how to analyze a script or show running order, they don't know how to apply the 4 properties of light, they don't know how to patch a light board, they don't know color theory, they don't know cuing techniques, etc.

Sound.

> The same applies to the sound equipment and sound board. Left to their own devices students can turn on the board and plug in the mics, but they were only adjusting volume levels. They had never adjusted for the varieties of sound quality, the optimal application and placement of equipment, feedback assessment, nor for balance.

Rigging.

> Left to their own devices students can fly in drapes and drops, but they do so without the proper safety protocol. Students can re-weight the battens when hanging or removing drops and scenery, but this involves hundreds of pounds of weight overhead and without the correct procedures and order of weighting, there is a great risk of malfunction.

Without a CTE class in existence the system in a lot of schools limits the number of students who may participate in technical theatre and limits diversity. Here's how this happens: when a student auditions for a show, they are typically asked on the audition form if they want to do tech if they are not cast, therefore the tech crew is mostly, and sometimes only, made up of students who have a primary interest in acting. The tech crew is also limited to those students (along with their parents – for transportation in some cases) who are available after school hours. Although the tech crew is presumably open to every student in the school, non-theatre students do not have a sense of what is involved, so they don't sign up. It's the students who have an aptitude towards wood work, metal work, math, art, film studies, science and engineering, computer programming, etc. who would benefit the most from technical theatre, yet they aren't encouraged to participate.

With a CTE program, a system is also in place in order to determine benchmarks and to measure expected outcomes of the program, which are different for each specialty (lights, sound, rigging), and to assess each student's knowledge base.

These assessments will be primarily formative, because of the "on the job training" nature of the work. For example, the teacher requires the student to set-up/run equipment, the teacher asks guiding questions, then the teacher modifies the student's level of involvement in activities based on feedback in terms of performance reflecting knowledge base and ability.

However, summative assessments can also be used. These can be in the form of written reflections and/or questionnaires (written assessment), mock show compositions and models (kinetic assessment), periodic assessment meetings (verbal assessment), etc. Written CTE tests assess recalled knowledge; the correct use of vocabulary, nomenclature, procedures, appropriate equipment usages, etc. For instance, my son comes home at the start of every year with tests about every piece of machinery and power tool in the woodshop at his school and has to pass those written tests with a 100% score and demonstrate a prescribed level of competence before being permitted to use any given piece of machinery or power tool. Such is not the case without a Technical Theatre CTE program in place.

For more information about CTE visit the U.S. Education Department's online Perkins Collaborative Resource Network (http://cte.ed.gov).

If your school does not have a tech theatre class usually the only way students are exposed to tech theatre may be during the two or three weeks (one week of tech rehearsals, two of three weekends of performances) that a show is in your theatre. Some students help build the sets or costumes beforehand. Students are given general information from the Drama teacher (who, despite a Theatre Arts endorsement, likely has limited technical knowledge), but mostly learn from shadowing other self-taught students throughout the process. This is one valuable way to learn, however it is a limited, and sometimes risky, way to learn.

At one high school I worked in the school did not offer at CTE class in tech theatre, so I started a Tech Theatre Club. This was before I knew about the Department of Labor and Industries strict restrictions about minors performing certain occupational activities (see the CTE Teachers section in the Safety chapter). After I found out about this restriction the district administration claimed that if an activity is performed while in a "club" rather than while in a "class" that the same rules do not apply.

I will talk about how the club was formed, but it should be noted that I advocate that even an after school Tech Theatre Club should be run by a CTE certificated teacher. I have since become CTE certification eligible myself. I strongly recommend that administrators closely examine the requirements in order to judge whether a club can get away without a CTE certificated teacher in charge. Regardless of who runs a club, if a student gets hurt the district is still liable and that liability will increase depending on the level of supervision provided.

In any case, our club started out as just an informal group of students, but was eventually formalized as ASB (Associated Student Body) clubs, which then entitled the club to some funding.

This was a program whereby students who are interested in learning about one of three aspects of technical theatre – lighting, sound, rigging/stagecraft – would work with a district theatre technician during set up, rehearsals, shows, and strikes, of outside events and district events. (Costume and make up was not included in the tech theatre club, because the school and outside events would do their own and this was not something they needed technicians to do for them.) We met once a month to learn about an aspect of technical theatre (both academically and hands on), went on a couple of field trips a year to places such as theatrical suppliers, other high schools' theatres and local colleges. In addition the students were given the opportunity to work as crew members on school events and outside events under the tutelage of the theatre technicians. In one school I couldn't keep the students away. There were three diehards who made up the core of the group and several others who worked events when they could, but in all I had 29 students signed up.

HOW DOES A TECH THEATRE CLUB OPERATE?

You can set up your Tech Theatre Club in a way that suits your unique situation at your school, but by way of example, here's how I set ours up.

Outreach to other students in the school can be in the forms of posted notices, announcements, 'blurbs' in school bulletins, etc.. Again, most students think of working in the theatre as acting, and don't realize that technical theatre employs and develops common skills and knowledge bases that are found in other areas such as wood work, metal work, computer programming, architecture, engineering, construction, science, people management, project management, computer drafting and design, art, etc. It's important to reach students who are interested in these fields. Relying on word of mouth will not reach these students.

Students agree to commit for the duration of the school year. However, a student may join at any time in school year if they discover they have an interest.

There should be a start of year information meeting for parents and students, which will cover: schedules, expectations, commitment level. It is particularly important that the parents are on board, because of the evening and weekend hours involved in working in a theatre. (The tech and performance weeks of big production invariably fall on the same weeks as a big test in school, and parents need to be ok with this probability.)

Students can participate in outside events and school events, as well as school plays and musicals. Events should have sufficient technical requirements to approach just below frustration level needed for learning. For example, sitting a sound board running two handheld mics for a band concert does not challenge the student. Substantial event examples include: one-day dance recitals, "Mr." shows (male 'beauty and talent' contests), Dancing with the Stars, prom fashion shows, etc. More complicated events include outside event variety shows, full length plays, and dance productions with several performances.

Hold quarterly group meetings where educational and relative topics are discussed and where students can collaborate and interact with other students.

Students should work at least one show at another high school in the district in order to experience another theatre.

No more than two students in each specialty (lights, sound, rigging) should be scheduled to attend a given show (other than school plays and musicals). These limitations are in order to allow all students enough experience time, and to limit overcrowding at the light board, sound board and fly rail. Scheduling of assignments will regulate this.

Whoever is acting as mentor or "advisor" for the Tech Theatre Club, be it a teacher, Theatre Manager, or technicians, should provide the best on-the-job practices and instructional strategies necessary to produce a positive student outcome. The mentor(s) should foster a caring and supportive one-on-one professional relationship with student, which encourages the student to develop their skills to the fullest potential. They also help to provide information that would be beneficial to the students future should they be interested in pursuing the entertainment industry, or other related fields, in college and/or in the work place.

In practice, while one person can oversee the club, they cannot oversee every individual student during an event or production because that would involve being in three places at once. Nor does any one person usually have enough specialized knowledge of the three main aspects of technical theatre; lighting, sound and stage/rigging. These are specialty areas with different skill sets and knowledge bases, and students tend to exhibit an affinity for one and not the others, so they should be mentored accordingly. You can have guest volunteers or technicians mentor the students, who have the education and real world knowledge and experience in the subject matter. If your theatre has technicians who are working the shows anyway, there is no added expense for the on-the-job instruction of these students.

Upon completion of the program each year each student may receive a Certificate and acknowledgement during any appropriate school awards ceremony. You can provide other documentation and recognitions as appropriate to your school's policies. In addition, a Tech Theatre Club provides a documented achievement that students can use on their college and/or job applications, regardless of what career they pursue.

EVIDENCE BASED ASSESSMENT

An evaluation will assess what are the student's expectations - what do they want to learn about, what do they want to be able to do, what is the tangible outcome that they expect. This program may be perceived as, but is in no way, an "easy A". Working tech on a show looks like "great fun" from the outside, and in part it is, but because of the dangerous nature of the theatre, and because of the long hours involved, theatre technicians can be some of the most safety conscious, procedure supporting, dedicated individuals. This is not a field to join for the image, it is hard work and a lot of it goes unrewarded from the outside.

If you want to include assessment as a function of your Tech Theatre Club, this can be developed in order to determine benchmarks and to measure expected outcomes of the program, which are different for each specialty (lights, sound, stage/rigging), and in order to assess each student's knowledge base and understanding. This is important in order to determine the level of autonomy in which each student may safely work, and the level of responsibility the student may take in the best interests of a production.

These assessments will be primarily formative, because of the "on the job training" nature of the work. For example, the technician requires the student to set-up/run equipment, the technician asks guiding questions, then the technician modifies the student's level of involvement in activities based on feedback in terms of performance reflecting knowledge base and ability.

However, summative assessments can also be used if desired. These can be in the form of written reflections and/or questionnaires (written assessment), mock show compositions and models (kinetic assessment), periodic assessment meetings with technicians (verbal assessment), etc. It's important, regardless, to have written tests that assess recalled knowledge; the correct use of vocabulary, nomenclature, procedures, appropriate equipment usages, safety etc. These can be developed from theatre curriculums and industry exams such as IATSE and USITT, or taken from CTE classes such as woodshop, where tests are required before a student may use the power tools and other equipment.

Sign-in forms, or "passport"-type books can be created in order to document the events worked, hours worked, duties performed, etc. In some schools a lanyard with beads is used. Each colored bead represents a level of competence in a given area. The teacher, advisor or technician only has to look at a student's lanyard to see what work they can do.

TECHNICIANS AS MENTORS

Many school districts think they cannot afford to hire professional technicians to staff their theatres, but consider this – technicians are generally paid even less than teachers. The technicians are your "guest teachers" – at much lower cost than the hourly rate of a teacher. The technicians have the education and real world knowledge of the subject that they can impart to the students. An educational situation without instructional strategies is akin to students in a wood shop or metal shop class or an art classroom without a teacher present – they can figure out how to paint a picture or make a sculpture, they could figure out how to use the equipment and come up with ideas of things to build and create, but they haven't been taught theory, techniques, tool usage, etc. In the theatre students inherently learn while "on the job", and you can set up programs that will maximize student learning; providing real-world experience and transferable personal and career skills for all performing students, and vocational training for tech theatre students.

Technicians work in the capacity of mentors for the student crews. This can often mean a lot of sitting around appearing to do nothing, so much so that non-theatre people wonder why they are paying the technicians and not just letting the students run the shows as they seem so capable. What non-theatre people don't understand is the 'hurry up and wait' nature of the theatre. There can be lulls in the action – the lighting people sit around waiting for a sound problem to be resolved, the sound people sit around waiting for a set moving issue to be rehearsed, everyone sits around waiting to take their cues at the right time, and so on. But the technicians need to oversee the students at all times, watching for "teachable moments", because by running tech themselves without a mentor the students do not learn the curriculum of the subject. At the very least, students should be supervised by one lighting technician, one sound technician and one rigging/backstage technician. Technicians in each area not only provide safety, but they also provide the students with a real world education that will serve the students with life skills no matter what profession they end up in.

CYA (Cover Your Administration) TRAINING PROGRAMS

In some of the schools I have worked the theatre department did not have technical theatre classes. One school had a drama teacher who just used scant sets, because he did not have the expertise nor the help. Another school had a drama teacher without technical expertise, who managed to drum up parent and teacher volunteers every year to build sets. These are obviously less than ideal situations. If your school is in this situation, do your best to CYA.

In a couple of high school theatres I set up several training programs, the very least of which was a safety and "etiquette" training that every performing arts student had to attend at the beginning of every school year. All of the band, choir and drama students (about 300 in each school) attended an assembly where they learned basic theatre safety (don't jump off the edge of the stage) to equipment protection (that cyc cost more than your parent's car – don't touch it). The student stage crews at those theatres went through more specialized training on the proper procedures and protocol of running a show and working together as an efficient technical team. You can read more about participant and crew safety in the Safety chapter.

Ideally it's best if your school can have a tech theatre class each year rather than a club. A tech theatre class would primarily be in charge of building the sets for the drama department's productions. In the process of doing this the students learn set building techniques, safety, and fulfill learning goals. There can also be units in lighting design, prop building, costume design and construction, and sound design. The other benefit to having a CTE class, other than student learning and safety, is that the school gets more funding for CTE classes.

Technical theatre also benefits those students who are not succeeding "academically", who need to find a reason, and passion, to stay in school. They discover a sense of value and gain the inspiration to succeed in school in general by working with dedication in the theatre discipline. A theatre education research study, cited in the Alliance for Theatre and Education's website states that students involved in theatre production outscored non-arts students in standardized testing and that there was a measurable correlation between involvement in the theatre and academic achievement. In addition, theatre helps to improve school attendance and reduce high school drop out rates. Not only that, but involvement in the theatre builds social and communication skills, and improves self-concept and confidence.

I have seen this first hand more times than I can count where technical theatre benefits those students who are not succeeding "academically", who need to find a reason, and passion, to stay in school. I once had a fifth grade student who was a wiz on the light board – you only had to give him half an instruction and he was off – yet I later discovered he could barely write a full sentence. I've seen high school students who come from unfortunate family situations who find personal power in tech theatre. I've seen students who were only scraping by in math, science and English totally understand how to design and build a set and communicate the process to others. One student at a school where I worked was barely scraping by in high school. He eventually graduated and in a local newspaper article was quoted as saying that the only thing that had made him want to come to school everyday and do his course work was his involvement in the Drama department. Without that, he would have left school. The list goes on and on. This isn't just regarding students today, this is a timeless problem. Even in my own high school there were students who were not doing well in school and excelled in technical theatre. For instance, one such high school classmate of mine is now a technician for Cirque du Soleil.

CHAPTER 15

PRODUCTION MEETINGS

EVERY event, no matter how small or large, and whether a school, district or outside event, should have a Production Meeting. This is where the Theatre Manager meets with the organizers of the event. The purpose of the meeting is to discuss concepts and practicalities for the show, and to go over in detail at least the following items:

- their tech needs; the practicalities of how the set, lights, sound and rigging will work together, and any specific requirements they have in any of those areas,
- their schedule,
- their expectations,
- your expectations,
- and any other details you need to know in order to make their show successful.

There is one exception to the rule of always holding Production Meetings, and that is for frequently recurring events where you all get used to what is expected and how they run. This might include band and choir concerts, traffic safety meetings or school assemblies, for example, which occur several times each school year. However, continue to be in touch with the teachers or organizers in charge, just in case any special requirements come up.

Always hold the Production Meeting in your theatre. It may be more inconvenient for an event organizer than for you, however if questions come up you can easily demonstrate or walk them around to help solve an issue. You may need to show them some equipment, or you may need to show them where a certain drape falls and how much space they have on stage. Some people have a hard time visualizing what you may be saying, so this is the best way to avoid misunderstandings. It's also essential for a group who has not used your theatre before to have the "Grand Tour". Ideally though, they have come for a prior Site Visit with you before committing to a booking.

Depending on the event – from a full length school play to a variety show to a lecture – you should request that the following people be present at the Production Meeting (as applicable).

- The person in charge of the event.
- The Stage Manager – in particular, the person who will be calling the show, if it's not one of your technicians.

- The Assistant SM – in particular, the person who will be heading the backstage crew, again if it's not one of your technicians.
- The Producer (if the event has one?)
- The design team: lighting designer, sound designer, set designer, costume designer
- Any additional student crew members who you feel would benefit from being involved in the process.
- Student organizers, if it's a student-run production (their supervising teacher should be there too).

Who you request from this list will be dependent on the complexity of the event. Sometimes it may just be the person in charge of the event – that may be all that is feasible, and that may be all that is necessary for some events. It's particularly valuable, if it's a show or event with students involved to bring the key students to the Production Meeting. Students often have valuable input and really benefit from being involved in the planning process – something they will encounter later on in 'real life' if they ever have to arrange a company event or give a presentation, etc.

Let the event organizer know that the purpose of the meeting is to discuss the concepts for the show (any metaphors you have for the design team to collaborate on), the practicalities of how the set, lights and rigging will work together, sound requirements, etc. It's particularly important to let non-theatre people know why you need a Production Meeting. In the past I've worked with teachers who wanted to have everyone arrive at 6:30 for a 7:00 show. They figured their students had been rehearsing and were ready to go. They did not, at the time, realize the amount of technical preparation that has to go into their show. The importance of technical preparation is addressed in detail in the Tech Rehearsals chapter.

PRODUCTION PACKAGE

At a Production Meeting the Theatre Manager should provide the event organizers with a packet of material, and go over the packet with the event planners. For liability reasons, consider having a signature page that lists what information they have received. For instance, one of the items included in my Production Package is the stipulation that no one should have bare feet in the theatre, there are just too many hazards. The only exception is when an actor has to be on stage barefooted, because of a dance, or because it is a part of their character. We'd attempt to keep the stage well swept and the backstage area clear, but if someone were to step on a wayward screw or nail, for instance, then the event can't hold you liable, because they have signed the signature page saying they received and read all the information you gave them, including the stipulation, in this case, that no one should be barefooted.

The information to provide to the event organizers includes:

- A sheet with your website address and a site map, so that they know what information they can find on your website.

- Responsibilities of the user (see below for a sample).

- Your safety policies (see the Safety chapter).

- Your policies about which tapes may be used in your theatre, and whether you provide them or not, and where they can purchase the correct kinds if you don't provide them (see the Tapes section of this chapter).

- A building layout plan.

- A seating chart.

- A copy of your Liability Waiver (see the Safety chapter).

- A strike checklist (a clean-up list they are responsible for).

- A sample running order form (see below).

RUNNING ORDER

One thing non-theatre people don't realize is how important it is to provide a Running Order to the people who will be working their event, and how important it is to rehearse the event in show order under show conditions whenever possible. This is particularly true of variety or recital-type shows. The participants know their show, but they don't think about the fact that the techs have never seen the show before and, in some cases, that the techs will be expected to run their show sometimes with only one rehearsal. It's also important for the performers, who have not been rehearsing in the space to do so in order to adjust their spacing and to know how best to get on and off stage. In order to help the rehearsal go as smoothly as possible ask the event to provide you with a Running Order.

There are a few events where it is not always possible to rehearse in show order, a dance recital for example. In a dance school's annual recital there can be over 100 performers, and instead of having everyone hanging around the whole time during tech rehearsals, it's easiest to have them come in groups. This is particularly important if there are children of different ages. For instance, it's best to rehearse all of the age two to ten dancers first, so that they can go home first. If this happens, ask the event organizers to give you two running orders – a rehearsal running order and a show running order. These should be cross-referenced by your technicians running the show.

It's also best if the Sound technician can be provided with a rehearsal CD and a show CD – this saves a lot of time in the long run. Ask their event planner to record the music or sound effects for the show all on one CD if possible. If not, then two CDs – one for the acts before intermission and one for the acts after intermission. The reason for this is that some CD players have to reconfigure themselves each time you insert a new CD and this can cause delays and awkward pauses for the audience if a separate CD is provide for each piece. Plus it's best not to have the show recorded and provided on any sort of music player, as the chances of pushing the wrong button or slipping your finger and selecting the wrong track is too high. Also, be sure ask the event planner to record the tracks all at the same sound level.

Some events will already have their running order prepared for you, but for those who don't, provide them with a spreadsheet that they can fill out. The type of information you should request includes:

- Name of Act/Piece

- Type of Act/Piece (dance, speaker, soloist, band, skit, etc.)

- Stage Usage (full state, half-stage, in front of main curtain)

- Number of Performers

- Mood of Piece (this is primarily for lighting)

- Costume Colors (again, primarily for lighting)

- Followspots (none, 1 or 2)

- CD Track Number

- Number of Vocal Mics

- Number of Instrument Mics

- Other (need a piano, for instance)

RUNNING ORDER FORM SAMPLE

(ELECTRONIC COPY IS AVAILABLE FROM THEATRE MANAGER FOR YOUR USE.)

PLEASE NOTE: If your music is recorded, please provide all music on one single CD if possible. Please, absolutely no iPods.

RUNNING ORDER FOR _____ (Event)

NAME OF ACT/PIECE	TRACK # (IF CD)	TYPE OF ACT/PIECE	STAGE USAGE	# OF PERFORMERS	MOOD OF PIECE	COSTUME COLORS	# OF F/S	# INST MICS	# VOCAL MICS	OTHER:
Sample 1	1	Dance	Full stage w/cyc	12	Classical ballet	Light pink				
Sample 2	2	Dance	Mid-traveler in	6	Up beat hiphop	Orange	2			
M/C		Speaker	SL Arm of stage	1	Comedy	Black tux	1		1	Piano.Set up band
Sample 3		Soloist singer	Front of main	1	Love song	Black w/silver	1		1	Piano
Sample 4		Band	Full stage w/black	5	Blues jazz	Multi		4	3	No mic-drums

Also advise the event planner to plan ahead for set changes. Nothing kills the energy of a show as much as the audience having to wait for set changes. If they are conducting a variety-type show that may need equipment (such as bands) or set pieces set up and taken down again, advise them to alternate small acts with larger acts. Smaller acts can be done in front of a closed main curtain while larger acts are being set up behind. This keeps their show running smoothly and keeps the energy level higher.

RESPONSIBILITIES OF USER

An event coming into your theatre, be it a school event or outside event, has the expectation that the theatre staff will be responsible for the technical success of their show or event. However, the user also has a responsibility to you and your facility. So that they understand your expectations before they arrive for their big day, they should be provided with a list of their responsibilities. Following are some suggested expectations of your users.

SAMPLE 'RESPONSIBILITIES OF USER' HANDOUT

1. **Supervision:** The user shall assume full responsibility for the supervision of their activity, as well as the conduct of all attendees and participants. Persons will not be admitted to the facility until theatre staff are present.

2. **Tobacco, Alcohol, Weapons:** The use of tobacco, alcohol and weapons are not permitted on district property. (The only exception is a prop weapon that is being used in a performance. The prop weapon must be viewed and approved by the Theatre Manager or designated Theatre Technician before it is brought into the building.)

3. **Set-Up:** The user is responsible for set-up of their event(s), under the supervision of the theatre staff required for production preparation. The user may not make adjustments to heating, light or furnishings/equipment without prior approval. No decorations or application of material to the walls or floors will be allowed without permission of the Theatre Manager.

4. **Clean-Up:** The user is responsible for clean up and must leave the facility in a clean and orderly condition with all furniture in the same location it was found.

5. **Large Events:** Large events require at least one Production Meeting with the Theatre Manager to determine the appropriate staffing, parking needs, fees and facilities for the event.

6. **Performing Rights, Licenses, and Royalties:** The user must agree to obtain all necessary performing rights and licenses and to pay any applicable royalties and other fees as they pertain to the event.

7. **Safety:** The school district does not allow flame of any kind in the Performing Arts Center. Also all materials and props must be self-extinguishing. Fog machines and equivalent are not permitted. All participants shall wear solid closed-toe shoes, unless sandals or bare feet are a part of performance.

8. **Food and Drinks:** No food or drinks are permitted on stage (unless they are a part of a performance) or in the house. Food is permitted in the backstage hallway and dressing rooms. This privilege will be revoked if food is not properly disposed of, or if there is a mess during or after the event.

9. **Live Animals.** Live animals should not be permitted in your theatre facility. The reasons for this – if they aren't already apparent – are addressed in the Safety chapter.

POST SHOW STRIKE

As well as pre-show planning with events, your users should also be informed of your post-show expectations. It's likely that the school custodians are the ones who will clean the theatre after an event, however all participants should be expected to clean up after themselves as much as possible. Cleaning up after show is commonly known as a "Strike", this includes taking apart any set pieces, restoring lighting, putting away sound equipment, putting away costumes, and so on.

SAMPLE STRIKE CHECKLIST

Stage deck
        All set pieces and props removed
        All tape removed from stage floor
        All draperies flown or back on rep spike
        Remove all show spike tape from fly ropes
        Ladders above head-height
        Stage has been swept with dust mop

Backstage hallway and/or scene shop
        All set piece and props removed
        Belongings collected
        Floor clear
        Any chairs used stacked on cart and stored
        Any stored set pieces stacked neatly out of the way
        Fridge/microwave emptied, cleaned
        Floor swept with dust mop

Catwalks
        Tidy – no extra equipment or personal items
        Headsets returned to storage in booth
        Equipment in storage bay neatly stored in correct
catagories
        Followspots are turned off

Dressing room
        Belongings collected
        Counters and mirrors clean
        Floor swept with dust mop
        Dressing rooms empty and clean
        Place garbage cans in hallway
        Microwave and fridge clean

Costume room
        Belongings collected
        Any borrowed costumes cleaned & replaced
        Counters clean
        Floor clean
        Place garbage cans in hallway

Wings
        SL tidy, all show items removed
        SR tidy, all show items removed

Booth
        Rep plot patch restored
        Garbage can placed outside of door
        Counter and Floors tidy
        Light board turned off and covered
        Equipment stored correctly
        Gels used for event are filed
        Sound board turned off and covered
        (hopefully your sound board is in the house,
        but I've included it in the booth section just in case)

Lighting equipment
        Event's gels, gobos, etc. collected
        Venue gels and gobos used for event are filed
        Lighting equipment returned to booth or storage bay

Sound equipment
        Event cd's and sound supplies collected
        Sound equipment returned to booth
        Stage monitors and cables stored
        Piano stored

Lobby
        All garbage and food scraps picked up
        Tables and chairs stacked
        Personal items removed
        Signs taken down from walls
        All tape and fastenings removed

Classrooms used as greenrooms
        All garbage put in garbage cans
        Floors swept
        All personal items removed
        Desks and chairs returned to original positions

Even if you mention clean up in general to your users, it's best to create a Strike Check List that you provide to your events. Also post this list in various areas around your theatre, such as the scene shop, dressing rooms and backstage. Include everything you can think of in your Strike Check List. Then, inform events that not everything may pertain to their event, but that you expect them to take care of what does. Following is a sample Strike Check List. It is divide up by area, so that it doesn't seem overwhelming and so that users can more easily see what pertains to them.

TAPES

Be sure to let your events know what sort of tapes you allow in your theatre. This may seem a bit nit-picky, but your theatre facility should not be left in a sticky mess. At one event I worked on, before we were aware of that they were doing, the participants used double sided clear tape to hold down a pathway across the stage made of construction paper. The tape came up at the end of the show but left little squares of sticky mess all over the stage. The only thing our custodians could get it up with was an adhesive remover, which then left oily patches all over the stage. They then had to bring in the ride-on mopping machine and mop the whole stage. A lot of time-consuming hassle that could have been avoided by using the correct tape.

At your production meeting – before the event sets foot in your theatre – be sure to provide them with a tape policy that reads something like this:

SAMPLE TAPE POLICY

ONLY TAPES APPROVED BY THE THEATRE MANAGER OR
THEATRE TECHNICIANS
MAY BE USED ON WALLS, FLOORS OR OTHER SURFACES OF
THE PAC.

NOT SURE? PLEASE CHECK WITH THE THEATRE MANAGER
OR A THEATRE TECHNICIAN BEFORE USING ANY TAPE NOT
ON THIS LIST.

*ALL TAPE USED MUST BE COMPLETELY REMOVED AFTER YOUR
EVENT.*

TAPES APPROVED FOR USE
SPIKE TAPE
GAFF TAPE
GLOW TAPE
PAINTERS TAPE

DO NOT USE
MASKING TAPE
DUCT TAPE
PACKING TAPE
SCOTCH TAPE
DOUBLE SIDED TAPE

CHAPTER 16

TECH REHERSALS

I cannot over-stress the importance of tech rehearsals for every event. If you are going to be running your theatre without a Theatre Manager you would soon find this out. But I'm sure you'd rather not compromise an event's integrity by finding out by trial and error, so here's some information about tech rehearsals. But, before I tell you about conducting tech rehearsals, let me tell you about a event I worked with who refused to hold a tech rehearsal, so you can see just what can go wrong. This was a dance recital for a dance school.

1. Although they refused to do a tech rehearsal for their recital, I wanted to show the dance school what we could do for them lighting-wise, so I spend nearly 2 hours in the theatre the prior afternoon pre-programming light cues for the running order that they'd provided me with. This way each light cue would come up smoothly at the start of each dance with the start of the music. Each of those looks had about 20 to 30 lights up at a time, and there's no way that a light board operator can bring up that many lights at one time unless they are pre-programmed for each dance during a tech rehearsal. Regardless, when the lights come up for each dance they would still be a bit choppy as the light board operator would never have seen the dances before and wouldn't be familiar with how each piece started or ended. Normally I would not spend 2 hours before a dance recital, but I wanted this one to run as smoothly as possible under the circumstances.

2. Because I had to guess at the mood and costume colors of the pieces, there ended up being inappropriate looks for the mood of some pieces. There also ended up being inappropriate lighting for some of the costume colors (for instance, warmer gels on a green costume makes it look black), because I could not see the costumes when I was "blind designing".

3. For most dances for a dance recital we do one light cue throughout – often there are 20 or more dances, so this is the practical thing to do. However, one dance in this dance recital started out traditional and turned into hip hop. Had we seen that in a tech rehearsal, we could have provided a dramatic lighting change with the change in mood half way through the dance.

4. When setting the lighting for a dance recital we try to have each piece look different than the previous piece. I had set the lights for this dance recital from the running order I was given, however when they dance school arrived they presented me with a different running order, which meant that

several dances with the same looks were now following each other. Again, something that could have been altered during a tech rehearsal.

5. Another time the lighting technician blacked out on a group of dancers who had started bowing after their dance – none of the other groups had bowed - but it was too late to stop the blackout. Again, a note could have been made during a tech rehearsal for any groups planning on bowing to hold the light fade for them.

6. Two dances had "false endings" – the music stops, but then starts up again - so both the light and sound technicians very nearly blacked out and turned the CD off when the music stopped in what would have been the middle of the dance, but luckily the music - and the dancers - started back up again in the nick of time and both board technicians were able to catch themselves. If there was a tech rehearsal, then the technicians would have made a note of "false ending" in their notes so there would be no risk of turning off the lights and sound on the dancers.

7. The dance company did not bring their own cable for their laptop, even though they were instructed to do so in their Production Package, so we were unable to show the video they wanted to show as the audience came into the house. Had we had a tech rehearsal, we would have found this out and probably would have had time to run to a local store to purchase the correct cable before the show. In watching the video on the computer screen, I thought it was a shame that it couldn't be shown.

8. On two pieces the dancers finished their dances but the music kept going. Again, if we'd seen that in a tech rehearsal we could have made a note to fade the music at the appropriate time, but in this case the music just kept playing while the dancers stood awkwardly on stage until we figured out they were finished. It wasn't long, but it was long enough to be awkward.

9. The dance company also provided us with a variety of CDs – although our Production Package had instructed them to provide one CD for each half of the show. This caused long pauses between CD's, while the CD player took it's own sweet time to recognize each CD before starting.

10. The sound technician put a CD in for one dance and it would not play. The director came storming into the house in a panic (the sound board for that theatre is in the middle of the house), motioned for the house lights to be brought up, and in front of the school's audience of nearly 500 parents was obviously agitated until the problem was sorted out and the dance could begin. Again, this would have come up in a tech rehearsal and been dealt with before the performance – and, his paying audience would have know nothing of it.

11. During the show we discovered that we needed to access the stage through the upstage right garage door, which, because we were in the middle of a show, we couldn't raise (it was very loud) and had to compensate for. Had we had a tech rehearsal we would have discovered this and we would have had the garage door raised before the show.

12. In the dance school's interests of saving as much time and money as they possibly could, they only allowed 15 minutes for the house to be open, which turned into 10 – instead of the traditional half an hour. Consequently

the audience of nearly 500 people had to wait uncomfortably out in the lobby, and then file through the one house door (bad theatre design), which can't really happen in a great hurry.

Luckily though, the show went ok overall and my technicians were good enough to "wing it". Some of the things that went wrong were minutia that only a techie would notice, but many of the faux pas were obvious to the audience. Not to say that mishaps don't happen in the best of times, but from my experience from the gazillion dance shows I've worked on, having a tech rehearsal all adds up to having a show run smoothly for the performers and for their audience, and gives the productions that professional edge that paying parents expect to experience.

THE START OF THE SHOW

Technical rehearsal (tech rehearsal for short) requirements vary from show to show. The purpose of tech rehearsals are so that the lighting technician can set the light levels and the timing of the cues, so that the sound technician knows when to play music or sound cues or when to bring up a mic level, so that the stage and rigging technicians know when to move a set piece in place or to raise or lower a drop or drape, and so that the actors can get used to working on the set, under the lights, with mics and sound, and with costumes (usually for the first time). The technicians and student crew need to do tech rehearsals so that they can learn the show. The actors have been practicing for weeks, now it's the technician and crew's turn. They don't know the show like the actors do.

A strict rule of thumb I go by is to go in show order whenever possible, and to conduct the rehearsal under show conditions. That means starting from the very beginning. Setting the house lights and the backstage lights, taking the house to half as if there was an audience there, taking the house lights out, opening the curtain, starting the first piece or act. I cannot count the number of times when a group has just started with their first act and not informed me and/or my technicians - they just start. We have to stop them and walk them through the start of show process. Shows don't just start like that, and if the performers and the technicians haven't practiced the start of the show during the tech, they are not going to know what to do in what order during the performance.

If you rent your high school theatre out to the public as well as host the schools in your district and your own school, and you host a variety of events such as concerts, plays, meetings, dance recitals, variety shows, lectures, etc. then you are essentially operating as a "road house". There are three basic categories of events that come into a "road house". It should be your policy to treat each event or show, regardless of whether it's a school event or outside event as professionally as possible. Any audience coming into your high school theatre should expect to be impressed by the quality of the work. Plus, running a show professionally is a 'real life' educational experience for all students involved. Each type of event or show has different tech rehearsal requirements. They are:

CATEGORY 1: CONCERTS/SPEAKERS

This category includes band concerts, choir concerts, lectures, meetings, school awards ceremonies and so on. These type of shows require minimal lighting – usually just a generic stage wash – where there are no light cues other than the house lights dimming at the start and raising at the end. There are no scenery or drapes that move during the show or event, and some are conducted entirely in front of the main curtain. The sound requirements may just be a mic or two, or fixed overheads, although for jazz band or choir there may be some solo mics needed. Because of these minimal requirements, although a Production Meeting is always in order, a tech rehearsal is not usually needed if everything is planned at the Production Meeting.

A word about band and choir concerts. If I can, I like to move them into the Variety Show category. It is not traditional to have lighting changes during a classical concert, but I've found over the years that subtle lighting changes for a jazz concert – one cue for each piece - can enhance the mood of each piece. If you are going to do lighting changes during a concert ideally it's best if you can hear each piece played or sung so you can adjust the light cue appropriately, but usually there is no time for this. So if you can catch the conductor or director before the show, go down the list of pieces and ask for the mood of each piece. That way you can give an educated guess at the mood of the lighting, and no tech is needed. This takes some experience, but a person well versed in lighting design can carry this off quite smoothly. With some practice, you can too.

CATEGORY 2: VARIETY SHOWS AND DANCE RECITALS

When an outside variety show or dance recital comes into your theatre, they usually know that they need a tech rehearsal. The ones that sometimes need some convincing are school variety shows or talent shows. However, once you've run a show with a tech rehearsal the teacher will never go back, as they will see the benefits when their show runs more smoothly than it ever has done before.

Usually variety and dance shows hold one rehearsal. This is sufficient if you are just creating one look for each piece and if the sound and staging requirements are minimal and straightforward – the curtain is opened to reveal the dancers in place on stage, the CD starts playing, the light cue is brought up. A good rule of thumb is to:

allow two times the expected running length of the show for the tech rehearsal.

One steadfast rule for these types of shows with one tech rehearsal is, whenever possible go in show order. The fact that I've just said "steadfast rule" in the same sentence as "whenever possible", indicates the ideal verses the reality. Ideally the show will run a lot smoother if the performers and technicians have practiced it in order and know what is coming next after what has come before. However, particularly for these types of shows it is not always practical to have everyone there at the same time or to have people waiting around. As mentioned in the previous chapter, many dance recitals have over 100 students performing. Sometimes is makes sense to bring in all the young children first (who can be as young as two or three years old) and practice their dances and then let them go home to rest up for the evening's performance, even if in the show their dances are interspersed between other dances. This is not ideal and there is a greater chance of a performance being compromised, but as long as the technicians know this ahead of time they can compensate for it as best they can during the tech and performance.

It's a bit easier to do a dance recital out of order, but when a variety show requires a band's instruments being set up after a dance, which came after a skit that had a few set pieces that needed to move on and off, then it's more important to do the tech rehearsal in show order. Dragged out set changes can kill the flow and energy of the show for your audience. For this reason, during your Production Meeting, encourage your event to alternate acts that are smaller that can go in front of the main curtains with acts that are larger or need more set up time. For instance, you can have a solo singer in front of the main curtain while a band strikes their instruments behind and a dance team gets in place. The curtains close on the band set up on stage, the solo singer sings, the curtains open on the dance team with an empty stage. The change in acts has run seamlessly for the audience.

CATEGORY 3: FULL LENGTH PLAYS AND MUSICALS

Full length performances must be carefully scheduled, and once the set is on stage the show should have exclusive use of the stage. For instance, a set cannot be moved to accommodate a band concert during the week. Let's talk about the schedule before we go into the actual tech rehearsal process.

In most of the high school theatres that I've worked in, all of which have functioned as road houses, time if of the essence, and each play loads in their set the weekend before tech rehearsals and loads it out the Sunday after a Saturday closing night. Some schools have the option – some would say "luxury" – of having a run through week on the set before tech week, and can take a few days following closing to strike the set and restore the rep plot. For our purposes here let's assume we have enough time – here's how a typical show schedule will look:

- Two weeks before tech – the lights are hung.

- Two Saturdays before tech week - the set is loaded in.

- Two Sundays before tech week – the lights are focused on the set.

- The week before tech week – run through for the cast on the set without lights or sound, sometimes with costumes.

- The Saturday before tech week – final touches on the set are made.

- The Sunday before tech week – dry tech, this usually takes about four to six hours depending on the show.

- Monday through Thursday - tech rehearsals through final dress, after school until about 10:00pm.

- Two or three weekends of performances.

- One "pick-up rehearsal" (this is a full tech) on the Wednesday or Thursday between the weekends.

- The Sunday or Monday after closing night – the set is struck.

- One day of the week following closing night – the lighting rep plot is restored.

This is quite a plush schedule. I have seen schools in districts that share a theatre at one school, where one set is loaded out and the next set is loaded in and the lights are hung and focused all on the Sunday following the first show's closing night on the Saturday and before the second show's first tech rehearsal on the Monday. Sometimes there is even a dry tech on the Sunday evening.

One last piece of the pie is if the show is a musical with an orchestra, and if your school has an orchestra pit cover that is supported by scaffolding (as opposed to a hydraulic lift). It can take about three hours for three to four technicians to remove and replace the pit cover each time, so you must also schedule this in.

HANGING AND FOCUSING THE LIGHTS

For full length plays and musicals you will also need to schedule time for the designer and crew to hang and focus the lights. Many non-theatre people understand how much time it takes to build a set and sew costumes before tech week, but assume that the lighting is just a question of turning on a few switches. This couldn't be further from the truth. And, unlike most of the sound preparation, which is mostly done during the tech rehearsals, there is quite a bit of lighting preparation has to be done before the tech week starts.

If possible the light crew needs time on the stage alone in order to hang and focus the lights. The reason for this is that they need to be able to bring down electrics, move around the stage on a ladder or genie, and for focusing lights, ironically enough, they need the stage in almost complete darkness. There's also a lot of yelling going back and forth (unless you have a wireless headset system), and the crew needs to be able to hear each other. This is not a situation conducive to concurrently building or decorating sets, or holding rehearsals.
However, that said, this ideal is not always the reality of the time constraints inherent in high school theatre. Most experienced lighting and set crews are used to working around each other during tech. As long as your set crew is willing to work under less than ideal conditions during this time the light crew can hang and focus lighting while a set crew is working on stage. One caution is to warn your set crew is that the stage may be going dark periodically. Because the set crew are working with hand tools and power tools, they must always be given a warning each time the stage has to go dark for the lighting crew.

Following is how much time you can expect to have to schedule for Hang and Focus. The times may vary depending on the experience of your light crew and how many "hands on deck", but this is a general rule for high school theatre.

Hanging, Circuiting, and Gelling Lights

Allow about 4 minutes per instrument.
For instance, if you have 60 instruments, you should schedule at least 4 hours for hanging.

Focusing Lights

Allow about 3 minutes per instrument.
For instance, if you have 60 instruments, you should schedule at least 3 hours for focusing.

TECH WEEK

Regardless of other time constraints or allowances, it's pretty standard for tech rehearsals to run Monday through Thursday (or through Wednesday with a Thursday opening) from right after school until about 10:00pm. Here's what to expect.

The Lighting Designer will ideally sit in the center of the house at the "Tech Table", with the Stage Manger and the Director. The Lighting Designer needs to see the lights as the audience would. The Lighting Designer and the Stage Manger will be in headset contact with the lighting technician at the light board, the sound technician at the sound board and the stage crew backstage (usually one person back stage has a headset and relays instructions to the rest of the crew). The Stage Manager will ask the actors to run through the show. The Lighting Designer will stop the cast in order to design and record cues, and to tell the Stage Manager when to call the cues, and to tell the lighting technician the timing of the cues. The light or sound board operators or the stage crew may need to practice the timing of a cue several times, and so the actors will have to run that part of the show over again. By dress rehearsal, the Stage Manager should be working together with all of the crew to execute the lighting and the designer's job is finished.

First Tech Rehearsal

This rehearsal is for the designers, Stage Manager and tech crew. The actors will have been rehearsing for 6 to 8 weeks, and now the tech need to set their "blocking and choreography". This will be a rehearsal with a lot of stopping, so warn your actors that there will be a lot of standing around on stage and hanging around back stage during this time (a good opportunity to get homework done or study for tests!). This is no longer a time for the director to stop to give directions, nor a time for actors to go over scenes. Each time this happens during a tech rehearsal it delays the process. Actors do not need to put on make-up or have finished costumes at this time.

For a Play

You should allow at least twice the length of the play.
So, if your play is 2 hours long, you should allow at least 4 hours for your first tech rehearsal in order to set the light levels and timing, and to practice set changes.

For a Musical

You should allow at least three times the length of the musical.
So, if your musical is 2 hours long, you should allow at least 6 hours for your first tech rehearsal in order to set the light levels and timing, and to practice set changes. Some directors choose to do this over the course of two days; Act I the first day, Act II the next.

Second Tech Rehearsal

Again, the actors have been rehearsing for many weeks, and now it is the tech crew's turn to rehearse their parts. The tech crew has now received their "blocking and choreography". The designers now need to refine their cues, and the tech crew need to "rehearse" executing their cues. Again, this will be a rehearsal with a lot of stopping, and sometime sections of the play will have to be repeated in order to get the timing correct on light cues, set changes, etc. It's best to have full costumes at this time, but make-up is not necessary.

The second tech rehearsal may go a bit quicker than the first, but it's best to allow the same time period.

Set Change Rehearsal

Usually around this time, it's best to let the set crew have the stage to themselves for a couple of hours before the Third Tech Rehearsal, in order to rehearse their set changes. A slow and awkward set change can kill the energy of a show. Set crews should be able to do the set change quickly, yet also safely. For instance, they should not run, but they shouldn't amble about either. They should be walking "with purpose", and each crew member should know what their job is for each set change. This takes some practice and should not be done under the added stress of actors moving about and lights and sound cues happening.

Third Tech Rehearsal

Not many schools and companies have the luxury of a third tech rehearsal, or some schools may decide to open their show a day early, but if you do have time, this should be a rehearsal with minimal stopping, while the crew practices their light cues and set moves in 'real time' as much as possible. Full costumes and make-up are a good idea by this point.

Final Dress Rehearsal

This is where it all comes together. The crews should know their light and sound cueing and set movements, and the actors should be in full costume and make-up. This rehearsal should be under performance conditions, and there should be no stopping for any reason. The director and designers can take notes during the rehearsal and make any refinements and/or changes after each act.

Between Techs

If possible, also schedule in time between the tech rehearsals for the crews to make adjustments. For instance, it may become obvious during a tech rehearsal that a light, or several lights, are the wrong gel color, the wrong focus, or in the wrong place. Or, extra lights may need to be hung, gelled and focused that weren't anticipated during the run-throughs. Sound technicians may discover they need to add another mic into the set, or that a monitor needs to be moved. The set crew may need to re-spike a set piece, and so on. This is what tech rehearsals are for, so there is nothing wrong with this, but the need for extra time should be anticipated and scheduled.

There is no point holding all the actors while adjustments such as these are done by the crews, so be sure to schedule in time between techs in order for the lighting crew to make these adjustments.

DRY TECH

A word about Dry Techs. If you've never done a Dry Tech, this is where the Lighting Designer, the Stage Manager, the technician operating the light board and the Director sit down together and design and record preliminary cuing without actors on stage. Set pieces need to be moved into place to set cues for each scene, so the set crew should be in attendance too. Adjustments can made to take into account the actor's and set's actual movement during the First Tech Rehearsal.

Although Dry Techs are not imperative, if you have time for a Dry Tech before your First Tech Rehearsal, this will make the whole tech process run more quickly and smoothly for the actors, as adjustments take less time than initial designing.

SAFETY ANNOUNCEMENTS

You can't really learn about tech rehearsals by reading about them in a book. If you've never run a tech rehearsal before, if possible see if you can attend a tech week at a neighboring high school. I've worked at many high schools and done many tech weeks. They're all pretty much the same process, and they all seem rather hectic and at times unorganized. But I assure you what you are experiencing in your high school theatre tech rehearsal is not uncommon. One thing that will help your tech rehearsals go a bit more smoothly and safely – no matter the type of event – is to set expectations right at the beginning. Start your tech with safety announcements, this way the whole process doesn't have to stop because one person is acting in an unsafe manner. Following are a few generic safety rules, which are addressed in the Safety chapter, but bear repeating here. You can change these to adapt to your own theatre space.

SAMPLE SAFETY ANNOUNCEMENTS FOR USERS/PARTICIPANTS

HOUSE

No food or drinks in the house.

Do not put your feet on the seats

Do not jump up on, or off of, the edge of the stage. Walk on the 'arm'.

Once the house is open, during intermission or after the show, don't peak around the curtain or walk on to the apron of the stage, or walk into the house from the stage.

IF THE ORCHESTRA PIT IS OPEN: do not lean over the pit from the house, or walk within 6' of the pit on the stage side (don't sit with your feet dangling over the edge) – unless... you've been blocked/choreographed to do so.

STAGE

Do not touch or play with the drapes. Oil from your fingers can erode the flame retardant finish.

Keep a 4' distance from the locking rail on stage left, don't touch the ropes.

Don't go up to the galleries or catwalks, even if the door is open. Unless it's a part of your act.

IF THE CYC IS DOWN: do not cross behind the cyclorama. If you need to cross go through the back hallway.

IF THE LIGHT LADDERS ARE DOWN ON STAGE LEFT AND STAGE RIGHT (MOSTLY IN THE CASE OF DANCE): do not touch the lighting instruments, even if they are off – they may have just been on and will be hot enough to cause a severe burn. When entering or exiting stay close to the legs as possible and don't stand in front of the light ladders as you will cast moving shadows on the stage.

PERSONAL BEHAVIOR

Student Crew must wear closed-toe solid shoes.

No bare feet, socks or slippers in any area of the facility. The exception is if it's a part of your character to be bare-footed or in socks or slippers, and then only when on stage. At all other times, wear shoes (even to walk to backstage).

Unless you are about to make an entrance, don't hang around in the wings or backstage. You may be seen by the audience, and you will be in the way of other actors trying to make an entrance and in the way of the tech crew. IF YOU CAN SEE THE AUDIENCE, THEY CAN SEE YOU.

During the tech rehearsals the lights might be changing or they might go to blackout in the middle of your act. Keep going unless you are asked to stop.

If you are backstage and the stage goes black, freeze and hold your position until the lights go back on again. Do not attempt to move around back stage during a blackout.

If you are onstage at the end of your act or scene where there is a blackout, hold your position until the lights are completely out. Do not break character until the audience can no longer see you.

During the tech rehearsals the sound levels for your mics and/or for sound effects and music might change, go silent, go loud, or have feedback. Keep going unless you are asked to stop.

No one, other than cast and crew directly involved with a performance, shall be allowed or invited backstage during any performance, between the time the house opens and until such time that the worklights have been turned on after the end of the performance. Performers and crew who wish to meet audience members after the show, should arrange to meet them in the lobby.

There are Strike Checklists posted in each dressing room. Before you leave the theatre please be sure that the dressing rooms and backstage area are left as you found them.

THEATRE TECHNICIANS AND STUDENT CREW HAVE BADGES – FOR YOUR OWN SAFETY AND THE SAFETY OF OTHERS, PLEASE DO WHAT THEY TELL YOU TO DO WHEN THEY TELL YOU TO DO IT.

PART 4 - SAFETY

CHAPTER 17

SAFETY AND
RISK MANAGEMENT

This chapter is the most important chapter of this whole book, and the longest, because it is the most serious and important aspect of designing and managing a high school theatre. This chapter is heavy on theatre safety operations, and knowing this information will substantiate the decisions that you as an architect or administrator will make. Everything that happens in a high school theatre takes a back seat to safety. Safety cannot be compromised in favor of form. Safety cannot be compromised just in order to put on an event or production to wow your audience. Or at the other end of the spectrum safety cannot be compromised in order to save money. Safety cannot be compromised even in the name of education. Without safety in a theatre, nothing else should happen. Plus, if your school is paid an impromptu inspection, your theatre could be shut down immediately if there are safety violations; they aren't going to care if it's an hour before opening night and that 60 plus students have been rehearsing and building for months in preparation for that night.

There is an excellent book on educational theatre safety that I highly recommend, titled *"Practical Health and Safety Guidelines for School Theater Operations : Assessing the Risks in Middle, Junior, and Senior High School Theater Buildings and Programs"* by Dr. Randall W.A. Davidson. If you think that title is long, wait until you start reading. The hardcover edition has 434 pages – all specifically about educational theatre safety.

In this chapter I can only give you an overview of high school theatre safety, but the overarching message is that it is imperative that schools have operational policies and procedures in place that safeguard personal safety, protect property, and mitigate liability. If policies are "do this" then procedures are "how to do this". Procedures are how your users implement your policies. It's also imperative that students are supervised by highly qualified personnel, trained to appropriately and safely use inherently dangerous equipment, and trained how to behave in inherently dangerous situations. Administrators need to understand these functions in order to provide adequate supervision of their students. Architects need to understand these functions in order to provide appropriate building functions that protect the students.

This falls under the category of Risk Management. This all said, one has to be realistic. It's called Risk "Management", not Risk "Elimination". The National Safety Council defines safety as

"the control of recognized hazards to attain an acceptable level of risk".

There is no way you can possibly prevent all accidents in a high school theatre, however this is the goal at all times.

A CONSTRUCTION SITE – IN THE DARK.

A theatre is like a construction site – in the dark. All high school theatres have specific designs and functions, but following are some universal dangers that can be found in the majority of high school theatres.

- Students moving hundreds of pounds of weight over the heads of other students – without safety helmets on.

- Students hanging scenery weighing hundreds of pounds on pipes – without certified rigging qualifications.

- Students in the catwalks and beams 30' in the air – without personal fall protection.

- Students working with electricity - without a license.

- Students using tools and power tools - without formal training and assessment.

- Students using hazardous chemicals such as foam and fog - without occupational-grade protection.

- Students at the edge of an open orchestra pit with a concrete floor 8' below - without a safety rail.

- Students being taught and supervised by parents and volunteers - without formal qualifications.

The inescapable fact is that these dangers, and more, are inherent in any school theatre. Nowhere in the 'real world' are people - let alone minors – legally allowed to work in these conditions without stringent safety policies and procedures, and without liability protection for the institution. And often times students are working under these conditions without their parents' knowledge or explicit permission.

School districts require employees to complete safety training on topics such as blood-borne pathogens, and allergies and asthma, and insist that funding is found for sports and science safety equipment, but it's just as important to impose safety standards on students in the school theatre who are moving hundreds of pounds of equipment above other students without safety helmets, operating equipment 30 feet in the air, working with electricity, using power tools and chemicals, and so much more. I've said it before and I'll say it again - safety-wise it's like allowing students into a wood shop or metal shop class without a teacher present – they can figure out how to use the equipment and come up with ideas of things to build, but they haven't been taught the safety procedures and aren't directly supervised.

ADMINISTRATION

So why do school administrations allow students to work under these unsafe and un-academic conditions in their high schools? It's not that administrators necessarily place more value on sports and science, it's purely that unless you were into tech theatre yourself in high school and/or college, you simply don't have the background knowledge to understand or assess the dangers inherent in theatres like you understand the educational value of, and more common life dangers inherent in, your swimming pool, football field, chemistry class or wood shop. This is because most people have had some real life experience with the dangers of sports, power tools, and chemistry, but a lot of people have no life experiences with theatres. When you go to a production as an audience member, all you see is the magical performance, not the dark backstage world of power tools, electricity, heights, heavy lifting, ladders, scissor lifts and the movement of overhead weights, to name but a few.

DRAMA TEACHERS ARE NOT TECHNICIANS

Another understandable misconception is that the Drama teacher can take care of the high school theatre's safety issues. This is based on the understandable assumption that because Drama teachers have likely taken college classes in technical theatre in order to fulfill graduation requirements for their degrees, they must be professionally trained in technical theatre. However, they are usually nowhere near highly qualified to correctly and safely operate the equipment in a theatre. This is especially true if a certificated English teacher is teaching Drama. Nor do most that I've met want to take on this sort of responsibility.

CTE TEACHERS

As well as a Drama teacher who teaches acting, some (but not enough) high schools also have a CTE (Career and Technical Education) teacher who teaches and supervises all of the technical aspects of a high school theatre. The Tech Theatre class's primary purpose is for students to learn through building sets and costumes, designing lighting and sound, and through providing these technical aspects for the school plays and musicals, as well as theoretical learning. Tech Theatre is a CTE subject, just like woodshop, culinary arts and some sciences.
In fact:

> **The Department of Labor and Industries prohibits children under 18 to be engaged in occupational activities, such as working in a scene shop, except for those enrolled in an educational program with a vocationally certified instructor. This not only goes for minors using power tools, but also for minors climbing to heights of more than 10', working with electricity, and moving heavy objects.**

That said, in the state of Washington (check in your state), if your school doesn't have a Tech Theatre class as a part of its credit-bearing curriculum, and all of the set building, light hanging, scenery moving for your shows is done under the auspices of an "after school club" of some sort (ASB or otherwise), and the club isn't funded with state or federal CTE funds, then the OSPI (Office of the Superintendent of Public Instruction) says that the requirement that the instructor be CTE certificated does not apply. Scary!

Regardless of the legal requirements, without instructional strategies the students could figure out how to use the equipment and come up with ideas of things to build, but they haven't been taught the safety procedures and aren't supervised. A Drama teacher might train students in safety as much as possible, but not to the level of CTE requirements. Safety is a life skill that is not generally taught. Learning about safety prepares students to be aware in whatever career they pursue. In addition, following CTE level requirements mitigate liability for the school district.

There is more about CTE tech theatre classes in the Education chapter.

TECHNICIANS

As well as the Drama teacher and CTE teacher, during a show students should be supervised by at least one lighting technician, one sound technician and one rigging/backstage technician. One misconception is that a school district doesn't need to spend money hiring highly qualified, professional theatre management and technicians because the Drama/Band/Choir teacher should be able to handle their own events in their own theatre. Nothing could be further from the truth. You wouldn't let students free in your *natatorium* (a building housing a swimming pool) without hiring life guards, so why allow students to use our *auditoriums* without "life guards".

As safety is the most fundamental concern in the theatre, even before the education of students, not only should the space not be overseen by one teacher, or by parent volunteers who don't always take theatre safety seriously, but no user (a district or outside event) should have free reign of the theatre without trained professionals present. If that were the case, then once the students are properly trained how to use the equipment and tools in a wood shop or welding class, why have any adults watch over them? Once kids know how to swim, why not just have volunteers sitting in the lifeguard chairs? Once the high school football team has practiced enough, isn't any teacher ok to coach them? School districts would never take that approach to safety in those disciplines, but a lot do regarding theatre safety.

In a contained classroom there are legal requirements for how many students (sitting in seats) a highly qualified teacher may teach. During a rehearsal or a production there are concurrently students in the booth, students in the house, students on stage, students in the galleries, students in the catwalks, students back stage right, students back stage left, students in the scene shop, students in the storage areas, students in the costume shop, students in the dressing rooms, students in the classroom and students in the lobby. For a straight play the average amount of cast and crew can be 30 or so students, for a musical the average amount of cast and crew can be 60 or more students, for a choir or band performance there can be 30 to 60 students involved. If one teacher is not legitimately allowed to have more than an average of 30 or so students sitting in seats in a contained classroom, how is it that too often one teacher is allowed to supervise 60-plus students who are spread out into several rooms and spaces in such a physically hazardous environment? It only stands to reason that in a theatre - where there can be so many students working on a show or event, roaming around many areas, using a variety of equipment, in the dark - that each area must be supervised by a highly qualified person. And, in the case of a school variety show for example, often times this is each of the performing student's first and only time in the theatre, and they are not aware of the dangers and therefore the protocols.

LAWS AND CODES

I start this section with a disclaimer. *What I say here is not enough, I've left a lot out, and what I have included may possibly not be accurate, so you should not believe a word I say about codes and regulations – I may be wrong. I am not a theatre safety expert, I can only providing you with a basic overview.* There are federal, state, local, and school district laws and codes that must be followed, and writing about them would fill another book. Therefore, it is essential that you familiarize yourself with all the federal and state codes that affect the operations of your high school theatre.

You should familiarize yourself with at least the following code requirements as they pertain to high school theatres from:

ADA	Americans with Disabilities Act
ANSI	American National Standards Institution
EPA	Environmental Protection Agency
L&I	Department of Labor and Industries
NEC	National Electrical Code
NFPA, IFC	National Fire Protection Association
OSHA	Occupational Safety and Health Administration
WISHA specifically)	Washington Industrial Safety and Health Act (check your state

In some cases these codes are only the minimum that is expected of you. On the other hand some of these codes apply to the school's employees, but not to the students. OSHA is one example of this. OSHA stands for Occupational Safety and Health Administration. Note the word "occupational". OSHA only applies to paid employees, not students or volunteers. Therefore a teacher may not stand within 6" of an open orchestra pit, but students and volunteers may, right? Perhaps technically, but the best and safest thing to do is for everyone to do everything in your high school theatre as if everyone were under OSHA's jurisdiction.

It's important to check to see what requirements pertain to your high school theatre. OSHA is a federal regulator. Some states have their own, such as WISHA in Washington State. Any states who do not have their own fall under OSHA.

MITIGATING LIABILITIES

It's likely that your school's Drama department is not the only user of your theatre, however. There are usually concerts, variety shows, class meetings, and so on from the school, but many high school theatres operate as "road houses" and have a variety of transient users that need constant monitoring and supervision.

Therefore as well as training your drama department staff, students and volunteers, it is imperative that the person running your theatre develop customized operational policies and procedures that improve personal safety, protect property, and mitigate liability in your high school theatre that pertains to all users – school, district and outside. You can do this by:

- Compiling a safety manual.

- Creating a Liability Waiver

- Creating customized signs, notices and handouts.

- Generating a safety inspection roster and timeline.

- Recommending changes or improvements to enhance safety.

- Engaging professional independent theatre technicians, inspectors, suppliers and/or subcontractors as applicable.

- Proactively informing the users of their responsibilities.

SAFETY MANUAL

Does your high school theatre have a Safety Manual? Employers are required by law to provide Safety Manuals, so your school theatre already has one, right? Plus, your school district administration are legally required to enforce OSHA and other safety standards for its facilities, so you're safe, right? What about Entertainment Industry standards, those exist specifically for the entertainment world, so you're covered there too, right?

Well, sort of…. None of these specifically or solely apply to high school theatres. Therefore, not only is it imperative to staff a high school theatre with qualified professionals, but also to create a safety program, enforce safety rules, and provide an on-site Safety Manual. That way if something does happen, you can provide documentation that you have been doing everything possible to mitigate dangerous situations. This applies to senior high school theatres, junior high school theatres, middle school theatres, and even some elementary schools that have theatres. Even if your performance space is an "auditorium" or "multi-purpose room" school theatre safety applies to you too! Regardless of the size or type of your theatre and the age of your students, it's essential to create and provide a School Theatre Safety Manual and to enforce school theatre safety rules to everyone who uses your school theatre.

Your Safety Manual should be a comprehensive policies and procedures document of safety standards intended to control and minimize the hazards typically found in your school theatre. It should address proper training, equipment maintenance, the dissemination of appropriate information, and enforcement of policies and procedures in order to maintain a safe and healthy environment for everyone in your school theatre. Admittedly it's usually the book that no one reads, but your Theatre Safety Manual will have practical implications in the theatre, because almost every document has information that can be posted, frequently taught and/or is constantly used in practice.

Every school theatre has its own unique operations, but here are a few fairly universal topics that should be in your Safety Manual. You can adapt these to suit your own needs and the codes and laws that affect your area.

SAMPLE SAFETY MANUAL CONTENTS

POLICIES

General Safety Policies
Theatre Safety for Performers
Safety Policies for Theatre Technicians and Student Crew
Responsibilities of the Outside Event User
Site Supervision Policies for School-day Events
Safety Rules for Workshops (scene shop and costume shop)
Noise Level Policy
Work Lights Policy
Pit Cover Removal and Replacement Policies
Fog Machine Policy

PROCEDURES

Theatre Safety Announcements for Classes, Auditions, Rehearsals and other
Non-performance use of the Theatre by district staff during the school day.
Counterweight System Operation Guidelines
Counterweighting Guidelines
Procedures and Safety for House Management
Announcements to Audience
Strike Check List
Liability Waiver for Students, Volunteers, and Outside Users

DOCUMENTATION

Copies of Signed Waiver Forms
Lists of Students Who Have Been Trained To Use Theatre Equipment
Equipment Incident and Repair Records
Completed 'Work Party' Maintenance Lists
Maintenance Schedule
MSDS Sheets

Some of this content may seem a bit repetitive, but your Safety Manual is essentially a compilation of rules for a wide variety of uses of your space. Although everyone needs to know not to jump off the edge of the stage and not to eat food in the house, house managers don't need to know the rules for using power tools and set builders don't have to worry about crowd management. So while each section of your Safety Manual will repeat common safety rules, it will also stipulate safety rules specific to each area's function, which allows people to specifically learn the safety rules and requirements of their own tasks, without having to read a whole tome in order to weed out what's important to them. Yet at the same time the Safety Manual acts as a "reference manual" just in case the set building student has to go and help out in the lobby on opening night.

Because you can't foresee every dangerous situation, following is a sample disclaimer you should have in your Safety Manual. You should consult legal counsel regarding wording for your unique situation.

SAMPLE DISCLAIMER FOR SAFTETY MANUAL

Please note: A theatre facility contains many mechanical, electrical and other physical hazards, which can constitute a risk of injury or in extreme cases, death, especially to those unfamiliar with the procedures and practices of the industry. In order to maximize safety, students, parents, district and outside users may not operate any equipment in the theatre until they have been trained and authorized. It is also important to obey the instructions of the theatre personnel. Failure to follow required safety rules, written or verbal, may result in immediate and possibly permanent removal from a given activity or production. This safety manual may not contain all the safety factors conducive to working in a theatre, and all staff and users should exercise personal caution at all times. All persons working in the theatre agree to hold harmless and indemnify the School District, its employees, officers and agents from all claims, liability, actions or lawsuits, except for acts or omissions involving the sole negligence of the school district.

There is no doubt that it is time consuming to create a Theatre Safety program and then to document it all in a Safety Manual, amid the shows, events, production meetings, repairs, maintenance, scheduling and the myriad of other administrative tasks involved in running a high school theatre. But, I urge you to get started and work on it when you can, because your next accident can happen tomorrow.

If you don't have time to create your own Safety Manual, standard and custom theatre safety manuals can be ordered at

www.RCDTheatreOps.com

Mention this book and receive 10% off.

Don't let the show go on without a Safety Manual!

SIGNS AND NOTICES

In addition to training your students and making your Safety Manual available, having a variety of signs that communicate each section of your Safety Manual is essential. You should post safety signs and notices everywhere around your theatre – backstage, in the booth, in the house, in the lobby - wherever people will be, as a constant reminder of all those "rules". To good technicians safety just becomes second-hand common sense, but most students will need reminding. This also serves as another "risk management" tool to mitigate liability. No student can say 'you didn't tell me that' when the safety policy is posted all around your theatre and has been for many years.

A few of the notices you should have posted in your theatre should include:

Food and drinks policy

General safety rules

Workshop rules

Counterweight system policies

Authorized entrance notifications (who can come into specific areas, such as the
catwalks)

Open pit notification and procedures

Departure checklist – for the last person to leave the theatre

What rules should be in your safety manual and on your signs?

Your Theatre Manager, technicians and CTE teacher will be able to come up with specific safety rules for people (students and outside events) performing in your theatre, but here are a few general rules to be aware of.

SAFETY RULES FOR PERFORMERS

SAMPLE RULES FOR PERFORMERS

HOUSE
No food or drinks.
Do not put your feet on the seats.
Do not jump up on, or off of, the edge of the stage.
Once the house is open, during intermission, and after the show, don't peak around the curtain or walk on to the apron of the stage, or walk into the house from the stage vestibule door.

STAGE
Do not touch or play with the drapes.
Keep a 4' distance from the locking rail on stage left, don't touch the ropes.
Don't place belongings or props in that area.
Avoid rolling heavy set pieces or pianos over the floor pockets.
Don't go up to the galleries or catwalks, even if the door is open.
Use only approved tapes. (If unsure, ask first.)
No one, other than cast and crew directly involved with a performance, shall be allowed or invited backstage during any performance, between the time the house opens and until such time that the worklights have been turned on after the end of the performance.

IF THE CYC IS DOWN
Do not cross behind the cyclorama – it causes ripples.
Always stay at least 3 feet away from the cyc.

IF THE LIGHT LADDERS ARE DOWN
Do not touch the lighting instruments, even if they are off – they may have just been on and will be hot enough to cause a severe burn.
When entering or exiting the stage stay close to the legs as possible and don't stand in front of the light ladders as you will cast moving shadows on the stage.

IF THE ORCHESTRA PIT IS OPEN
Do not lean over the pit from the house.
Do not walk within 6' of the pit on the stage side.
Do not sit with your feet dangling over the edge of the pit.

PERSONAL BEHAVIOR
Any student or adult crew must wear closed-toe solid shoes and black/dark clothing.
No bare feet, socks or slippers in any area of the facility. The exception is if it's a part of your character to be bare-footed or in socks or slippers, and then only when on stage. At all other times please wear shoes (even to walk to backstage).

SAFETY RULES FOR TECHNICIANS AND STUDENT CREW

Your techs need safety policies too, the same for your student crew. Here are a few basic rules for them.

SAMPLE RULES FOR TECHNICIANS AND STUDENT CREW

Never work in the theatre alone.

Do not operate any equipment or perform any tasks for which you have not been trained.

Student crew may not operate any equipment or perform any tasks unless you have a signed liability waiver on file and you have been trained.

Unplug equipment and instruments before: changing a lamp, trouble shooting, repairing, or other activities requiring caution.

When in the galleries or catwalks all loose items in your pockets must be left in the box provided.

Do not stand on anything – chairs, ladders, etc – in the galleries or catwalks/beams.

Gaff tape all cables on the stage deck, back stage and in the galleries and catwalks/beams.

Know the location of fire extinguishers and first aid boxes.

Always return tools and supplies to their proper place and leave work areas clean.

When on headset, don't talk during a standby.

When on headset, don't say anything you don't want the world to know.

When going off headset, announce "Name going off headset" and turn off the talk button before you set the headset down. When returning to the headset, announce "Name on headset".

Technicians and crew members may eat and drink in the booth, at the sound console or at the production tech table if they are working a rehearsal or show and are not able to leave for more than two hours (if a mess is left, this privilege may be revoked.)

Always follow, and enforce with others, the safety and etiquette rules posted in the theatre and listed in the Safety Manual.

MORE SAFETY RULES

Fire Use for Productions

Most theatres, particularly high school theatres do not allow flame of any kind in their theatres. The only exception may be the use of flash paper, but even then the use must be supervised and authorized by a theatre technician. At any time any open flames are in use, at least one crew person should stand by offstage with a fire extinguisher at hand the entire time the open flame is present, and that should be that person's sole duty at that time.

Smoking

Smoking is prohibited on high school campuses. Therefore, only smokeless, powder- or water-vapor "stage-cigarettes" and "stage-cigars" should be used in a production. That said, you should be aware of the risk of the powder or vapors being carried into the air and the particles setting off your fire alarm system.

Prop Weapons

District policies prohibit the carrying, possession or use of a firearm – or anything that looks like a firearm - on school premises, which includes, but is not limited to, guns, knives and swords. Prop weapons are usually permitted in the theatre for the purposes of use during rehearsals and production only. Prop weapons are not toys, and because a student who is caught even carrying something that looks like a weapon could be expelled you should ensure that the following procedures must be followed:

- Theatre staff should be informed prior to the event if the event includes the use of any prop weapons.
- Theatre staff should meet the student at their car and accompany them into the theatre.
- All prop weapons shall be treated as real weapons; handle prop guns as if loaded, and handle prop knives and swords as if they are sharp.
- Prop weapons should only be available when required for a rehearsal or performance.
- Only the performer who is using the prop weapon, the Props Master, assigned Weapons Handler, event manager, or a PAC technician should handle any prop weapons.
- All prop weapons should be secured in a locked room or cabinet when not in use.

Stage Combat

Likewise, because stage combat can look real, safety procedures should be followed.

- The Theatre Manager should be informed prior to the event if the event includes stage combat.
- All stage combat should be practiced under the supervision of a Fight Director or appropriately trained individual.
- All stage combat should only be performed by those specifically trained by a professional.
- No stage combat should be practiced or performed outside of the rehearsal or performance area, or outside of rehearsal or performance times.

LIVE ANIMALS

It's a good idea to prohibit all live animals in your theatre. I'll digress here with a few of stories.

I was working a (actually pretty amazing) community variety show in a high school theatre. We got through three days tech rehearsals and we were on the last number on opening night, which was a barn dance. I was engrossed in something in the booth, and I didn't look up until the last number had started, and there on stage were three llamas standing by the cyc!!! What?! Where had they come from?! Unbeknownst to me they had loaded them in backstage at the last minute without a by your leave. My first concern was that one would spit on the cyc. But then my concerns grew as the llamas were lead forward during the dance, by now obviously freaked out by the noise, lights and people. One llama was being tended to by a young child (I later found out, the owner's child) and was lead down to the apron of the stage. This llama was prancing around, getting more and more freaked out. All I could think of then was that it would accidentally take a step off the edge of the stage, falling on an audience member in the front row and breaking its leg. Fear not, dear reader, none of these concerns came to be, but after that I banned all live animals from the theatre.

When I informed the group that they couldn't bring the llamas the next time, they said they always had an animal of some sort. One time they had a rooster who pooped on the stage in the middle of an act. Who knew it would do that (!), so they had nothing prepared to clean up the poop with and the technicians had to use their hands. But, suddenly there was a cue to take with the fly system, so they just had to pull the ropes, poopy hands and all.

On a prior occasion I was working on a high school play that called for a live cat. All through rehearsals the cat had been pretty mellow, but on opening night it sensed the audience and became nervous. In addition the owner had changed the cat's food that very day. You can imagine what happened on opening night. Not just poop, but diarrhea. Somehow the cast managed to hold it together during the scene and get the cat off the stage, but they changed to a stuffed toy cat after that.

They say actors should never work with animals because they upstage them. That's the worst of your problems if you allow live animals in your theatre. My stories could have been a lot worse, and I'm sure there are a lot of worse stories out there.

A FEW MISCELLANEOUS SAFETY TIPS

Blocked doors are an egress hazard.

Hallways and other areas that are legal exits cannot be used for storage.

Backstage lighting is essential.

A lot of painting goes on in the theatre. Make sure that the areas where this happens are properly ventilated – try blowing soap bubbles to check the air flow. On nice days painting and foam carving can be done outside, but on rainy days when you are working enclosed in the scene shop, make sure that your scene shop has a ventilation fan. Be careful about which doors you open, fumes or sawdust can be blown onto the stage or into dressing rooms.

FLY SYSTEM (COUNTERWEIGHT SYSTEM)

The fly system won't be addressed in the safety chapter. Because it is one of the most dangerous parts of the theatre, it has a chapter all of its own addressing operations and safety.

ORCHESTRA PIT SAFETY

Back on the stage - another code worth mention is OSHA' requirement for people to stay 6' away from an open orchestra pit. Not only this, but a guard rail must be in place, and a pit net installed. Right away any theatre person can see a problem with these requirements. How can the audience watch play through a railing? So, OSHA does allow for circumstances such as performances before an audience.

There are cases galore of injuries and death of people falling into orchestra pits. These include:
a dancer falling into a pit and suffering spinal injuries, a stagehand falling into a pit breaking his leg, another stagehand falling into a pit and suffering brain injuries, and even more tragic, a director backing into an open pit who died from head injuries, and a musician who fell into a pit and died from his injuries. The list goes on and on. Most of these people were professionals. You are dealing with students. These safety requirements are not to be taken lightly.

In lawsuit situations some courts have in the past ruled in favor of the theatre, because actors and crew have been working in the space for a long time and know the pit is open during a performance, and therefore should be taking precautions accordingly. Even the outside users of your space take upon these liabilities themselves. It is however, imperative that this is in writing in their contract. In the case of educational theatre a lawsuit for negligence is more likely to be upheld. Regardless, you don't want a serious injury or death on your conscience. When it comes to safety my motto is:

BETTER PARANOID THAN SORRY.

In the educational setting, it's up to whoever is running your theatre to train the students. It is therefore essential to have guidelines concerning an open pit, whether you have a hydraulic pit cover or scaffolding pit cover. For instance, the movement of the hydraulic lifts, or the removal and replacement of the pit covers must be done by trained staff, usually the Theatre Technicians. I recommend a minimum of three technicians to remove and restore a scaffolding pit cover system, however four is optimal for safety. In the case of a hydraulic system there should be one person operating the lift, while one person guards below the pit and one person guards the growing pit hole from the stage deck. A student or outside event crew member may assist Theatre Technicians in the removal or replacement of the pit covers, but only after turning in a signed liability form and only under the direct supervision of the Theatre Technicians. Keep copies of the pit cover plans and procedures in the safety manual, in the booth and at the Theatre Manager's district office. Under no circumstances must the pit be removed or replaced without the plans at hand.

CATWALKS FALL PROTECTION

Safety up above the stage is a bone of contention for theatre folks. There is an OSHA code that says that anyone working above a 6' drop (7.5' in California as of this writing – you see how you must know your local codes) must use fall protection, that is: harnesses. Catwalks and beams can be 30' above the house floor. Anyone – student or professional - who has ever had to move around in the catwalks and beams hanging and focusing lights, running cable or operating a followspot will tell you that they couldn't functionally do their job if they kept having to fiddle with a safety harness. Luckily there are other "equivalent" methods that may be acceptable. One other method of possibly acceptable fall protection is having guard rails at appropriate heights that will withstand specified forces. Therefore it's imperative to ensure that your safety railings in your catwalks are up to code, and to have your district install additional railing if not, because in the theatre working with a harness is impractical. In addition, if there is any chance that something might be kicked off a work surface – as in the platforms of a catwalk, for instance – that there must be a toe board installed to prevent this. Check your codes for the height of the toe boards. And always remember to gaff tape down any cables crossing a walkway.

The safety risks of your school theatre needs to be assessed by your Theatre Manager. In one theatre I worked in I had to put in work orders to fix many physical safety problems with the space that had gone unresolved for years prior to my arrival. At another theatre I was able to prevent a lot of problems that were in the plans before the equipment and building features were installed. One example was hand rails for stairs. In the first theatre mentioned, at the point in the catwalks where there are stairs down to the followspot platform – just where someone is most likely to trip or fall in the dark – there were no cables across the opening under the lighting pipe, leaving a hole about 3' wide and 4' high – plenty of room for a person to fall through. I was able to put in a work order for the district to remedy this at the existing theatre and I seeing the same situation in the plans for the theatre under construction, I was able to remedy it before the catwalks were even completed.

An in-depth study of OSHA codes as applies to fall protections in the theatre can be found at http://s15.a2zinc.net/clients/USITT/USITT2013/Custom/Handout/Speaker0_Session445_1.pdf

NOISE LEVELS

One safety issue that people rarely consider in high school theatres is sound safety. Noise is measured in decibels (dBA), which are units of sound pressure. Decibels are measured on a logarithmic scale, which means a small change in the number of decibels is a large change in noise level. Exposure (sudden or repeated) to high noise levels can cause temporary or permanent hearing loss. Loud noises can also cause an accident if it's difficult to hear a warning signal. If you have to shout to be heard, noise may be an issue in the theatre.

OSHA sets legal noise limits in the workplace, but as mentioned before students and volunteer are not covered by OSHA, but you should act as if everyone is. NIOSH (the National Institute for Occupational Safety and Health) recommends that workplace noise be below 85dBA. Consider that a table saw in your scene shop has a noise level of over 100dBA, and musical instruments in your orchestra have noise levels of between roughly 70 – 130dBA. A sound technician who is working at a sound board in the middle of a house during an event, especially one with music, or who is checking sound cues through headsets, can be exposed to sound levels as high as 85dBA for applause, and much higher if the sound technician is forced to turn up the volume of her headset to hear the Stage Manager calling a cue over the applause. The same goes for any technician trying to communicate on headset.

While your students are not likely to be exposed to long term loud noises in your school theatre – think of a construction worker who uses a jack hammer 8 hours a day for days in a row – you still should attempt to control the hazardous exposure of noise, just as you would attempt to control the hazardous exposure to falls and chemicals.

There are several ways to control the hazardous exposure to high noise levels. Make sure that items that make a loud noise are well maintained and replaced when they get too old. If purchasing new equipment and tools, be aware of noise levels and choose the best noise level that you can. Limit the amount of time students and others spend working at a noise source. If possible, relocate students and others who are not working at the noise source to another area while the noise source is in operation. If it's not possible to relocate bystanders, create as much space as possible between them and the noise source.

Place speakers on stands instead of on the floor. Low frequencies prefer to travel through solid surfaces than the air, so if you put your speakers in the air the low frequencies are forced to travel through the air, thereby will be louder, which allows the balance of the overall sound to be reduced. Also, aim speakers so that performers are not exposed to the open backs. Use baffles as needed.

Provide suitable Hearing Protection Devices (HPDs). These may be ear muffs or ear plugs. These can be used when it's not feasible to implement the above precautions.

Above all, inform all staff, students, volunteers, and theatre users about the hazards related to noise exposure.

HOUSE MANAGEMENT

It's also imperative to have written policies and procedures for House Management activities in your school theatre. House Management includes anyone working in the lobby, selling concessions, selling tickets, taking tickets and ushering people to their seats. A lot of the safety precautions are the same as any where else in the theatre, but some are different, so it helps to have a written policy in order to train your own people, or to hand to events using your theatre, so that they have been informed of certain safety issues and can assist with crowd management.

Sample policies and procedures that your house staff should enforce include:

SAMPLE POLICIES FOR HOUSE MANGEMENT

OCCUPATION OF THE SPACE

Users may not enter any part of the PAC, including the ticket booth and lobby area, unless an authorized district employee is in attendance, even if the doors are unlocked.

CROWD MANAGEMENT

Food and drinks are not allowed in the house.

Audience members and users must not put their feet (even bare feet) on any part of the seats in the house.

Due to fire codes, sitting or standing in the aisle or stairways is not permitted.

Do not allow audience members to walk up on, or sit on, the edge of the stage.

No one, other than Cast and Crew directly involved with a performance, shall be allowed backstage during any performance, between the time the house opens and until such time that the worklights have been turned on after the end of the performance.

If the orchestra pit is open: do not allow audience members to lean over the orchestra pit wall.

CONSESSIONS

Users are responsible for all set up and cleaning up of concessions.

Users should do their best to clean up any spills and messes, but then report the incident to the Theatre Manager or PAC technical staff.

MEDICAL EMERGENCIES, ACCIDENTS AND FIRST AID

If an injury, accident or other incident is serious or life-threatening call 9-911 immediately. Render whatever first aid can be applied until emergency services arrive to relieve you.

If an injury, accident or other incident occurs during the school day, choose an individual to go to the front office to get the school nurse.

Never move a person suspected of serious injury unless it is a life-threatening situation such as a fire.

All injuries, accidents and other incidents must be promptly reported to the Theatre Manager technicians.

Location of First Aid Kits

FIRE

In the event of a fire:

Activate the fire alarm. Evacuate the building, await the arrival of the fire department. Try to account for everyone in the building.

Do not re-enter the building until you are told to do so by a member of the fire department.

Location of Your Fire Alarm Pulls, Fire Extinguishers and Eye Wash Stations

REPORTING SAFETY CONCERNS

It should be the policy of your theatre that no safety concern is trivial and that contributing to the health and safety of all is everyone's responsibility. All theatre personnel, teachers, students, and other users of the facilities should be encouraged to report any concerns without fear of retribution.

ASSEMBLY OCCUPANCY

One code that bears mentioning is the NFPA (National Fire Protection Association) 101.12.7.6.1 and NFPA 101.13.7.6.1. This codes says:

"Assembly occupancies shall be provided with a minimum of one trained crowd manager or crowd manager supervisor. Where the occupant load exceeds 250, additional trained crowd managers or crowd manager supervisors shall be provided at a ration of 1 crowd manager or crowd manager supervisor for every 250 occupants..."

It goes on to say "...unless otherwise permitted (by the authority having jurisdiction)" This could apply to your school district, so you should check with your administration. If your district doesn't have any exceptions to the rules this means that your high school theatre will likely need at least one or two trained crowd managers. Find out if this rule applies to sporting events. If it does, then it applies to your school theatre. Teachers are not "trained crowd managers". If you google Crowd Management Training, you can find online courses or courses in your area.

In addition, it's actually illegal to sell tickets for over capacity – standing room only – yet many cash strapped Drama departments and other events frequently ignore this on the assumption that there will never be a fire, earthquake or other reason why the theatre would have to be evacuated. That's the same as saying why wear a seat belt because it's unlikely you'll get in a crash.

SCENE SHOP

Moving backstage, another area that your students use is the scene shop. A theatre scene shop is essentially another woodworking shop on a high school campus, and is just as dangerous. Each high school is different, and following are some examples of who typically supervises in a high school theater scene shop, and the pros and cons involved.

DRAMA TEACHERS

Might supervise building.
Some (most?) don't know how to use power tools, and don't teach correct and safe usage.
Students are left unsupervised in the scene shop while the Drama teacher is directing rehearsals on stage.

PARENT SET DESIGNER AND BUILDER

Intermittent - parents come and go, they leave after their child graduates, and you can have years where there is no interested parent.

Usually competent to use and teach usage of power tools – usually have had some experience in construction, hence their interest to help out. The drawback is that sets use different building techniques than house construction.

STIPENDED PROFFESSIONAL

The stipend can be very low, not encouraging a good person to return.
Not all professionals have experience in, or the patience for, working with children.
Stipended professionals are not likely to know about or enforce CTE requirements for safety testing.
Some professionals are also parents and may stay on for a year or two after their student graduates.
Stipended professionals cost the Drama department money – usually from the proceeds of the ticket sales.

ANOTHER TEACHER

A teacher who has an interest in building and construction could over see the scene shop, but they do not usually have experience in set design, set building and stagecraft. Nor are they CTE highly qualified. The set gets built but the students do not learn any stagecraft.

THEATRE TECHNICIAN

Theatre Technicians have the knowledge to do the job.
Theatre Technicians love to pass on their craft to others.
Theatre Technicians can work at a high school for years, forging rapport with the students.
Theatre Technicians have a knowledge about how each production fits in with the rest of the theatre's annual schedule (such as not leaving the stage in a mess, when there is a dance recital coming in).
Not all theatre technicians have teaching skills (although most are happy to share their craft!).
Not all high schools have theatre technicians on staff.
Theatre Technicians are not highly qualified teachers.

CTE (CAREER AND TECHNICAL EDUCATION) TEACHER

CTE teachers have the knowledge to do the job.
CTE teachers create a formal program with learning goals and assessments.
CTE teachers can work at a high school for years, forging rapport with the students.
CTE teachers don't always have any say as to other events that come into their theatre.
Not all school districts have a career and technical education program in their theatres.
Most CTE teachers are specialists in lighting, sound, sets and rigging, but not all.

Most importantly, it bears repeating, the Department of Labor and Industries prohibits children under 18 to work in a wood or metal work occupation, except for those enrolled in an educational program with a vocationally certified instructor.

The tools commonly used in a scene shop include table saws, band saws, electric drills, routers, welders and spray paint, foams and other flammables. L&I also requires that as well as having a certified instructor, that students must demonstrate written and skills proficiency before they can use any equipment in a theatre. Your school theatre must also provide appropriate protective equipment and have regular inspections. In addition, as per OSHA, there must always be one staff member present who is trained in first aid and CPR, plus theatre staff themselves must be provided with a safe work environment.

The best way to run your high school theatre scene shop is to have a professional of some sort supervising, teaching and mentoring your students. If there is no CTE program requirement in your area, still follow the same rules, policies, procedures that your CTE woodshop teacher has to follow. Also give your students the same equipment and tools operations tests that your CTE woodshop teacher has to.

FIRE TREATING

Another safety issue which is usually the domain of the workshops (scene shop, prop shop, costume shop) is that of fire treating materials. This section does not address pre-installed drapes and flame testing those, this addresses materials that you bring into the theatre. My official advice to you is that every piece of wood, material, foam, etc that is used in your theatre must be fire treated.

Now I'm not saying "Fire Proof" because there is no such thing, even steel studs are considered flammable at some point. However, all scenery, props and costume materials should be treated with fire retardants. Items that will burn but extinguish themselves after the fire source is removed are considered "Flame Retardant".

In some cases we use residential building materials to build sets, and they may already come in as fire treated for flame retardancy. Pressure treated wood, for instance, has a higher fire rating and may be considered 'fire treated' under some residential fire codes, although theatrical fire codes can be different. If, however, the wood you purchase for your sets is not considered to be 'fire retardant' then you must 'fire treat' them yourself – particularly after painting them, regardless of their inherent fire resistance. Another fact to know is that some theatrical paints have a higher fire rating that most household paints.

Foams are another material commonly found in the theatre. Some foams actually have quite a high fire rating, and have to actually be heated up before it catches fire. Some foam insulations, for example, can have a flash point of 615 degrees.

And, of course, you definitely want to fire treat every costume piece that every actor – who has the potential of standing too close to a very hot theatrical light without noticing until it's too late – is wearing.

There are different fire hazard classifications that indicate flame spread, fuel contribution and smoke development. These details are beyond the scope of this chapter, other than to let you know that as the person who is in charge of your theatre (be you a district administrator, Drama teacher, or professional Theatre Manager), you must educate yourself in the matters of fire treating materials. A good place to start is your local theatre safety inspection company, such as Stagecraft Industries on the west coast.

MSDS

Yet another detail you have to be aware of in scene shops is all the chemicals – in this case that mostly consists of paint, paint and more paint. You may have heard of MSDS – Material Safety and Data Sheets – in other areas of your life. Technically you must have on hand an MSDS sheet for every single chemical you have in your work place – yes, this includes white-out and pens! This is almost logistically impossible, although most companies have no problem providing you with them. So, my official advise to you is to take an inventory of every chemical you have in your theatre and have a binder in your scene shop for MSDS's. There is a sensible reason for this – if someone accidentally swallows, inhales or touches a dangerous chemical, you can look at the sheet for the make up of the chemical and other safety information. In one district I worked for the MSDS sheets were all kept in the district offices, so in the safety manual and scene shop rules I stated that "MSDS's are available at the district offices". But, again, officially, I am advising you to have those sheets on hand in your theatre.

COSTUME SHOP

Don't forget that your costume shop can also have potentially dangerous equipment and chemicals in it too, and should follow the same safety policies and procedures as a scene shop. In addition, Costume Design is a CTE subject (at least in the state of Washington – check for your state), just as is Fashion Design, and therefore the same requirements apply.

SAFETY TRAINING

Safety is not a 'thing' you get, nor something to be read about in a book - it has to be the culture of your high school theatre. It's not enough to have a Safety Manual and handouts and signs. You have to train all users of your high school theatre, whether they be performers, student crew, parent volunteers or outside users. Following are some suggestions for trainings in the high school theatre.

Annual Theatre Safety Talk for all Performing Arts Students

Once a year hold a basic Theatre Safety talk that all Performing Arts students must attend, whether they are in drama, band, choir, a performance club or tech. This training should be held near the start of the school year, before any performances have begun. This can add up fast and you can find yourself talking to 200 – 300 students, so have a syllabus prepared for yourself. Present a general safety overview that includes rules such as no jumping off the stage, don't touch the cyc, no visiting friends and family members may come back stage, if the door to the catwalks is open it doesn't mean you can go up there, an so on. It's pretty dry information, so keep the mood serious but light. Admit to them that this is the 'boring meeting', but let them know that they, as the Performing Arts students, need to be safe, but also that they are stewards of their theatre, so that when a non-Performing Arts student uses the space - say for a variety show or school pageant - that they must act as role models and peer-mentors.

Student Crew Trainings

Students who are going to be using the theatre at a deeper level – the tech crew for school productions – need to a more in depth training and are expected to be role models for all other students who work in the theatre. All students should be taught not to wipe their hands on the flame retardant covered drapes as they walk by and not to enter a door just because it is unlocked, but those who are actually operating your lighting, sound and fly systems, or going up into your catwalks or beams to operate the followspots, or push sets around in the dark need specific training and practice. These trainings should be held shortly before each tech week of each show begins. Don't schedule this training too far out so that they forget what you've taught them when it comes time to use the equipment, but not too close to the first day of tech that the training is rushed. You will need full use of the stage, so on the day of your training the actors will have to rehearse elsewhere. If you have theatre technicians working at your high school theatre, then you can have a training session with stations, in which you split the group up into smaller groups and rotate every half hour or so. If you acquire new tech students at any time throughout the year they must be trained too.

Scene Shop Trainings

Most likely your state has a Career and Technical Education (CTE) program, but that doesn't mean all school districts enforce those requirements – this is especially true for school theatres, because there is little understanding about the dangers. It is likely that your state stipulates that students may use the hand tools and power tools only if there is a CTE teacher present and if the students have been trained and tested. Otherwise, an adult has to do most of the work. Regardless of whether you have a CTE program, students should be trained and tested at the CTE requirement level - there should be a specific training for any student who will use hand and power tools in the shop. Although I understand the practicalities, I do not advocate students doing anything in a scene shop without a CTE teacher present.

Set Building Workshop for Volunteers

Another group it is imperative to teach theatre safety and protocols to is your parent volunteers, especially the set builders. Mothers and fathers who want to volunteer in a high school scene shop usually have some sort of background and interest in construction. When I started working at one theatre there were a group of dads who were already building a house set for "The Sound of Music". And that's just what they did – they built a house on stage. That thing was never going to budge. As luck would have it, throughout the year they were able to repaint it and use it as a factory in "The Pajama Game" and later a community variety show used it as a brothel!

This isn't standard practice in set building though, we were just lucky with the choices of shows that year. There are techniques to building sets so that they can be modular, portable and also safe for student actors to stand on. If you have parents who want to build sets, it is best to instigate an annual set building and rigging workshop, which is mandatory for anyone (teachers, parents and students) who will be building sets to attend. Teach about modular set pieces, general theatre construction techniques for flats, platforms, stairs, etc, and how to safely hang drops and flats using the correct rigging hardware with the correct techniques (although a rigging technician must be present to supervise any hanging of scenery). If you don't have anyone on your theatre staff who can teach this, hire a professional from the community, such as www.theatricaltraining.com in the Seattle area. Spending the money on training set builders will be less than spending the money on lawsuits down the road. Consider the cost of hiring a professional as a form of insurance.

Here's a suggested list of topics for your set building workshop for volunteers:

CONSTRUCTION AND APPLICATION

FLATS

PLATFORMS AND WAGONS

STAIRS AND STEPS

CROSS BRACING

CONNECTIONS

RIGGING

HARDWARE

PAINTING

TYPES OF PAINT

BASIC TECHNIQUES

SAFETY

Outside Users

It's likely that your school's Drama department and other school groups are not the only users of your school's theatre. Many high school theatres operate as "road houses" and have a variety of transient users that need constant monitoring and supervision. Therefore, you should have written safety policies that you provide to them before they arrive for their event, and you should do a short safety training when they arrive. In reality it may not be practical to get everyone in one place at one time – for instance most dance schools tech their little ones' dances first so that they can go home, and dancers are coming and going all throughout the tech rehearsal period – so in that case require that the Outside User make each participant aware of the safety rules. Have them sign a document that says they agree to this and other requirements of using your theatre, that way if an accident or incident occurs you have proof you did the best you could to provide them with the safety information.

LIABILITY WAIVER

You may have noticed that people don't always read notices, or sit down with a cup of coffee to spend a pleasurable afternoon pouring over their company's safety manual, or even remember what they've been trained on half the time. For liability purposes, you should also have students and other users who are using any equipment in your school theatre sign a safety liability waiver.

Following is a sample Liability Waiver, which is specifically geared towards students who are working tech (again, you should consult your own legal counsel and adopt wording that suits your specific space and situation).

SAMPLE LIABILITY WAIVER FORM

I, _____, parent/legal guardian of _____(student or self), do hereby give my permission for my student/self to operate the equipment in the theatre, which includes but is not limited to:

Operate the counterweight system for the purposes of flying scenery and electrics in and out.

Work under the supervision of a theatre technician in order to re-weight pipes.

Enter the galleries and/or catwalks for the purposes of rehearsals or performances, and specific show-related purposes.

Operate a followspot, hang and focus lights, set up and operate sound equipment.

Operate hand tools, power tools, in order to build or repair scenery, set pieces and/or props.

Use and/or operate other equipment inherent to the theatre and/or to the production therein.

I understand that a theatre facility contains many mechanical, electrical and other physical hazards, which can constitute a risk of injury or in extreme cases, death, especially to those unfamiliar with the procedures and practices of the industry, and that my student may not operate any equipment in the theatre until they have been authorized by the theatre technical crew. I also recognize the importance of following the instructions of the theatre personnel and my student agrees to obey such instructions. Failure to follow required safety rules may result in immediate and possibly permanent removal from a given activity or production. I agree to hold harmless and indemnify the School District, its employees, officers and agents from all claims, liability, actions or lawsuits, except for acts or omissions involving the sole negligence of the School District.

No matter what safety precaution trainings you have and what notices you post, and how many liability waivers are signed, there is always that litigious parent. A parent's signature on a liability waiver is not necessarily going to stop them from suing the school district if their child is hurt, but it shows that you have done your best to inform the parent of what activities the student will be involved in and the precautions they must take, and the trainings you have provided. One such incident happened while my daughter was in tech theatre at her high school (where there was no Safety Manual or liability waiver). A student was walking backstage in the dark and broke her ankle. Of course the parents sued the school district. I believe this was settled out of court, but, like some court rulings about people falling into orchestra pits, students and their parents have to accept the dangers of working in a theatre. I myself am a parent of three children who have been in high school tech theatre, so I get where parents are coming from, but the theatre is not a safe place, and if you want your child to live in a bubble, you should not allow them to work in their high school theatre.

STUDENT CREW IDENTIFICATION

After training your student crew *and* after they've turned in their waivers(!), you'll need a way to indicate who has been trained to other school and theatre staff – because no one should be allowed to use the equipment in your theatre without proper training and a signed waiver. There are many ways to do this. One way is to post a list on the wall where you, or whoever trained the student, writes the student's name, and then initials under the areas in which the student has been trained. Another is to create lanyards with colored beads indicating areas of the theatre the student has been trained on. Yet another way to identify student crew is to have them wear badges, much like your own district employee badge. Your HR person at your district offices probably has a badge making machine and can make some badges for you that read "STUDENT THEATRE CREW".

It's probably not necessary for a student crew members of a school play to wear badges, as this is a closed community and everyone usually knows who everyone else is and what their job is, but if a student crew member is working on a school event where there might be a variety of students involved, say a Variety Show, then it's good for the participants to know that number one, the students with badges are allowed to operate the equipment, and number two, that the students with badges do have a knowledge about the theatrical process and therefore should be respected if they ask another student to do something – particularly as it could be a safety issue. Another situation in which students should wear badges is if they are helping out at an outside event, such as perhaps a dance recital. The users renting the space should know that these students aren't just 'hanging out' and that they are there to work and be relied upon.

It's probably not a good idea to let each student have their own badge. Theatre isn't the only thing they do, and badges can get lost or forgotten. Plus, it sometimes goes to some students' heads when they're given a symbol of 'authority', so it's best not to create that sort of a situation around campus. Instead, have a supply of about 8 badges (usually about the maximum you might need) that live in your scene shop or booth – wherever is most convenient – and have a checkout sheet. This not only saves on having to make a lot of badges and risk losing the, but it also serves for liability reasons – in case you ever need to go back and see who was working a show.

MAINTENANCE

One part of safety is keeping your physical space in good working order and in safe condition. Some maintenance is performed as issues crop up during the school year, but there is some maintenance that should be done on a regular basis – this includes safety inspections.

Following is a generalized list of maintenance items (also repeated in the Maintenance chapter). Some of these items should be ongoing at all times – such as always check that your line weights are balanced, however this list is for the purposes of formal inspections as well.

SAMPLE SUGGESTED MAINTENANCE SCHEDULE

THEATRE TECHNICIANS

Check all Line Weights are balanced.	Twice a year
Clean filters of dimmer racks.	Once a year
Clean and inspect lighting instruments.	Every 2 years
Paint the stage deck.	Once a year

DISTRICT CUSTODIAL

Vacuum drapes.	Once a year
Vacuum out floor pockets.	Once a year

DISTRICT MAINTENANCE

Test smoke vents.	Every year
Operate smoke vents.	Twice a year
Fire inspection.	Once a year
Charge or replace fire extinguishers.	By date on tags

THEATRE SAFETY INSPECTION COMPANY

Counterweight System Inspection	Every 2 years
Drapes Flame Testing	Every 2 years

Your theatre may have specific needs that you can add to this list. In the high school theatre a lot of the planned maintenance such as these activities take place during the summer when the school theatre is less likely to be constantly in use. You should perform at least these maintenance items at least as frequently as listed, ideally more if district funds allow.

Some maintenance can be done by your technicians, and some by your district custodial and maintenance staff. There is other safety maintenance that should only be done by a professional company that specializes in theatre safety. On the west coast, such a company is Stagecraft Industries (www.stagecraftindustries.com), a manufacturing, installation and inspection company based in Portland, Oregon. Stagecraft not only has done thorough rigging and theatre safety inspections for me in the past, but also installs and repairs equipment in new and existing theatres. The products they produce can be found in high school theatres in the States and even overseas.

DOCUMENTATION

And finally, it is important to document every accident, incident, and equipment maintenance performed in your theatre. It's important to document accidents, incidents and equipment malfunctions that adversely affect people. Stagecraft Industries recommends a logbook for *"keeping a detailed record of all incidents relating to the maintenance of, or malfunction & repair of, any stage rigging, curtain & track or electrical systems, as well as all other stage/studio & house related rigging hardware and equipment."*

Your school district probably has standard report forms, however you should create additional specialized documentation specific to your theatre. This record can be in any format that you create, however at least the following information should be included:

Date of Incident/Accident/Maintenance.

Time of Incident/Accident/Maintenance.

Location of the Incident/Accident/Maintenance.

Person injured/equipment broken.

How the injury or incident happened.

Witnesses.

Actions taken at the time.

Further steps taken to resolve the issue.

And remember – no detail is too detailed.

CONCLUSION

Regardless of detailed details and prepared preparations, you can't possibly anticipate every accident and incident. And, as said before, even if a student's parent has signed a waiver allowing their student to use that power tool or fly that cyc, it doesn't mean they won't sue the school district if their child gets hurt. But remember, it's called Risk "Management" not "Risk Elimination" and even the

National Safety Council defines safety as *"the control of recognized hazards to attain an acceptable level of risk"*. There is no way to completely eliminate risks in a theatre - however you must attempt to at all times.

In order to do so it is imperative that you provide appropriate supervision, have operational policies and procedures that safeguard personal safety, protect property, and mitigate liability in your high school theatre, and these should pertain to all users. It's also imperative that you train your students to appropriately and safely use inherently dangerous equipment and how to behave in inherently dangerous situations. Safety isn't something that can be taught in a few hours in a classroom, safety policies and procedures must be continuously practiced. Your theatre is one of the most dangerous places in your school that students have access to. Plus a theatre has many different physical areas and job specialties and it's important to have people who are qualified to work in those areas. For instance, a sound technician would probably not be the person to re-weight a pipe, someone trained on rigging should be doing this. A Stage Manager would not be re-wiring a lighting instrument plug, and so on.

If you can show that you have provided the safest possible environment, complete with policies, procedures, trainings, notices, supervision and documentation of acceptance of risk, and have people with the necessary skill sets running the theatre operations, then you can mitigate liability, and more importantly perhaps prevent what could have been a more serious accident from happening.

Why standby, when your next accident could happen tomorrow. Go!

FINALE

FINAL ACT

If this book has thoroughly overwhelmed you by now and you've come to realize that there is much more to designing and running a high school theatre than you previously thought, then I've done my job.

I was once working in a high school theatre when the principal came through with a group of people in tow. I later discovered that this was the administration and architects from another school that was building a theatre. The principal proudly showed them around the impressive-looking state-of-the-art theatre facility, but what he didn't realize was the functional problems that existed behind the façade.

In that particular theatre the issues ranged from a tech booth counter that was too low, such that when the light board operator and Stage Manager sat down they couldn't see the stage, to a scene shop that had been placed alongside the back wall of the stage with no hallway in between, such that it was the only entrance to upstage right (think: little girls in ballet shoes entering the stage through a nail and screw ridden scene shop). Another major functional issue with that particular high school theatre was that in order to save money at the time of building there was no access to the stage right galleries – where lights are hung, and directors are fond of putting actors. If you were up in the galleries focusing lights and you discovered you needed a gel frame, you would have to walk up to the catwalks, across the catwalks, down three stories of the stairs behind the stage left galleries, through the house, up to the booth, get the gel frame, walk back down through the house, up the three stories of stage left gallery stairs, across the catwalks and back down the stage right galleries. A simple ladder under the stage right galleries would have sufficed and not broken the budget. It would have been much more helpful to the visitors to be able to sit down with my theatre staff and the tech theatre students that I worked with in order to help them avoid many function pitfalls such as these. But it was simply because the principal had never worked 'in the trenches' of the theatre in his building that he was unaware of these issues and wouldn't have known to mention them to his visitors.

If you are designing a high school theatre, or will soon be the administrator in charge of managing a high school theatre, I strongly encourage you to sit down with the technical staff of local high school theatres. Plus, don't discount tech theatre students. I can't count the amount of times I've heard a tech theatre student exclaim "what were they thinking?!" It's simply the cry of a person who has to work in a space designed and managed by people who, through no fault of their own, don't have the experience of being 'in the trenches'. I hope this book has helped you experience the trenches of technical theater somewhat, and given you a more in depth look at the operational requirements of high school theatres.

I recently came across some proposed plans for a new high school's black box theatre. These plans did not include a second level if there was one, nor specs on the equipment, so I could not assess the situation completely, but I had a glance. Speaking from experience, while the school would like a theatre, schools are usually under capital budget restraints, which are passed on to the architect to take into consideration in their designs. However, also speaking from experience, I find that too many school districts trying to save money in the initial construction stages only cause themselves perpetual operating expenses after construction.

Here are the proposed plans for the new black box theatre that were posted publically on the school district's website:

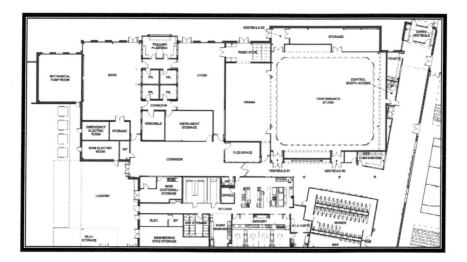

Some questions that I think this school district should consider, which would affect operational costs in the long run include:

- is there a scene shop in which to build and paint sets,
- is there a costume room large enough for several people to spread out in,
- is there sufficient storage space for sets and costumes,
- in the existing storage space is the door between the storage space and the performance studio (black box theatre) high enough to move large set pieces through,
- are there dedicated dressing rooms for the male and female performers,
- is there an office space for the Drama teacher,
- is there an office space for a Theatre Manager?

Because of my experience 'in the trenches' I could foresee some changes that would be beneficial to the functionality of the space and that would save the school district money in the long run:

198

- move the door of the "Flex Space" to the opposite wall and make this the Costume Room,
- put the Riser Storage space at the other end of the Drama room space and putting double doors at each end of the Riser Storage room,
- turn the now adjacent Costume and Riser Storage rooms 90 degrees for easier movement of the risers into the theatre,
- do away with the Drama room – Drama classes can be held in the Performance Studio,
- turn the Drama room into a Scene Shop, with a pedestrian door and a garage door in the exterior wall and in the wall between the Scene Shop and the theatre,
- reduce the number of stalls in the Women's and Men's restrooms to allow for space for dressing room(s),
- create an office space (really, two are needed) out of the end of the existing Storage room (with a window – theatre people spend too much time in dark boxes as it is),
- and finally, be sure not to install windows in the Black Box Theatre (I've seen that happen).

BLACK BOX VS. SMALL PROSCENIUM

There are also some general pros and cons to consider for the long term when considering investing in a black box theatre as opposed to a small fixed proscenium theatre. A black box theatre has a high versatility factor; it can be re-configured to a proscenium stage, a thrust stage or theatre-in-the-round. But, with versatility comes expenses.

To begin with, masking flats (walls) or drapes would have to be purchased or constructed to create a "backstage" space. Each time the acting space is reconfigured the lighting instruments and drapes would have to be moved to new positions. This would be on top of the usual set construction that is needed for a performance. Every school district should look at their theatre operations plans and look at the costs, time constraints and safety factors, and assess some questions, such as: Who would be doing this, a class of students lead by a CTE teacher and/or professional technicians hired by the district? Are students allowed to go up on a genie or ladder to rehang and refocus the lights? Are the students trained in how to safely rig flats and/or drapes from the grid?

One school I worked at had a black box theatre and they hired me to create a lighting rep plot for them. Theatre-in-the-round and thrust stages require about twice the number of lighting instruments than a proscenium stage does because the actors and the sets must be lit from several sides. This theatre had been given a lighting package, but it was insufficient for the space potential, so the Drama teacher decided to create a fixed proscenium stage within the black box space with flats as the proscenium walls. In another black box school theatre I worked in there were an ample amount of instruments but there were no lighting positions to allow for lighting the sides of the stage, so we had no choice but to structure the theatre into a permanent proscenium configuration. In these circumstances it would perhaps have been better to provide that school with a small 100-seat theatre, had the administration assessed future operations, budget and time restrictions ahead of time.

On the other hand, there are some plusses to a black box theatre. For instance, a black box theatre's floor space can be cleared for classes and rehearsals to be held in there. Plus a black box theatre is great for learning environments where tech theatre skills are a part of the curriculum. For instance, set design and construction techniques have more liberty, and lighting techniques can be created for class exercises. It all depends on the administration's vision for their theatre operations.

A TO A TALKS

As you can see it's so important for the architect and the administrators to understand high school theatre operations, and to have the conversation about how the school's theatre will be operated (and funded!) in the long run, because this vision will determine the design decisions made now.

It's my passion to help architects, administrators and academics to be able to understand the behind the scenes operations that they normally wouldn't have a chance to see. If you don't have access to a theatre professional who can facilitate a collaborative dialog that will reveal approaches where high school theatre design can alleviate unexpected operational costs of educational theatre operation, then I hope this book has given you an advantageous peek into the world of high school theatres.

High school Theatre Managers and Tecnicians can only accomplish their mission with your help. If the facility is appropriately designed, and the administration are supportive of the operations, and academics are well educated in the operations, then the students will be the stars!

Break a leg!

GLOSSARY OF THEATRE TERMS

* indicates that the definition of this term can be found in the Glossary.

Spelling: you will see hyphens and spaces and compound words used interchangeably. For example: off-stage, off stage, offstage or stage-right, stage right or stageright.

APRON
The part of the stage deck* that is downstage* of the proscenium*.

APRON STRIP LIGHTS
This is a band of lights – usually blue - that goes from one side of the stage to the other, just upstage of the stage deck that covers the pit, so that when the pit is open they warn a performer (who can be blinded by the production lights shining in their eyes) where the edge of the stage is. Some apron strip lights have a small red light in the middle, which dancers can use for spotting, and to let all performers know where the center stage line is.

ARBOR
The framework that holds the pig irons* that counter balance the weight of anything hung on the battens* in the counterweight system*.

ARM
The strip of stage deck* that protrudes out along the wall of the house* alongside the front part of the seating.

BACKSTAGE
The area of the stage deck* that is hidden from the audience's view, either by drapes* or set pieces.

BATTENS or PIPES
The pipes that hang above the stage and hold lights, mics and scenery. The pipes that hold the lights are called Electrics* and the pipes available for scenery hanging are called GPs*. Another common pipe is the Cloud Truss*.

BEAMS or CATWALKS
The beams or catwalks are the area above the house* where lighting instruments are hung, and sometimes followspots* are located. The term "beam" actually refers to a closed space built above the ceiling of the house, while the term "catwalk" actually refers to a metal walkway structure that hangs below the ceiling of the house. However, in the industry, the terms are loosely interchanged.

BLACK BOX
Short for "Black Box Theatre", which is a small theatre that is usually just one large, windowless room. The walls are painted black and the drapes are black, hence the name. The audience is usually set up on risers, which allows for different configurations for the stage space – proscenium*, thrust* or theatre-in-the-round. The backstage space is created with drapes or flats*.

BLACK MASKING
When the "Black Masking" is referred to it is specifically indicating the black masking* that hangs upstage and covers the length of the stage. It usually hangs just in front of or just behind the cyc*.

BLACKOUT
This is the term for when all of the stage lights are turned out at one time. It usually depicts the end of a scene or a dance.

BLACKS
Technicians* working backstage must wear dark or black clothing, so that if they happen to move within sight of the audience they will be less noticeable than a flash of white or light color clothing. The general term for their dark clothing is "blacks", as in "Don't forget to wear your blacks, it's opening night."

BLOCKING
Blocking is the term for where the actors move. Setting the blocking is like choreographing a dance. Actors have to learn their blocking as well as their lines.

BOOMS or BOX BOOMS
This is a lighting position, typically recessed into the side walls of the house* near the stage, which typically run vertical. The booms can either be accessed from the front from a ladder set in the house, or from behind via a walkway.

BOOTH
The term "Booth", when used alone, refers to the small room at the back of the House* where some of the Technicians* sit during a rehearsal or show. It usually consists of a light board, sometimes the Followspot * can be in there, a projector, and a place for the Stage Manager* to sit. The sound board is typically (or should be!) in the House*. Not to be confused with the term Ticket Booth*.

CABLE
A cable is a conduit that houses sound or lighting wiring. In the theatre they are almost always black. They are not, as in the 'outside world', referred to as "extension cords".

CAST
A collective term for the people who are performing – it may be a play or a ballet. Musicians are usually referred to as "performers", however in general the cast refers to the group of performers you see on the stage, as opposed to the crew* who work backstage and run equipment, who you don't see.

CATWALKS or BEAMS
The catwalks or beams are the area above the house* where lighting instruments are hung, and sometimes followspots* are located. The term "beam" actually refers to a closed space built above the ceiling of the house, while the term "catwalk" actually refers to a metal walkway structure that hangs below the ceiling of the house.

However, in the industry, the terms are sometimes loosely interchanged. The catwalks are also referred to as the "cats".

CLEAR!
A word called out when someone on stage is responding to a warning that a pipe* or batten* is about to fly in or out. Clear should not be called until the person on stage has ascertained that the area is actually clear.

CLOUDS
Clouds are hard shells that are usually permanently hung from a batten*. They hang vertically, but once flown in to the appropriate height they open up to hang horizontally. They create a "ceiling" above a band or orchestra that bounces the sound into the audience. Some clouds have lights installed in them and some hang between light battens*, in both cases to provide down light for musicians to see their music.

CLOUD TRUSS
This is the batten* on which the clouds* are hung. This batten is different in that it usually consists of three pipes* hung in a triangular formation, which can better carry the heavy weight of the clouds*.

CONCESSIONS
This term refers to the food and drinks which are sold at a performance, typically during intermission, however some places sell concessions before and after a performance as well.

COSTUME SHOP
This is the room backstage where the costumes are created, sewn, fitted and stored.

COUNTERWEIGHT SYSTEM or FLY SYSTEM or RIGGING
This is the system of ropes that you typically see back stage in a theatre. The term "counterweight" comes from the fact that the scenery* or lighting instruments* are in some way counter weighted so that the weights on one end of the ropes weigh as much as the scenery* or lighting instruments* on the pipes, so that they are easy for one person to move in and out. These days it's most common to find pig irons* providing the counterweights, however some theatres still use sand bags. Some rigging systems use winches, which can adjust to the weight of the scenery* or lighting instruments*, and do not require physical re-weighting by technicians*.

CREW
A collective term for the people who work backstage and run the equipment needed for a show. In order to avoid confusion, in a high school, the crew usually refers to the students, while the technicians* usually refers to the district employees that staff the theatres.

CUE
This is the term for the action a technician* takes when executing their job and usually denotes a change of some sort. For instance: a lighting cue can be a change in the lighting "look" or intensity; a sound cue can be a change in volume; a set cue can be where the set crew moves out one or more set pieces and moves in one or more others.

CYC
The cyc is the large piece of white (or off-white) material that is hung towards the back of the stage (upstage*). The full term is "cyclorama", and it is so named

because the single piece of material used to circle the sides and back of the stage – you still sometimes see this in film. The cyc costs as much as a car. This is because it is one seamless piece of material which can have dimensions as long as 40' or more. As of this writing, there are only 3 places in the world that manufacture cycs. The cyc is used to project colored and/or patterned lights on, in order to create mood, or to depict time of day, or location. Such as a dark blue cyc is a sky at night, a green cyc might depict a forest. An amber cyc might be used for an up-beat jazzy piece of music and a lavender cyc might be used for a mellow jazz piece.

DECK
This is the common term for the floor surface of the stage.

DOWNSTAGE
Most people have no trouble remembering stage left* and stage right* as being from the actor's perspective, however remembering which is upstage* and downstage is harder. Downstage is towards the audience and upstage is towards the back wall of the stage. Here's how to remember: These days our stages are usually, mostly level, while the house* is raked*. In Shakespearean times the floor where the audience stood or sat was level, while the stage was raked. So when the actors walked towards the audience, they were literally walking down hill (down the stage) and when the actors walked away from the audience, towards the back wall of the stage, they were literally walking up hill (up the stage). Hence the terms upstage and downstage.

DRAPES
Short for draperies. Sometimes called the "soft goods*". This usually refers to any permanently hung pieces of material, such as the legs*, the mid-traveler*, the masking* and the cyc*.

DRESS REHEARSAL
This is the final rehearsal (or sometimes two) before opening night. The actors are in full costume and make-up and know all their lines and blocking*, the technicians* and/or crew* wear their blacks* and know all their cues*. The dress rehearsal is traditionally run without stopping in order to simulate a real performance. If someone makes a mistake it is dealt with as if an audience were watching.

DROP
A drop or "backdrop" is a painted piece of material that is hung across the stage. It usually depicts a location of the whole play or of a specific scene.

EDISON or STAGE PIN or THREE PRONG TWIST
These are the there most common types of lighting instrument* plugs and outlets that you will find in the theatre. Edison refers to your standard household plug. Stage pin also has three pins or prongs, but they are in alignment. Three prong twist has three pins or prongs that form a circle, one prong has a tab and once the plug is inserted into the outlet it is twisted to secure it.

ELECTRIC
The electric is a term that collectively refers to the pipe* on which the lighting instruments* are hung along with the raceway* into which the lighting instruments* are plugged.

FLAT
This refers to the wall of a set*. It is made of a wooden framework in the back, and is either covered with muslin (a "Broadway flat") or luaun plywood (a "Hollywood flat").

FLOOR POCKET

This is a square hole in a stage deck* that is covered with a trap door. The floor pockets can be backstage – these usually contain outlets for lighting instruments – or on the stage – these usually contain outlets for sound equipment. Both typically also contain an Edison* outlet.

FLOWN vs. TRAVELED

The terms traveling and flying usually pertain to a drape* that goes across the full stage, such as the main* or the mid-traveler*. Most of these drapes hang from a pipe, and also have curtain pulls like a curtain in your home. So, when the pipe is lifted vertically this is called flying, or that the drape or set piece is flown. When the curtain is flown in such that the bottom is touching the stage deck* then when you pull the curtain ropes to open the curtain horizontally, half to the left, half to the right, then this is known as traveling.

FLYING

You may think of Peter Pan when you think of "flying", however in the case of technical theatre "flying" is what the flyman* does. It refers to moving the hung scenery* and lighting instruments* in* and out* of the stage space. A crew member may be told to "fly* in* that flat*".

FLYMAN

This term refers to the person (male or female) who operates the fly system*/counterweight system*/rigging* during a show.

FLY RAIL or LOCKING RAIL or RAIL

The fly rail/locking rail/rail is generally referred to as the area where the ropes of a fly system*/counterweight system*/rigging* are located. A flyman* is said to be "working on the rail". Specifically it refers to the length of metal railing where the rope locks are affixed.

FLY ROPE

This is the actual rope used in a fly system*/counterweight system*/rigging* system. It has properties that allow it to carry hundreds of pounds of weight. It is the part of the system that the flyman* pulls in order to move the scenery*.

FLY SYSTEM or COUNTERWEIGHT SYSTEM or RIGGING

This is the system of ropes that you typically see back stage in a theatre. The term "counterweight" comes from the fact that the scenery* or lighting instruments* are in some way counter weighted so that the weights on one end of the ropes weigh as much as the scenery* or lighting instruments* on the pipes, so that they are easy for one person to move in* and out*. These days it's most common to find pig irons* providing the counterweights, however some theatres still use sand bags. Some rigging systems use winches, which can adjust to the weight of the scenery* or lighting instruments*, and do not require physical re-weighting by technicians*.

FLY TOWER

This is the tallest part of your theatre building. It houses the counterweight* system, and allows lighting instruments* and scenery* to be pulled up out of sight of the audience. Many high schools opt to have a ¾ fly tower. This not only saves money in construction materials, but in a ¾ fly tower the proscenium* opening is smaller and therefore a fire curtain is not required. The curse of a ¾ fly tower is that the scenery cannot fully be pulled out of sight of the audience and there is usually a few inches that hang down below the sight lines, and when the scenery is flown in often times the pipe it is hanging from is visible. Another drawback to a ¾ fly is that the grid is flush up against the ceiling, instead of being about 6' below it, so access to the cables of the counterweight* system is limited in case a repair is needed.

FOCUS
Focusing the lights is the process whereby the lighting technicians* aim the lighting instruments* in the correct position and in the correct format as decided by the lighting designer, in order for them to fulfill the purpose for which they were intended.

FOLLOWSPOT
The followspot, or spot light as some Muggles* call it, is a large lighting instrument* usually mounted on a pole at chest-height, that can be moved around by an operator. The purpose of the followspot is to highlight a specific performer, usually a main character during a song of a musical or possibly a stand-up comedian alone on the stage. Because the performer moves around the stage the followspot operator can "follow" the movement and "spot" the performer with the light*.

GAFF TAPE
This tape is as wide as duct tape and is usually black (it comes in other colors, but black is the most practical for the theatre). It is used in the theatre for all sorts of uses, including securing items and cables. This tapes lifts off fairly easily and doesn't leave a sticky mess. NEVER use duct tape in the theatre.

GALLERY
This is a recessed walkway along the side of a house* that allows for lighting instruments* to be hung, which are easily accessible. There can be one, two or three levels. It's also a favorite place for directors to want to place performers.

GARAGE DOOR
As the name suggest – unlike most things in a theatre – a garage door is like a garage door; just not in a garage. It is a large roll-up door, usually made of metal, that is tall enough and wide enough to move large pieces of scenery* through. There is usually a garage door from the scene shop* to the loading dock of the theatre, and another garage door from the scene shop to the backstage hallway, and then another garage door from the backstage hallway to backstage. Some theatres which have their scene shop directly behind the backstage wall (not recommended!) have the garage door leading directly from the scene shop to backstage.

GEL
This is the colored filter that is put in front of a lighting instrument and held in place by a gel frame*. Gels actually used to be made of gelatin, which is how they got their name. They held up ok under the hot lighting instruments*, but if you put them in water they were reduced to a soggy mess. These days gels are synthetically made of a type of polyester. There are hundreds and hundreds of gel colors, each one varying slightly from the next – and yet Lighting Designers complain there are never enough colors.

GEL FRAME
This is the metal frame that holds a square of gel* in place in front of the lighting instrument*. There is a slot in the front of the lighting instrument* where the gel frame slides into.

GENIE
Not the kind that comes out of a lamp or bottle. If there were that kind of genies in theatres, technicians' jobs would be obsolete. So we don't allow them. But we welcome "genie lifts", which are scissor, or vertical mast lifts that allows a technician to work high in the air – usually above 20' in order to work on a set* piece or to focus lighting instruments*. "Genie" is actually a brand name, but in the theatre "genie" has become a common term for any lift, much like a "Kleenex" can refer to any tissue.

GHOST LIGHT or NIGHT LIGHT
This is the light that is typically left on when a theatre is unoccupied. It is so that the first person next entering the theatre can see in order to reach the switches for the worklights. The theatre is a very dangerous place, and not somewhere that someone should be walking around in in the pitch black. Night lights are sometimes traditionally called ghosts lights, so that there is some light left of for the traditional theatre ghost to see by. The night light can be just a lamp on a stand that is wheeled out to center-stage and plugged in, or it can be a fixture hardwired into a lighting system and usually situated in the beams* or catwalks*

GLOW TAPE
When activated by bright light, this tape glows in the dark. It is primarily used backstage* (sometimes on stage) at the edge of platforms, stairs, etc, so that actors, crew* and techs* can see the edge and don't trip and fall during a black out. Glow tape is very expensive and should be used sparingly.

GOBO
This refers to a pattern that is inserted into a lighting instrument*. It can be made of metal, glass or can be a photographic image much like a slide. Metal gobos can be "break up patterns" which looks like dappled light coming through trees, to more specific shapes such as a window, a castle, snowflakes, and so on. Glass gobos can be used to create fire and water effects.

GP
GP stands for General Purpose, and is a pipe* that is not designated to hold lighting instruments* or clouds*. GPs are typically used for hanging scenery* on.

GRAND or MAIN
This is the large curtain that hangs just upstage* of the proscenium arch*. It is the curtain that separates the stage from the house*, the actor from the audience. It is commonly referred to as just the "main" or the "grand".

HANDHELD
This is a shortened term for a handheld wireless microphone*.

HANG AND FOCUS
This is the term used for the process whereby the technicians* hang the lighting instruments* in the positions where the lighting designer determines where they need to go, patches* where the lights are plugged in into the light board and then focuses* the instruments* for the correct function.

HEADSET
You will hear of two types of headsets spoken about around a theatre. One type belongs to the theatre's communication system that the crew uses and the other kind are mics* that performers wear. Usually if you just hear the term "headset" used by

itself we are talking about the communication system. Also, you will hear the whole arrangement, which includes the headset, beltpack and cables referred to as "the headset". Technically the beltpack carries the power and the headset itself is plugged into it, but we call the whole thing "the headset". When a Stage Manager tells her crew to "set up the headsets" she means to plug in or put in place the headsets, cables and beltpacks.

HOUSE
The house is where the audience sits.

HOUSELIGHTS
These are the fixtures that light up the house*. In a full theatre they are on dimmers so that they can be adjusted slowly or partially.

IN, OUT, ON, OFF
In the theatre you fly pipes* "in" (down) and "out" (up), and you move scenery or actors "on" (into the view of the audience) and "off" (away from the view of the audience).

INSTRUMENTS
This primarily refers to the lighting instruments. Instruments are movable – usually installed on a pipe* with a C-Clamp. As opposed to fixtures which are the lighting fixtures you would find in your house or office – these are hardwired in or "fixed".

LADDERS
In this case the ladders don't refer to the things you climb, but the lighting pipes and raceways that hang on either side of the stage in more recently built theatres. These allow for side lighting, especially important in dance (in order to light the whole body, not just the face). Most theatres that have light ladders have one upstage* of each leg*, and there are usually 3 or 6 instruments on each ladder.

LAMP
"It's called a *lamp!*" is a favorite theatre cry. Never a "light bulb". The "bulb" is just the glass part. A "lamp" is made of the bulb, a filament, the gas and a base.

LLAMA
An example of live animals that are often not permitted in theatres. Not only do live animals draw attention away from the actors, but their behavior can be unpredictable. They can poop, throw up and spit. If you have a tens of thousands of dollars of drapes on your stage, you may wish to consider animals carefully. Animals can also "freak out" and run or fall into the audience, risking harming themselves and the audience. Allow the use of llamas or any live animals at your peril.

LEGS
These are the narrow (usually black) drapes that hang on either side of the stage. They are usually parallel to the front edge of the stage, sometimes they are angled slightly. These serve to hide the view of backstage* from the audience, yet allow performers to enter and exit the stage at various places. They also allow set pieces to be moved on and off stage, without the audience seeing them being stored off-stage*, and also allow for the stage to be lit from the side.

LIGHT
The stuff that comes out of a lamp.

LOBBY
The area where the audience waits to be let into the house*. Concessions* are usually sold in the lobby.

LOCKING RAIL or FLY RAIL or RAIL
The fly rail/locking rail/rail is generally referred to as the area where the ropes of a fly system*/counterweight system*/rigging* are located. A flyman* is said to be "working on the rail". Specifically it refers to the length of metal railing where the rope locks are affixed.

MAIN or GRAND
This is the large curtain that hangs just upstage* of the proscenium arch*. It is the curtain that separates the stage from the house*, the actor from the audience. It is commonly referred to as just the "main" or the "grand".

MAINSTAGE
In a performing arts center that has more than one theatre, the main stage refers to the largest theatre. The main stage is usually a proscenium* theatre, while a second theatre is usually black box* theatre.

MARLEY
This is a "rubber"-like floor that is laid down over the stage deck* for dancers. It usually comes in long strips about 6' x 40'. The strips are taped together with marley tape.

MASKING
The masking refers to a drape* - usually a black drape* - that masks the audience's view to the backstage* area. This is usually the legs*, mid-traveler*, side masking and upstage* masking.

MIC
Short for microphone. There are several types of mics, the most common being the vocal mic, the instrument mic, the condenser mic, the floor or plate mic, the wireless handheld mic. Each type of mic has a different polar pattern*.

MID-TRAVELER
The mid-traveler, as the name suggests is a drape that usually hangs in the middle of the stage*, and travels* open and closed, although it can also be flown*.

MONITOR (SOUND)
When a part of a sound system, this refers to a speaker that is placed on stage or in the pit so that the performers can hear music or other performers that are usually hard to hear from where you are. For instance, dancers on a stage find it hard to hear music coming from speakers that are only in the house*, and orchestra members in the pit* find it hard to hear the actors' lines from up on the stage. Usually just the word "monitor" is used and the specific item is inferred from the context of the conversation.

MONITOR (A/V)
When backstage* this refers to a video screen in a dressing room or classroom that is hooked up to a camera in the house* that is aimed at the stage. This is so that performers can be watching what is going on on stage, so that they know when to enter, without being in the way backstage*. Usually just the word "monitor" is used and the specific item is inferred from the context of the conversation.

MUGGLE

What's a Muggle? According to Dictionary.com, a "muggle" is a term originating from around the 1920's to describe a person *"who is ignorant or has no skills"*. Oxforddictionaries.com defines a Muggle as *"A person who is not conversant with a particular activity or skill"*. Both refer to the meaning popularized in the Harry Potter series: "a person without magical powers". In the theatre, where we create the "magic", a Muggle good-naturedly refers to a non-'theatre person' who does not have a knowledge of what goes on behind the scenes in order to make the "magic of theatre" happen.

NIGHT LIGHT or GHOST LIGHT

This is the light that is typically left on when a theatre is unoccupied. It is so that the first person next entering the theatre can see in order to reach the switches for the worklights. The theatre is a very dangerous place, and not somewhere that someone should be walking around in in the pitch black. Night lights are sometimes traditionally called ghosts lights, so that there is some light left of for the traditional theatre ghost to see by. The night light can be just a lamp on a stand that is wheeled out to center-stage and plugged in, or it can be a fixture hardwired into a lighting system and usually situated in the beams* or catwalks*

OFF-STAGE

This refers to the part of the stage deck* that is hidden behind the drapes* or masking* - the part that the audience can't see. It is also a directional command – the actor walks "off-stage".

PAC

Performing Arts Center. This term interchangeably refers to the whole building housing the theatre (house* and stage) and classrooms, or just the theatre itself. The meaning can be found in the context of the conversation.

PATCH

Patching is a lighting and a sound term. Instead of the first fader on the light or sound board, for instance, controlling the first circuit where the lighting instrument* or mic* is plugged in, the technician may prefer for the first fader to control a lighting instrument* or mic* that is operating in a certain area of the stage. So the technician will patch the appropriate instrument* or mic* into an appropriate fader. A similar concept to old patch boards that telephone operators used to control.

PIG IRONS

Pig irons are the metal weights that are used to counter balance the scenery* or lighting pipes* so that they can easily be flown in* or out*. There are three general sizes (or weights), the larger is fondly called a Pig, the next is called a Half-pig, and the smallest are called Piglets. Some people call them "bricks" instead, as they look somewhat like bricks.

PIPES or BATTENS

The pipes that hang above the stage and hold lights, mics and scenery. The pipes that hold the lights are called Electrics* and the pipes available for scenery hanging are called GPs*. Another common pipe is the Cloud Truss*.

PIT

The pit refers to the orchestra pit, which is a large space in front of the stage and usually about 8 or so feet below the stage deck* level. This is so that the orchestra can play and be heard, but not block the view of the stage from the house*. During

210

shows when there is no orchestra, the pit is usually covered up with a pit cover, which looks like an extension of the stage deck*.

POLAR PATTERN
This refers to the direction from a mic* picks up sound. Some pick up sound from only one direction (uni-directional) and some pick up sound from more than one direction (bi-directional).

PRODUCTION LIGHTS
Production lights refer to what most people think of as "stage lights". They are the lights that are used during a performance. As opposed to work lights* which are used for rehearsals, classes and for technical purposes.

PROP
This is any item that a performer carries on stage with them. Anything else – such as a chair or picture frame – is considered a set* piece.

PROSCENIUM or PROSCENUIM ARCH
The proscenium arch is the opening in the front wall of the house*, which frames the stage.

RACEWAY
This is the long 'box' with circuits that runs along a lighting pipe or electric*, into which the lighting instruments are plugged.

RAIL or LOCKING RAIL or FLY RAIL
The fly rail/locking rail/rail is generally referred to as the area where the ropes of a fly system*/counterweight system*/rigging* are located. A flyman* is said to be "working on the rail". Specifically it refers to the length of metal railing where the rope locks are affixed.

RAKE STAGE or RAKED STAGE
A raked stage is a stage that is angled. The front of the stage (literally downstage*) is lower than the back of the stage (literally upstage*).

RE-WEIGHTING
This is the process whereby the weights on a counterweight system* are either added or removed in order to match the weight of the scenery* or lighting instruments* added or removed from a batten*.

RIDER
This is a document from an event coming into the theatre that instructs the theatre technicians* what technical requirements they will have for the event.

RIGGING or COUNTERWEIGHT SYSTEM or FLY SYSTEM
This is the system of ropes that you typically see back stage in a theatre. It is also called the counterweight system* or the fly system*.

RISERS
The steps that a choir stands on so that you can see all performers and so that all performers voices can be projected.

RUN THROUGH
A run through is when the cast rehearses the whole play in one go, instead of just focusing on particular scenes or acts.

RUNNING ORDER
This is a list of what happens when in a show – such as for a variety show, the Running Order might start: M.C. welcomes audience, dance #1, song #1, M.C. talks, dance #2, skit #1, and so on. All technicians* need to have a copy of the Running Order of a show that they are rehearsing so that they can make notes about what they need to do for the performance.

SCENE SHOP
This is the room backstage where the sets* are built, painted and stored.

SCENERY or SET
A piece of scenery or a set* piece refers to an item on stage that a performer does not carry or move – as opposed to a prop* - such as a wall, stairs, a tree and so on.

SET or SCENERY
A set piece or piece of scenery* refers to an item on stage that a performer does not carry or move – as opposed to a prop* - such as a wall, stairs, a tree and so on.

SHELLS
Shells are movable walls that can be place behind musicians so that the sound is better bounced into the audience. It helps the audience better hear a group of instrumental or vocal musicians, while a mic* helps the audience hear a specific musician.

SHOP
A shop in the theatre is the place where items are built and stored.

STAGE MANAGER (SM)
The Stage Manager is the person in charge of the smooth running order* of a performance. While each technician* knows what their job is for any specific cue*, the SM makes sure that all of the cues* happen at the right time.

SOFT GOODS
This refers to any of the drapes* in a theatre.

SPIKE
To spike something means to place a small piece of spike tape* on the stage deck* to indicate where the item should be placed. For instance, during a set change a technician* may have to set a table exactly where a focused* lighting instrument* will hit it during a following scene. In order to be sure to place the table in the same location night after night the table is spiked. Another thing that is spiked can be the ropes of the counterweight* system. Often times a technician* pulling the ropes during a performance may not be able to see when to stop, so the rope is spiked at the location where the set* piece is in place. In either case, this is called being "on spike".

SPIKE TAPE
Spike tape is a special type of tape used to spike* the set or ropes. It is fairly thin, comes in a variety of colors and is easily removable once the show it done (almost nothing created in the theatre is permanent). The different colors are useful to spike*

the set* pieces for different scenes – for instance, the furniture locations for scene one can be done in green spike tape and the furniture locations for the second scene can be done in orange spike tape, in order to not cause confusion as to what needs to be placed where and when.

STAGE LEFT
This is from the actor's perspective. If you are sitting in the house watching a show, stage left would be on your right.

STAGE PIN or THREE PRONG TWIST or EDISON
These are the there most common types of lighting instrument* plugs and outlets that you will find in the theatre. Edison refers to your standard household plug. Stage pin also has three pins or prongs, but they are in alignment. Three prong twist has three pins or prongs that form a circle, one prong has a tab and once the plug is inserted into the outlet it is twisted to secure it.

STAGE RIGHT
This is from the actor's perspective. If you are sitting in the house watching a show, stage right would be on your left.

STANDBY
When a Stage Manager* calls a standby it is to alert the technicians* that they have a cue* coming up. Typically once an SM* calls a standby no one must talk over the headsets* until the cue* is complete, because the timing of the cues* can be essential and the technicians* need to hear the SM say "Go."

STRIKE
This term refers to the taking down, dismantling disposing, and/or storage of the set, lights, sound equipment and costumes once a show is over. Some plays will strike after the closing night performance, which can take into the wee hours. In educational theatre, students aren't allowed to stay up that late, so some pieces may be struck on closing night, but the majority of the strike will happen the next day.

TECH REHEARSAL
This refers to the final rehearsals prior to opening night where the technical aspects are integrated into the show. Prior to tech rehearsals the actors will have been rehearsing with minimal costumes and props*, and perhaps just large blocks or classroom chairs as set pieces. They also do not have lighting cues* or use mics*. The tech rehearsals are for the actors to get used to working with all of the technical aspects of the show and for the technicians* to have a chance to "rehearse" their parts – such as when does a light cue happen and when does a set piece have to move. Tech rehearsals can be boring for the actors who have been used to running their show non-stop by that time, while the technicians* move at a slower pace as they record their cues*, sort out any problems and get used to their jobs.

TECHNICIAN, TECH, TECHIE or TECH CREW
This refers to a person who helps with the technical, non-acting, side of a show. Good technicians are never noticed by an audience.

THREE PRONG TWIST or EDISON or STAGE PIN
These are the there most common types of lighting instrument* plugs and outlets that you will find in the theatre. Edison refers to your standard household plug. Stage pin also has three pins or prongs, but they are in alignment. Three prong twist has three

pins or prongs that form a circle, one prong has a tab and once the plug is inserted into the outlet it is twisted to secure it.

THRUST STAGE
A thrust stage is a stage with audience members on three sides – the stage "thrusts" into the audience.

THEATRE-IN-THE-ROUND
Theatre-in-the-round is where the audience surrounds the stage on all sides. Despite the name "round" this is usually a square stage.

TICKET BOOTH
Most people are familiar with this term because most people have been to a production or sporting event where they've had to purchase or pick up tickets from the ticket booth. Some theatres use their ticket booths solely for that reason, and some ticket booths also do double duty as an office. This is not to be confused with the term Booth*, which is used by itself.

TRAVELED vs. FLOWN
The terms traveling and flying usually pertain to a drape* that goes across the full stage, such as the main* or the mid-traveler*. Most of these drapes hang from a pipe, and also have curtain pulls like a curtain in your home. So, when the pipe is lifted vertically this is called flying, or that the drape or set piece is flown. When the curtain is flown in such that the bottom is touching the stage deck* then when you pull the curtain ropes to open the curtain horizontally, half to the left, half to the right, then this is known as traveling.

TWO-FERS
Two-fers are a Y shaped lighting cables that allow two instruments to be plugged into one outlet. Two "fer" one. Very useful in a theatre that doesn't have enough circuits.

UPSTAGE
Most people have no trouble remembering stage left* and stage right* as being from the actor's perspective, however remembering which is upstage and downstage* is harder. Downstage is towards the audience and upstage is towards the back wall of the stage. Here's how to remember: These days our stages are usually, mostly level, while the house* is raked*. In Shakespearean times the floor where the audience stood or sat was level, while the stage was raked. So when the actors walked towards the audience, they were literally walking down hill (down the stage) and when the actors walked away from the audience, towards the back wall of the stage, they were literally walking up hill (up the stage). Hence the terms upstage and downstage.

USHER
An usher is a person who takes tickets and helps audience members find their seats.

WINGS
This refers to the space backstage* from the legs* or masking* to the backstage* wall. The wings traditionally refers to just the sides of the backstage* space, hence the term "waiting in the wings".

WINCH
An electric winch can be used instead of a counterweight* system. Winches can automatically adjust to hundreds of pounds of weight without the need for the

technician* to re-weight*. The pipes are then moved by pressing a button instead of pulling on a rope.

WIRELESS MIC
A mic that transmits a signal to a receiver which then relays the information to the sound board, as oppose to being wired into the system and then physically patched* into the sound board.

WORK LIGHTS
These are lights that are to be used anytime someone needs to be in the theatre for any reason, other than there being a show in progress. In that case, Production Lights* are used. Work Lights are always a white light, and are usually mounted on the electrics*, the beams* and/or the side walls of the stage.
A word about Work Lights. Some theatres have been known to use their Production Lights* because they have no Work Lights. Consider this – if all of the Production Lights are on, that adds up to about 120,000watts of power used, not to mention the replacement cost of the lamps and gels that are being burned through. LEDs are the best Work Lights because they are energy saving, have a long lamp life and turn on and off immediately. HIDs also save energy and have a long lamp life, but take about 10 minutes to warm up, and if you turn them off and then need them on again immediately they can take up to 20 minutes to warm back up again (this is another common reason for people turning on Production Lights – impatience). Fluorescents have a longer lamp life than Production Lights, but a much shorter lamp life than LEDs and HIDs. It is worth the money to get work lights installed if you don't have them, and worth your effort to insist they're used if you do have them.

Made in the USA
San Bernardino, CA
04 September 2016